T0212503

Lecture Notes
in Business Information Processing   **259**

More information about this series at http://www.springer.com/series/7911

Ulrika Lundh Snis (Ed.)

Nordic Contributions in IS Research

7th Scandinavian Conference
on Information Systems, SCIS 2016 and IFIP8.6 2016
Ljungskile, Sweden, August 7–10, 2016
Proceedings

 Springer

Editor
Ulrika Lundh Snis
Department of Economics and IT
Hogskolan Vast
Uddevalla
Sweden

ISSN 1865-1348   ISSN 1865-1356 (electronic)
Lecture Notes in Business Information Processing
ISBN 978-3-319-43596-1   ISBN 978-3-319-43597-8   (eBook)
DOI 10.1007/978-3-319-43597-8

Library of Congress Control Number: 2016947769

Printed on acid-free paper

This Springer imprint is published by Springer Nature
The registered company is Springer International Publishing AG Switzerland

Preface

The 7th Scandinavian Conference on Information Systems, SCIS 2016, hosted in Ljungskile, Sweden, was jointly organized by the LINA (Learning in and for the New Workplace) research center at University West and the Digital group (Learning in a Digitalized Region) of University West and the University of Gothenburg.

SCIS 2016 highlighted the digitalization of society, that has proceeded and entered almost all aspects of our lives. Digitalization refers to the way in which many domains of social life are reshaped around digital communication and media infrastructures, and what constitutes a worker, a student, and a citizen in a digitalized society as it has consequently evolved to be. In parallel, new research interests concerning the use and design of digital services and devices have emerged. The 7th SCIS conference had the theme "Living in the Cloud" emphasizing three aspects in particular; First, it refers to "the cloud" as the increasingly ubiquitous digital data storage "up there," which makes digital information appear to be detached from physical location and thus available anytime, anywhere, connecting everything with everyone. This has a profound effect on contemporary practices and on the way humans construct and perceive our understanding of information and information systems. Second, it refers to how boundaries appear blurred and vague and it is unclear where things start and end. For example, digital services today are often open-ended systems, resembling containers or infrastructures, which are changed by users during use as a dynamic evolution. Finally, it illustrates the tension between contrasting aspects related to the consequences of digitalization, such as how to handle the diffusion of private versus professional roles, relations, services, or information systems and how to balance benefits versus challenges of being constantly connected.

A total of 25 manuscripts were submitted to the conference. The evaluation was a careful double-blind review process with at least two reviewers for each paper. Finally, nine papers were accepted for presentation at the conference and in these proceedings (with an acceptance rate of 36 %).

SCIS 2016 invited three keynote speakers: Margunn Aanestad from Oslo University (Norway) Carsten Sørensen from the London School of Economics and Political Science (UK), and Viktori Kaptelinin from Umeå University (Sweden).

As in previous years, the SCIS conference was arranged in conjunction with the Information Systems Research Conference in Scandinavia, known as the IRIS conference, which began in 1978 and which with its 39th annual gathering is the oldest consecutive information systems conference in the world. IRIS is today organized as a working seminar between established researchers and doctoral students. The young researchers and their interest in information systems boded well for shaping the future of the field.

We would like to thank the supporters and sponsors of this conference. We are grateful to all those people who contributed to this conference, whether as organizers, Program Committee members, reviewers, scientific contributors, or otherwise. Finally, we would like to extend our warmest thanks to all those volunteers who contributed in so many ways to making this conference a successful and memorable event.

May 2016

Martin Gellerstedt
Ulrika Lundh Snis
Johan Lundin
Lena Pareto
Lars Svensson
Dick Stenmark

Organization

Conference Chairs

Lena Pareto   University West, Sweden
Lars Svensson   University West, Sweden

Program Chair

Ulrika Lundh Snis   University West, Sweden

Proceedings Chairs

Johan Lundin   University of Gothenburg, Sweden
Ulrika Lundh Snis   University West, Sweden

Cloud Chairs

Anna Sigridur Islind   University West, Sweden
Tomas Lindroth   Gothenburg University, Sweden

Web Chair

Stefan Nilsson   University West, Sweden

Sponsorship Chairs

Martin Ljungdal-Eriksson   University West, Sweden
Monika Hattinger   University West, Sweden
Ann Svensson   University West, Sweden

Program Committee

Ivan Aaen   Aalborg University, Denmark
Margunn Aanestad   University of Oslo, Norway
Magnus Bergqvist   Halmstad University, Sweden
Fredrik Bergstrand   University of Gothenburg, Sweden
Erik Borglund   Mid Sweden University, Sweden
Morten Brandrup   Roskilde University, Denmark
Tone Bratteteig   University of Oslo, Norway
Katerina Cerna   University of Gothenburg, Sweden
Esbjörn Ebbesson   Halmstad University, Sweden

Sisse Finken	Linneaeus University, Sweden
Martin Gellerstedt	University West, Sweden
Kerstin Grundén	University West, Sweden
Amir Haj-Bolouri	University West, Sweden
Monika Hattinger	University West, Sweden
Ilona Heldal	University College Bergen, Norway
Ola Henfridsson	Warwick Business School, UK
Harald Holone	Østfold University College, Norway
Karin Högberg	University West, Sweden
Netta Iivari	University of Oulu, Finland
Will Jobe	University West, Sweden
Lars-Olof Johansson	University West, Sweden
Leona Johansson-Bunting	University of Gothenburg, Sweden
Viktor Kaptelinin	Umeå University, Sweden
Joakim Karlsson	Østfold University College, Norway
John Krogstie	Norwegian University of Science and Technology, Norway
Arto Lanamäki	University of Oulu, Finland
Jonas Landgren	Chalmers University of Technology, Sweden
Susanne Lindberg	Halmstad University, Sweden
Tomas Lindroth	University West, Sweden
Berner Lindström	University West, Sweden
Jesper Lund	Halmstad University, Sweden
Mona Lundin	University West, Sweden
Anita Mirjamdotter	Linneaeus University, Sweden
Judith Molka-Danielsen	Molde University College, Norway
Christina Mörtberg	Linneaeus University, Sweden
Stefan Nilsson	University West, Sweden
Livia Norström	University West, Sweden
Urban Nuldén	University of Gothenburg, Sweden
Jacob Nørbjerg	Copenhagen Business School, Denmark
Henry Oinas-Kukkonen	University of Oulu, Finland
Torbjörn Ott	University of Gothenburg, Sweden
Samuli Pekkola	Tampere University of Technology, Finland
Esko Penttinen	Helsinki School of Economics, Finland
Noora Pinjamaa	Aalto University, Finland
Tero Päivärinta	Luleå University of Technology, Sweden
Ada Scupola	Roskilde University, Denmark
Sofia Serholt	University of Gothenburg, Sweden
Anna Sigridur Islind	University West, Sweden
Maria Spante	University West, Sweden
Dick Stenmark	University of Gothenburg, Sweden
Susanne Stigberg	VUT, Austria
Frantisek Sudzina	Aalborg University, Denmark
Reima Suomi	University of Turku, Finland
Ann Svensson	University West, Sweden

Carsten Sørensen	London School of Economics and Political Science, UK
Michel Thomsen	Halmstad University, Sweden
Virpi Tuunainen	Aalto University School of Business, Finland
Tuure Tuunanen	University of Jyväskylä, Finland
Kristian Tørning	Danish School of Media and Journalism, Denmark
Helena Vallo Hult	University West, Sweden
Sara Willermark	University West, Sweden
Thomas Winman	University West, Sweden
Lena-Maria Öberg	Mid Sweden University
Christian Östlund	University West, Sweden

Contents

Preface

This book contains the proceedings of the IFIP Working Group 8.6 Conference, which was organized by University West and held in Ljungskile, Sweden, in August 2016.

The aim of the IFIP Working Group 8.6 is to foster the understanding of and improve research in practice, methods, and techniques involved in the transfer and diffusion of information technology within systems that are developed and in the development process itself.

The theme of the 2016 conference was "Diffusion of IS for Learning New Practices." The theme aims to encourage research into the challenges for learning and competent acting with regards to diffusion, adoption, and implementation of various forms of information technology. We aimed to address issues related to learning new practices from both the organizational and societal perspectives traditionally covered by IFIP Working Group 8.6.

A total of 11 manuscripts were submitted for the conference. The Program Committee undertook a double-blind reviewing process with at least two reviews for each paper. The four chairs used the reviews as well as their own evaluation to select four research papers to be included in these proceedings. Further, one panel was selected for presentation at the conference. Two keynote speakers were invited for the conference: Eleanor Wynn from Portland State University (USA) and Carsten Sørensen from the London School of Economics and Political Science (UK). Their talks were associated with the conference theme.

Our warmest thanks go to the research contributors and the sponsors of this conference, whether as organizers, Program Committee members, keynote speakers, or others. You made this a successful event.

May 2016

Ulrika Lundh Snis
Anna Sigridur Islind
Jan Pries-Heje
Jacob Nørbjerg

Organization IFIP 8.6 2016

General Chair

Jan Pries-Heje   Roskilde University, Denmark

Program Chairs

Ulrika Lundh Snis   Högskolan Väst, Sweden
Jacob Nørbjerg   Copenhagen Business School, Denmark

Organizing Chairs

Ulrika Lundh Snis   Högskolan Väst, Sweden
Anna Sigridur Islind   Högskolan Väst, Sweden

Proceedings Chair

Ulrika Lundh Snis   Högskolan Väst, Sweden

Working Group at Högskolan Väst/University West

Lars Svensson
Lena Pareto
Ulrika Lundh Snis
Stefan Nilsson
Anna Sigridur Islind

Program Committee

David Wainwright   Northumbria University, UK
Peter Bednar   University of Portsmouth, UK
Deborah Bunker   University of Sydney, Australia
Mohamamd Hossain   RMIT University, Australia
Michael Myers   University of Auckland Business School, New Zealand
David Wastell   Nottingham University, UK
Eleanor Wynn   Portland State University, Intel Corporation, USA
John Persson   Aalborg University, Denmark
Carsten Sørensen   London School of Economics, UK
Peter Axel Nielsen   Aalborg University, Denmark
Nancy Russo   Malmö University, Sweden
Björn Johansson   Lund University, Sweden
J.P. Allen   University of San Francisco, USA
John Venable   Curtin University of Technology, Australia
Amany Elbanna   Royal Holloway University of London, UK

Contents

SCIS 2016

Evolution of the Blog Genre: The Emergence of the Corporate Personal Blog

Noora Pinjamaa[(✉)]

Aalto University School of Business, Helsinki, Finland
Noora.pinjamaa@aalto.fi

Abstract. Drawing on existing findings on blog genres, this study contributes to previous research on blogs as virtual communities and computer-mediated communication channels. Excluding Herring et al.'s [5] research on blogs as a single genre and their importance in the internet ecology, further research is needed to understand specific developments within blogging technology. More specifically, there is a gap in examining the uses of blogs in a corporate context. With a case study of corporate communication through a blog, the aim of this research is to further the knowledge of corporate blogs and to advance the theoretical understanding of that particular type of blog.

Keywords: Blog · Blogging · Genre · Magazine · Word-of-mouth · Corporate blog

1 Introduction

Developed in the 1990s, blogs remain a pioneering social and technical innovation of the web 2.0 era. Blogging has evolved from the resemblance of a form of a diary, to being a highly valued collaborative social communication outlet [1]. Users writing blogs often focus on a specific topic such as technology, fashion or food [2]. As blogs have become more popular, some companies have seized the opportunity and either used independent blogs for commercial purposes or established corporate blogs [3, 4]. While studying blogs as an Internet genre, Herring et al. [5] observed that blogs could even be hybrids with both personal and professional characteristics.

There is evidence of successful corporate [6], private [7] and entrepreneurial bloggers, and their business models [8], but different types of blogs have often been studied in silos. Despite some examples of information systems research focusing on corporate blogging [9] a vast amount of research has mainly focused on user-generated blog platforms in which users update their personal blogs [7]. In a corporate context, blogs are often used for word-of-mouth (WOM) effects and information dissemination. However, blog communities are highly attentive and sensitive towards corporate or sponsored content. Previous research has identified various community responses when studying WOM communication and the knowledge exchange occurring between blogger and community [10]. When exposed to commercial content, blog communities are found to respond with positive and negative comments, or with supportive or accepting reactions [11, 12].

© Springer International Publishing Switzerland 2016
M. Gellerstedt et al. (Eds.): SCIS 2016, LNBIP 259, pp. 3–15, 2016.
DOI: 10.1007/978-3-319-43597-8_1

Apart from Herring et al.'s [5] research on blogs as a single genre and Dennis et al.'s [13] framework of corporate blogs and their visibility, further research is needed to understand specific developments within the blogging technology. Through a case study of a media company's blog community, the aim of this research is to further the understanding of the corporate uses of personal and professional blogs and to advance the theoretical understanding of corporate blogs by addressing the following research question:

RQ: How have corporate blogs changed over time?

2 Related Literature

2.1 Evolution of Blog Genres

Defined by Yates and Orlikowski "genres are typified communicative actions invoked in recurrent situations and characterized by similar substance and form" [14]. The users enacting the communicative actions within the blog genre, bloggers, are identified as early adopters [1] opinion leaders [15], [16] often motivated by gratification [7]. Bloggers are willing to experience, and pursue opportunities to share their experiences [17]. Readers of blogs seek enjoyment in various forms such as community membership [18], entertainment and inspiration [19] and are described as opinion seekers [20].

The blog genre is as a form of social media, which provides a media for argumentation and even to some extent, a substitute for traditional media [21, 22]. When compared to traditional media, especially professional bloggers are more prone to include product placements in their blogs. Despite containing less commercial information than for example magazines, blogs are often more effective due to the blogger's ability to provide information that is perceived as relevant to the blog readers [23].

As a way to deal with marketing challenges, companies have been collaborating with bloggers and paid them for consulting activities, for speaking at various events [24, 25], for publishing blog posts or for writing or appearing in corporate communication channels [24]. More specifically, there are several types of blogs within the blog genre, which provide different benefits to companies. The Table 1 below lists and describes blog types scholars have identified.

Table 1. Table of blog types.

Types of blogs	Description of blog
Corporate blog [4, 6, 10, 25–27]	• Internal use between company employees • External use to communicate company news and marketing messages to stakeholders • Updated by company employees
Professional blog [8, 28]	• The blogger is the owner of company • Main revenue originally based on blog success
A-list blog [29–31]	• Has high visitor rates, often employed by businesses • Maintains a freelancer-status (compensated on a commission-base)
Personal or private blog [7, 11]	• Engages in consumer-to-consumer WOM marketing • Transforms commercial information into a form suitable for the community
Mixed blog [5]	• Is a hybrid of private, public, personal and professional

Excluding corporate blogs and entrepreneurial bloggers, previous research finds that bloggers have commonly maintained a personal status in their blog communities. Personal, A-list blogs spare the effort of marketing the blog to companies as they only need to accept commercial content that they consider as suitable for their blog's narrative [11, 32]. One of the earliest examples of corporate blogging emerged from the software company Sun Microsystems. As the company's CEO started a corporate blog he challenged both the company's customers and employees to communicate with him directly and to provide unfiltered feedback [27].

2.2   Blogger Narratives and Their Business Value

The blog genre has a communication substance, which consists of a log history and a narrative that appeals to a specific audience. This constantly creates community expectations from the blogger. Unlike in traditional media in which the narrative of the stories is based on one-way communication, blog narratives are based on the premise of a two-way communication within the social online community. Depending on the blog's communication style, researchers have distinguished various narrative strategies amongst blogs [11, 32].

In a study on blogger narratives, Kozinets et al. identify four alternative blogger communication strategies as well as consequent responses to bloggers' commercial content [11]. The strategies are evaluation, explanation, embracing and endorsement. (1) Evaluation, conceals the blogger's participation in a campaign and explicitly acknowledges the community's norms, while (2) the narrative of explanation reveals the details of the campaign by even discussing the communal potential for conflict. (3) Embracing, is explicit about the commercial collaboration, uses professional, marketing language and often reflects polarized responses. (4) Endorsement, is characterized by a blogger's enthusiasm towards marketing promotions, whilst acknowledging that the content may not appeal to the whole community. From the four strategies, (3) embracing and (4) endorsement strategies are most often employed in brand communities and are more favorable towards commercialism [11].

Blogs with large communities may provide several benefits to companies. For a slowly digitalizing industry such as the media industry, blogs represent a forum for direct communication with consumers, allowing consumers to participate in the company's content creation [33]. Whilst media companies acknowledge the potential in incorporating social media features, such as bloggers to their websites, they still struggle with understanding the actions that the change requires as well as the necessity to measure engagement [33]. When using blogs for corporate communication, a manager should have an understanding of the form (observable linguistic features of communication) [14] and mechanics of the blog [34].

3   Netnographic Method and Case

This paper adopts a qualitative, interpretive approach to collecting and analyzing the data. Similarly to prior blog research [8, 11, 35, 36], netnography or online ethnography is used to study an online community and its computer-mediated discussions [37]. Netnography is suitable for an object of research such as a blog in which one expects to find a social tie amongst all members of a group [38]. Similar to interview data, netnographic data can be perceived as complex social, cultural and psychological expressions of the experiences of the individuals of a community [39]. The method "adapts the open-ended practice of ethnography to the contingencies of the online environment" [40]. Unlike surveys or interviews in which one would be constrained by their own choice of language and the questions presented, netnography offers a more complete understanding of the social and cultural environment [40]. The method provides tools for capturing the natural context and participative nature of a blog [11].

3.1 Case

Despite companies being slow in reacting to the change caused by digitalization they have strived to respond to the changes in demand by further emphasizing the role of advertising and by providing new types of digital goods and services. One of such successful endeavors results from cooperating with bloggers.

This paper focuses on a novel case study of a Finnish online magazine's TV show called Style Day. The case represents an innovative way for a traditional media company to offer digital content. The Style Day TV show was conceptualized with and marketed by the Strictly Style blog and was sponsored by advertisers. With around 12 000 unique monthly visitors [41], the 4-year-old Finnish Strictly Style blog [41] is today (in 2016) an employee of the women's lifestyle media and is blogging on the media's website [42]. The blog was awarded the title of Fashion Blog of 2014, in the Elle Style Awards [43].

The blog released a total of eight episodes of the online TV show Style Day. The episodes were originally published on the video-sharing platform Youtube. Each time a video was uploaded on Youtube, the blogger published a blog post related to the released episode, with the video embedded in the text-based blog article. In each episode ranging from a length of 5:26 min to 9:36 min, the blogger, in the role of a stylist and show hostess, together with a guest assistant (usually another A-list blogger) does a makeover for a reader. Readers could apply for a makeover in the show earlier in 2013. Each makeover consists of various clothing and accessories, provided by sponsoring advertisers. In addition to the product placements in the videos, the advertising brands were separately mentioned in the blog posts. During the release of the episodes, the blog's readers were also able to participate in sweepstakes in which they could win prizes from the sponsors. The TV show is the first show produced by the company.

Studying the blogger's posts and the readers' comments, with the focus on narratives permits uncovering both parties' motives [44] and better understanding the blog as a two-way communications forum. More importantly, the method allows for analyzing the blog genre's substance (topics expressed in the communication) and form [14]. The explored discussions include symbolic data such as emoticons and text. Although the blog is a lifestyle blog and cannot be compared to all blog categories such as political or technological, it is representative of A-list blogs [29, 30].

3.2   Blog Data Collection

The primary data consists of the Strictly Style blog's log from a two-month's period, from August 2013 to October 2013. The blog archive data for the research was collected in retrospect, with the consent of the blogger. The method of analysis included thematic coding and was divided into manual and semi-automated iterations to maximize result accuracy (Myers 2013). The semi-automated iterations were completed with the Leximancer software.

   The data collection time was selected on the basis of the online TV show. The data includes all the blog posts and comments from the beginning of the launch of the online TV show, until the release of the last episode. As seen in the upper right hand corner of the Fig. 1 below, The Style Day (Tyylipäivä in original language) online TV show is a product of Olivia, branded with the magazine's name (Olivia is mentioned under the show's name).

Fig. 1. Screenshot from the Olivia magazine's website with the TV show in the upper right corner

   Although the core interest is the communication about the show, all other blog posts and comments from the two-month (average 30 posts per month and 72619 words) data set were analyzed and inductively interpreted to uncover thematic categories [45]. When translating the blog data from Finnish to English, particular attention was paid to the original meaning, to ensure a truthful representation of the users' original intent.

3.3   Iterations

In addition to manually processing the data, the data mining tool Leximancer was used to further explore the data and verify assumptions from previous iterations [46]. The software permitted to generate a thesaurus highlighting connections between concepts in the blog's content. The semi-automated method of textual data mining supported the subjective perspective of the netnography and decreased the likelihood of researcher bias.

During the analysis, distinction was made between blog posts comprising and or lacking call-to-actions (CTA), and amid commercial and non-commercial posts. The complete data set was analyzed and interpreted various times during all of which, one or more categories were identified leading to new interpretations and modifications of existing meanings. Overall, twelve separate thematic categories were identified, six categories of blogger posts and six categories of reader comments (see Sects. 4.1 and 4.2).

4 Findings

For simplicity and confidentiality, the posts of the Strictly Style blogger and the comments from quoted readers are designated with pseudonyms *Blogger* and *Reader* (with an arbitrarily assigned number). Analyzing through Kozinets' et al.'s (2010) framework of narrative strategies, the blogger's narrative had most commonalities with endorsement and embracing strategies. The blog's communication consists of a soft-sell approach with embedded advertising. When the blogger first introduces the concept of the online TV show and reveals the show's developer, she uses the pronoun "we", referring to herself and her media company-employer, instead of "I".

> *Blogger: "...With pride **we** bring you Style Day, which is the first community-based online TV show produced in a fashion blog in Finland! ..."*

Such transparent embracing of the collaborating media company is a common characteristic of a brand-centered community.

4.1 The Blogger's Narrative Strategy

Ever since the blog was established in 2010, and throughout the two months of collected data the blog's narrative style remains authentic and faithful to its value proposition, described in the sidebar of the blog's webpage as follows:

> *"Mrs. V. A wife, a mother and a woman, who loves being one."*

Whilst the blog is portrayed with the following description:

> *"This blog is dedicated to fashion, beauty, healthy living and to all feminine. I strictly hold on to my privacy, therefore, this blog only scratches the surface of the wonderful thing we call life."*

The portrayal is consistent with the blog's narrative. When not blogging about the show she publishes posts about trends, fashion, as well as shares her travels and special events with her readers. The description suggests that the blogger does not intend her content as personal, and therefore gives a justification for including sponsored or company-endorsing content in her posts. However the analysis finds that the blogger's narrative does not change if posting commercial content. The following blogger's quote (categorized as category 4 in Table 2) exemplifies how instead of endorsing a brand with an explicit sales objective- and persuasion-orientated communication [11], the blogger maintains an interactive and rather informational narrative.

Table 2. Categories of blog posts (adapted from [2, 47])

Description of blogger communication	Frequency (%)
1. Blogger showing her appreciation of or thanking the readers	50 %
2. Blogger promoting Style Day (or magazine company)	20 %
3. Other (e.g. blogger empathizing with a reader or explaining herself)	12.5 %
4. Blogger endorsing or mentioning a brand/sponsored content	10 %
5. Blogger call-to-action (asking for readers' comments/opinion)	5 %
6. Blogger posting about or discussing fashion/trends	2.5 %

*Blogger: '...Great to also hear that **the store's staff** is also reliable. The letter exchanges that I've been pursuing with the London office have indeed left me with a positive impression. So you wont be upset if **good offers or tips** to the store are shared;)'*

The Table 2 below demonstrates six categories emerging from the blogger's posts and comments (the frequencies were derived from a total of 40 posts and comments). Most of the comments and posts consisted of several themes, from which the most dominant were counted. For example, when a reader enquired about a hat that the blogger is wearing in a picture and the blogger responds:

*Blogger: 'Thank you! I wear those way too seldom when thinking about how good they look and how comfortable they are! Unfortunately I cannot come up with an answer right now. But you can find black and Bordeaux-rouge ones in the **e-commerce store of Supertrash**! They ship to Finland!'*

The blogger's comment is categorized as category 4, a brand mention as she finishes by emphasizing that the Supertrash brand could be a solution for the reader. Overall, category 1 was the most common with a 50 % frequency. Below is an exemplar quote in which the blogger responds to a reader's feedback about the Style Day show.

*Blogger: '**Thank you so much** for the encouragements! You know, the beauty of this concept is that you don't have to "settle" for just my (and in this episode Mimmi's) [another A-list blog] styling, but **you get to also give YOUR own solutions** and tips for the challenge! :) More about that tonight! :)'*

Although the blogger persistently blogged about the online show, in each of the episodes and the sponsored competitions related to the show, her narrative consistently supported communal norms. This was reflected in the primarily positive response from the community. Also, the commerciality of the posts is softened with the use of emoticons, giving emotional cues on the blogger's intentions [20].

The blogger's narrative strategy explicitly exposes her warm relationship with the media company while strongly complying with communal norms. The narrative shifts between endorsement and embracing strategy [48]. The blogger is explicit about her involvement in the project but at the same time, highlights the online TV show's meaning for her community. She expresses her gratitude to the users for giving the idea of the show's concept. The blogger emphasizes that the reason why Style Day was executed was to fulfill the needs of her community. The following is a quote from the promotional blog post of the online TV show (representing category 2).

*Blogger: '...Tomorrow will launch the first episode of Style Day, which has been **inspired by you**! During the years, I have come to receive more and more email requests from you regarding various beauty and style issues... The problems were very typical and interesting. **We** wanted **to provide you** with useful solutions. That is how we came up with Style Day...'*

4.2   Characteristics of the Community

The more popular a blog is, the more is expected of her [19]. During both of the observed months, the blogger posted on a daily basis. The only exception surfaced at the end of the second month, during which the blogger had a short gap without a post, for which she immediately apologized for, and to which the readers reacted with approving comments in her next post.

From the iterations it was apparent that the blogger acknowledged the necessity of both asking questions from her audience and responding to at least 50 % of their questions. Table 3 displays the categories that emerged from the readers' comments. The frequencies are based on a total of 70 comments. Five out of the six categories represent positive responses to the blogger's posts.

Table 3.   Categories of reader comments (adapted from [2, 47])

Description of blog reader communication	Frequency (%)
1. Reader endorsing the online TV show, the blogger or her style	57.1 %
2. Reader sharing a tip or giving advice to the blogger/community	14.3 %
3. Reader giving feedback to/criticizing the blogger	11.4 %
4. Reader asking for advice/opinion or specific blog post content	8.6 %
5. Reader interacting with the community or responding to another reader	7.1 %
6. Reader defending blogger	1.4 %

An example of the interactive character of the blog emerged when the blogger announced the commencement of Style Day. Various readers commented by congratulating (category 1) her with the new project to many of which she politely responded by thanking for the kind words and supporting attitude.

*Reader 1: "Hey Hanna you are so **super!!** **Lovely** new conquest to which **you fit** better than **well! Congrats** and **good luck** for the future :D"*

The comment above demonstrates the nature of comments analyzed when evaluating the blogger's authenticity. There were no significant findings suggesting that the community would not approve the show or the blogger's endorsing attitude. Instead various readers were enthusiastic about the blogger's new commitment. Despite 20 % of the blogger's content being endorsements the blog community did not perceive the blogger as the magazine brand's ambassador but rather as a highly accomplished blogger with her TV show.

The readers' endorsing behavior (category 1) with 57.1 % of the comments was reinforced by the blogger's appreciative narrative. Some of the blogger's answers written to the readers were personified by thanking the reader by using his or her pseudonym. The blogger distinctly shows that she recognizes and appreciates the individuals in her community, which resonates well with the readers.

The Strictly Style blog has a warm tone across all her posts and comments, which depicts a close, friendly relationship with readers. Amongst the analyzed comments, the majority has thanked the blogger for her enjoyable writing style as well as for her mature reactions and responses to reader feedback. Examples of such comments:

> Reader 3: '**Thank you** for writing from your heart'
> Reader 4: '**Thank you** for a **sophisticated** blog. It is **nice** to read a blog that isn't a battlefield'

In addition to analyzing the patterns of communication of the blog, the reader comments were screened for evidence about the reactions to the product placements included in the Style Day online show. There were only a few comments addressing the brands included in the episodes, the type of which is sampled in the quotes below.

> Reader 5: '...In the future, it would be nice if you could **mention from which store/which brand's** clothes were selected to the model. I'm assuming that **Junarose's** clothing line was used in this first episode?'
> Reader 6: 'In the future I would also wish for longer episodes, this one gave me a sense of rush and I've also been missing details, why it would be good to focus on some aspects of dressing and **what clothing brands and accessories** were used :)'
> Reader 7: 'Hi! Do you have any idea whether that **Only's sweater** is coming **to the stores** in for example a week/month? ...'

Overall, most of the readers' comments were found to respond to a CTA of the blogger in the corresponding blog post. Similarly to previous research on A-list blogs [29, 30], this would suggest that the blogger has the power of an opinion leader in her community. There were a few comments that did not fit to any category, the amount of which was not however significant. One such an example is a comment, which only consists of a reader's hyperlink to his or her blog. Based on the data analysis, a pattern of the blogger-reader communication was recognized (see Fig. 2).

The most common pattern of communication started with (1) the blogger publishing a blog post usually containing a CTA to which (2) the reader responded with a comment either addressing directly the CTA or one of the pictures included in the post and the discussion ended approximately 50 % of the time with (3) the blogger still replying to the reader.

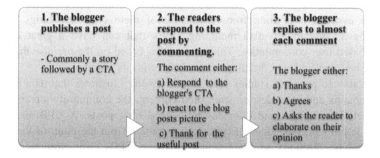

Fig. 2. The process of the blogger-reader communication

5 Discussion and Implications

With a netnographic method, this study analyzed the substance, linguistic features and communicative actions of a particular type of blog within the blog genre [14]. The most frequent type of communication consisted of the blogger expressing her appreciation and acknowledging the community. While the blog readers were found to respond to commercial content in six different ways (see Table 3), out of which only one represents a tempered, negative response. Based on the analysis of the blog and the rapport of the blog and her audience, it can be argued that the blog does not comply to the definition of a corporate blog, as presented in prior literature (see Table 1).

Corporate blogs are defined as channels which' discourse is primarily company-centered [6]. Despite some similarities, with only 20 % of the communication focusing on company brand communication, it is not representative of corporate blogs. The analysis shows that the audience does not perceive the blogger as equal to the media brand. Rather, the blogger is closer to the audience than a corporate blogger, such as the blogging CEO of Sun Microsystems [27]. The Strictly Style blog has a more personal relationship with her community.

The findings suggest that the blogger has characteristics from various types of bloggers. When compared to a priori defined blog types (see Table 1), this case study identifies an evolution within the blog type of corporate blogs. This corporate blog has characteristics similar to personal blogs and therefore is defined as a corporate-personal blogger (CPB). Despite her corporate employee status, the blogger has maintained the warm, personal relationship with her community that she established when she still was a personal blogger. Having such a personal relationship with her community provides her with an exceptional advantage. Unlike corporate blogs that are less personal and highly brand-focused, the discourse of a CPB is similar to branded storytelling. As such, CPBs provide information valued by and relevant to their audience.

5.1 Implications

In 2005, Herring et al. predicted that in the future blogs would become more diverse. This research confirms their prediction and argues for a need to revise the definition of corporate blogs. Due to the increased pressure for companies trying to stay relevant online and experienced bloggers becoming professional content creators, corporate blogs have evolved over time from consisting of mere corporate blogs officially managed by a company to also including CPBs that can have a great effect on consumer-based user communities. This argument is based on the premise that a CPB has established itself a loyal, trusting relationship with its community.

Comparably to previous studies [11, 32], this study illustrates that as a blogger's narrative remains authentic despite sponsored content, the community's responses do not vary between organic and company-influenced blog posts. A CPB such as the Strictly Style blogger, considers all commercial content from the point of view of the blog community. Similarly to professional bloggers, CPBs only promote ideas and brands that they can relate to [7]. The 12 categories of blog communication identified in this study provide a useful taxonomy for researchers to compare with other campaign communications within blog communities.

For practitioners, the taxonomy could be further extended and used for other purposes, such as to provide guidance for data analysts when assessing community responses to commercial blog communication. This case study highlights the benefits of employing personal blogs. Especially in the media industry, few companies have yet invested in developing forms of online collaboration that would go beyond traditional banner advertising. In order for managers to provide attractive online channels to advertisers, they should identify successful bloggers and collaborate with CPBs already from the beginning of the process of planning an online campaign.

6 Conclusion and Future Research

Blogs are a valuable tool for corporate communication when the content fits the stakeholders' needs [13]. This case study describes how a company proactively listens to their customers through a blog and embraces the customers' contributions to their new online product. This study has two key contributions to previous research on the blog genre. One, it argues for an evolution within the blog category of corporate blogs, a mix of corporate and personal blog, a CPB. Secondly, it analyzes linguistic features and develops a taxonomy consisting of two categorizations of blog and community communication patterns in a corporate context. Overall, the study provides insight into the evolving blog genre and yet growing blogging landscape as well as the possibilities for future research on further emerging categories and their implications.

The research has specific limitations. The data was collected from only one blog and focused primarily on the blogger-community communication. There are other aspects such as blog layout design features that could be considered and that could offer further explanation as to what impacts blog communication. Also, the data set is relatively small if compared to the number of blogs some researchers have studied [5]. Having a comparative case from another corporate context and using the taxonomy developed in this paper to guide content analysis could be fruitful.

References

1. Li, F., Du, T.C.: Who is talking? An ontology-based opinion leader identification framework for word-of-mouth marketing in online social blogs. Decis. Support Syst. **51**(1), 190–197 (2011)
2. Vaast, E., Davidson, E.J., Mattson, T.: Talking about technology: the emergence of a new actor category through new media. MIS Q. **37**(4), 1069–1092 (2013)
3. Baek, H., Ann, J.: Chronological analysis of the electronic word-of-mouth effect of four social media channels on movie sales: comparing Twitter, Yahoo! Movies, Youtube, and Blogs. In: Pacific Asia Conference on Information Systems (PACIS) (2014)
4. Orzan, G., Macovei, O.I., Orzan, L.M., Iconaru, C.: The impact of blogs over corporate marketing communications: an empirical model. Econ. Comput. Econ. Cybern. Stud. Res. **47**, 79–96 (2013)

5. Herring, S.C., Scheidt, L.A., Wright, E., Bonus, S.: Weblogs as a bridging genre. Inf. Technol. People **18**(2), 142–171 (2005)
6. Smudde, P.: Blogging, ethics and public relations: a proactive and dialogic approach. Public Relat. Q. **50**, 34 (2005)
7. Sepp, M., Liljander, V., Gummerus, J.: Private bloggers' motivations to produce content – a gratifications theory perspective. J. Mark. Manag. **27**(13–14), 1479–1503 (2011)
8. Pihl, C., Sandstrom, C.: Value creation and appropriation in social media - the case of fashion bloggers in Sweden BT - special issue on opening up innovation and business development activities. Int. J. Technol. Manag. **61**(3–4), 309–323 (2013)
9. Jackson, A., Yates, J., Orlikowski, W.: Corporate blogging: building community through persistent digital talk, pp. 1–10 (2007)
10. Baehr, C., Konstanze, A.-B.: Assessing the value of corporate blogs: a social capital perspective. IEEE Trans. Prof. Commun. **53**, 358–369 (2010)
11. Kozinets, R.V., De Valck, K., Wojnicki, A.C., Wilner, S.J.S.: Networked narratives: understanding word-of-mouth marketing in online communities. J. Mark. **74**, 71–89 (2010)
12. Quinton, S., Harridge-March, S.: Relationships in online communities: the potential for marketers. J. Res. Interact. Mark. **4**(1), 59–73 (2010)
13. Dennis, A.R., Minas, R.K., Lockwood, N.S.: Mapping the corporate blogosphere: linking audience, content, and management to blog visibility. J. Assoc. Inf. Syst. **17**(3), 162–193 (2016)
14. Yates, J., Orlikowski, W.: Genres of organizational communication: a structurational approach to studying communication and media. Acad. Manag. Rev. **17**(2), 299–326 (1992)
15. Summers, J.O.: Media exposure patterns of consumer innovators. J. Mark. **36**, 43–49 (1972)
16. Shoham, A., Ruvio, A.: Opinion leaders and followers: a replication and extension. Psychol. Mark. **25**, 280–297 (2008)
17. Guadagno, R.E., Okdie, B.M., Eno, C.A.: Who blogs? Personality predictors of blogging. Comput. Hum. Behav. **24**, 1993–2004 (2008)
18. Porter, C.E., Donthu, N., MacElroy, W.H., Wydra, D.: How to foster and sustain engagement in virtual communities. Calif. Manag. Rev. **53**(4), 80–111 (2011)
19. Baumer, E., Sueyoshi, M., Tomlinson, B.: Exploring the role of the reader in the activity of blogging. In: CHI 2008 Proceeding Twenty-Sixth Annual SIGCHI Conference on Human Factors in Computing Systems, pp. 1111–1120 (2008)
20. Xun, J., Reynolds, J.: Applying netnography to market research: the case of the online forum. J. Target. Meas. Anal. Mark. **18**(1), 17–31 (2010)
21. Straubhaar, J., LaRose, R., Davenport, L.: Media now: understanding media, culture, and technology. Cengage Learning, Boston (2013)
22. Tremayne, M., Weiss, A.S., Alves, R.C.: From product to service: the diffusion of dynamic content in online newspapers. J. Mass Commun. Q. **84**(4), 825–839 (2007)
23. Balasubramanian, S.K., Karrh, J.A., Patwardhan, H.: Audience response to product placements: an integrative framework and future research agenda. J. Advert. **35**(3), 115–141 (2006)
24. Müller, S., Goswami, S., Krcmar, H.: Monetizing blogs: revenue streams of individual blogs. In: European Conference on Information Systems (2011)
25. Hsu, C., Yang, S.O.: Achieving online relationship marketing via tourism blogs: a social network perspective achieving online relationship marketing via tourism. Pac. Asia J. Assoc. Inf. Syst. **5**(4), 1–25 (2013)
26. Lockwood, N.S., Dennis, A.R.: Exploring the corporate blogosphere: a taxonomy for research and practice, pp. 1–10 (2008)
27. Barker, P.: How social media is transforming employee communications at Sun Microsystems. Glob. Bus. Organ. Excell. **27**(4), 6–14 (2008)

28. Pinjamaa, N., Cheshire, C.: Blogs in a changing social media environment: perspectives on the future of blogging in Scandinavia. In: Twenty-Fourth European Conference on Information Systems (ECIS), Istanbul, Turkey, pp. 1–16 (2016)
29. Colliander, J., Dahlen, M.: Following the fashionable friend: the power of social media - weighing the publicity effectiveness of blogs versus online magazines. J. Advert. Res. **51**(1), 313 (2011)
30. Ko, H.-C.: Why are A-list bloggers continuously popular? Online Inf. Rev. **36**(3), 401–419 (2012)
31. MacDougall, R.: Identity, electronic ethos, and blogs: a technologic analysis of symbolic exchange on the new news medium. Am. Behav. Sci. **49**, 575–599 (2005)
32. Kulmala, M., Mesiranta, N., Tuominen, P.: Organic and amplified eWOM in consumer fashion blogs. J. Fash. Mark. Manag. **17**(1), 20–37 (2013)
33. Wikström, P., Ellonen, H.-K.: The impact of social media features on print media firms' online business models. J. Media Bus. Stud. **9**(3), 63–80 (2012)
34. Thorson, K.S., Rodgers, S.: Relationships between blogs as eWOM and interactivity, perceived interactivity, and parasocial interaction. J. Interact. Advert. **2000**(June), 39–51 (2004)
35. Kretz, G.: 'Pixelize Me!': a semiotic approach of self-digitalization in fashion blogs. Adv. Consum. Res. **37**(2003), 393–399 (2010)
36. Brodie, R.J., Ilic, A., Juric, B., Hollebeek, L.: Consumer engagement in a virtual brand community: an exploratory analysis. J. Bus. Res. **66**(1), 105–114 (2013)
37. Kozinets, R.V.: The field behind the screen: using netnography for marketing research in online communities (1999)
38. Kozinets, R.: Netnography (2010)
39. Moisander, J., Valtonen, A., Hirsto, H.: Personal interviews in cultural consumer research – post-structuralist challenges. Consum. Mark. Cult. **12**(4), 329–348 (2009)
40. Kozinets, R.V.: Click to connect: netnography and tribal advertising. J. Advert. Res. **46**(3), 279–288 (2006)
41. Blogilista: Strictly Style (2014)
42. Olivia osti suositun muotiblogin. Taloussanomat (2009)
43. Hirvonen, V.: "Elle Style Awards 2014: Ja palkinnon saa…"
44. Tsoukas, H., Hatch, M.J.: Complex thinking, complex practice: the case for a narrative approach to organizational complexity. Hum. Relat. **54**, 979–1013 (2001)
45. Walsham, G.: Doing interpretive research. Eur. J. Inf. Syst. **15**(3), 320–330 (2006)
46. Myers, M.D.: Qualitative research in information systems. MIS Q. Discov. **21**, 241–242 (1997)
47. Mishne, G., De Rijke, M.: A study of blog search. In: Advances in Information Retrieval, p. 12 (2006)
48. Kozinets, R.V., de Valck, K., Wojnicki, A.C., Wilner, S.J.: Networked narratives: understanding word-of-mouth marketing in online communities. J. Mark. **74**(2), 71–89 (2010)

'It Has to Be Useful for the Pupils, of Course'
– Teachers as Intermediaries in Design
with Children

Netta Iivari[✉] and Marianne Kinnula

INTERACT Research Unit, Faculty of Information Technology and Electrical
Engineering, University of Oulu, P.O. Box 3000, 90014 Oulu, Finland
{netta.iivari,marianne.kinnula}@oulu.fi

Abstract. We explore ways by which teachers act as intermediaries in information technology (IT) design with children through analyzing three of our
design projects conducted with schoolchildren and their teachers. In our projects
the teachers acted as informants and evaluators, but not as IT design partners,
albeit they had a lot of decision-making power as steering-group members of the
projects. The teachers offered valuable understanding of children through their
general knowledge about child development and their knowledge of their class.
Teachers also acted as valuable facilitators in the design process, enhancing
children's participation in the design process. They also acted as advocates of
children and their learning. They considered children's learning goals and fit
with the curriculum and developed their own skills and knowledge to serve
children's learning. Occasionally, they also acted as advocates of children's
interests more generally; however, not in the sense of critical tradition.

Keywords: School · Children · Teachers · Intermediary

1 Introduction

When designing information technology (IT), it is pivotal to invite users into the design
process. In information systems (IS) research, user participation has been one of the
central themes for decades [18]. Especially user participation has been highlighted in
the Scandinavian tradition [8] and more recent participatory design (PD) tradition [30].
The whole existence of the discipline of Human Computer Interaction (HCI) has also
been legitimized through the rhetoric on 'representing the users' [2]. These disciplines
and traditions share the assumption that users need to be involved in the design process.
Another shared assumption concerns the need of various kinds of intermediaries to
cater for users' needs and to facilitate users' participation in the design process. In HCI,
PD and IS research, there is on-going discussion related to such intermediaries. Even
during the early days of IS research, not only workers and systems designers were
expected to collaborate but trade unions were also needed [8]. In the more recent
literature a variety of intermediaries has been brought up [14, 30, 31].

Today, systems are no longer designed only for workers, their work practices, and the
workplace, but instead for a variety of people with a diversity of needs within an array of
contexts of use (e.g. [16, 18, 30]), e.g. for children [4]. The Interaction Design and

M. Gellerstedt et al. (Eds.): SCIS 2016, LNBIP 259, pp. 16–28, 2016.
DOI: 10.1007/978-3-319-43597-8_2

Children (IDC) research community has specifically concentrated on the research topic of IT design for and with children. Within this community, IT solutions and design methods suitable for children have been introduced, allowing and supporting children's participation in the design process [33]. IDC researchers have also contemplated on the role of other parties potentially needed in the design process. One such party is teachers, related to whom a number of benefits and problems has also been identified. However, a careful consideration of teachers' role as intermediaries in IT design with children is still missing in the IDC literature. For such, the existing IS and HCI research offers useful insights, enabling a systematic and nuanced examination of the topic.

This paper contributes by exploring ways by which teachers act as intermediaries in design processes with children. By examining three of our previous projects in which we have carried out design together with children and their teachers, we identify a number of activities teachers have been involved in as intermediaries as well as different roles teachers have adopted in the design process with children.

Next, we review the existing IDC literature addressing IT design with children and teachers' role in that. Thereafter, we present an analytical lens for making sense of the intermediary position of teachers, built on the existing IS and HCI literature. Then, the research design and cases involved in this study are described, after which the empirical results are outlined. We conclude by summarizing the results, discussing their implications and limitations, and identifying paths for future work.

2   IT Design with Children and Teachers

In IDC research the main aim is to create high quality IT for children, with children [33]. Especially children's participation in IT design has gained attention. The significance of the school context and teachers in design work with children has also been acknowledged long ago. Especially when designing or evaluating educational technology, school environment is a natural field setting and teachers a suitable expert group to be involved [7, 22, 23, 27, 32]. More generally, IDC researchers have recognized that teachers are 'significant adults' in children's lives [4, 21, 24]. Teachers are needed for allowing design sessions in their classrooms [6]. This may involve teachers making changes into their teaching plans [4, 6]. Collaboration with teachers is important for fitting the design activities with the existing curriculum so that the classroom time can be justified [4, 7, 28].

Part of the IDC community is relatively critical regarding teachers' participation: they warn that teachers' participation may hamper children's possibilities to take part in design as equal members [3–5, 9]. Teachers usually are in charge in the classroom and children are used to following orders and being tested by teachers, and this may be detrimental from the viewpoint of design in which everyone's expertise is to be valued on an equal basis and all are to contribute equally [3–5, 9]. Because of this, there have been suggestions for changing the power structures between teachers and children e.g. by placing the design activities somewhere else than school, or by letting children start projects before teachers and thus to become 'experts', able to teach teachers when they join the projects [6]. A similar type of approach has also been utilized when giving children a possibility to teach teachers in use of new IT [22].

Positive findings regarding teachers' role in the design process can also be found. Teachers can be invited as informants or evaluators into the design process: they can offer information for the basis of defining suitable learning goals for a design solution, and they can evaluate achievement of those later on [23, 29, 32]. Teachers can also take care of practical arrangements [25] and help children to focus on design tasks [19, 20, 22]. They can collect data [4] and help children and designers to understand each other [19, 20, 22]. They can comment on the planned activities and used language [19, 23, 26, 28] and participate in evaluating project results [20].

3   Analytical Lens

In the existing IS and HCI research, intermediaries have been called for to cater for users' needs and to facilitate user participation in the design process [13, 14, 30, 31]: e.g. in the HCI literature HCI professionals have been positioned as needed advocates of users, who are to 'represent the user' both in presentational and political senses, i.e. to know the users and deliver this knowledge to design and to speak if not fight for the user in the design process, as well as to facilitate collaboration among users and designers [1, 2, 10–13]. In the Computer Supported Cooperative Work (CSCW) literature, ethnographers have been seen as essential for systems design: they are to acquire thorough understanding of users' work practices through their ethnographic fieldwork and to communicate this understanding to the design [15]. In the CSCW literature, user advocates, i.e. people having thorough understanding of users, have also been called for to 'speak for the users' in the development [17]. In the IS literature, change agents have been called for to enable and facilitate user participation [18]. Clearly divergent positions can be identified, however: while the mainstream IS literature argues for enabling and facilitating user participation to serve the needs of the organization and the management, critical IS literature influenced by the Scandinavian tradition calls for facilitating user participation for the purpose of emancipating the users and for combating the organization and management goals [31].

Particularly HCI professionals' intermediary position between users and developers has received attention during the past years. In addition to different activities these intermediaries are to perform in the design process (see above), the literature has also identified a number of HCI professionals' roles in the design process: they have been positioned as informants, evaluators, design participants, or authoritative designers [11]. In an informant position, HCI professionals merely offer information for developers; the information may be based on their empirical user studies or on some general HCI theory or guidelines. As evaluators, HCI professionals comment on the design solutions, again relying on their empirical user feedback or some general HCI guidelines. However, HCI professionals may also be invited into design teams as active participants, having some decision-making power. On some occasions, HCI professionals may even be allowed to act as actual, authoritative designers, having the power to make influential design decisions regarding the design solution [11].

As a summary, various kinds of intermediaries have been recommended for 'representing the user' in the design process and for enabling users' participation. Some of them are expected to offer understanding of users to designers (e.g. HCI professionals, ethnographers), others to stand for or to speak on behalf of users during the design process (e.g. HCI specialists, user advocates), while some are to facilitate cooperation among users and designers during the design process (e.g. HCI professionals, IS change agents) [31]. Equipped with these tools and distinctions, we will make sense of teachers' roles and contribution as intermediaries in the design process with children.

4   Research Design

This study was initiated in cooperation with a national LUKUINTO ("Joy of Reading") programme in Finland, to encourage children to increase their literacy skills and interest in reading. IS/HCI researchers were invited to contribute. They, together with their Masters' level students, initiated small-scale research and development projects, which also included representatives from the LUKUINTO programme and local schools, including some teachers and pupils. The projects included designing games for young people for the purpose of increasing their literacy skills and reading interest, while later the focus was broadened to educating children in game design and more generally in IT design. In this paper, we study three projects. They are similar in many respects but also offer versatility as regards possible teacher roles and activities as one was organized during the LUKUINTO programme, while two have been conducted afterwards with teachers initiating the cooperation.

4.1   Project A

The project was initiated by the IS/HCI researchers and the LUKUINTO representatives and it aimed to increase the literacy skills and reading interest of children by letting children design a game, to develop a game editor to enable children to develop games and to educate and empower children in IT design. It was essential to allow children to participate as much as possible. A teacher volunteered to take part and she was invited into the steering group of the project. The project work was part of normal schoolwork for the pupils: it was integrated into their Finnish language lessons.

The participants were one class of 7th graders (13–14 years) in a local comprehensive school. The Masters' level students worked extensively with the class: they organized workshops on game ideation, design, evaluation and editor evaluation. The children acted as design partners and evaluators.

Data of the project includes multimodal data of workshops with children, game and editor development related data, project management data, results reports, short interviews with children, and a teacher interview.

4.2   Project B

This project was initiated after the LUKUINTO programme ended. A teacher familiar with the work of the IS/HCI researchers initiated cooperation. A Masters' level student project was established. The teacher acted as the customer and set the project aims: to develop a game supporting children's learning in different school subjects (history,

English language, Finnish as native language) and to involve children as much as possible in game development. The teacher chose the theme of the game so that it served children's learning related to the historical phenomenon of immigration and made collaboration between different school subjects possible. Several teachers responsible for these subjects were involved in the project, while the customer teacher was part of the steering group of the project. The project work was integrated in the normal schoolwork of the pupils.

Altogether, 58 8th graders (13–14 years) and 37 7th graders (12–13 years) from different classes from a local comprehensive school took part in the study. All 7th and 8th graders took part in game design. They created the base story for the game that the Masters' level students implemented. In addition, they created mini-games to complement the main story line. Ten 8th graders also coded parts of the game. Six 7th graders tested the final game, three 8th graders arranging the tests. The game is currently in use at the school history and English subject classes for 7th and 8th graders. Overall, the children acted as design partners and evaluators of the new game, and as participatory designers when arranging the tests for the younger children.

Data of the project includes game development related data, interviews of 8th graders arranging the testing of the game, project management data, results reports, and two teacher interviews.

4.3   Project C

This project was also initiated after the LUKUINTO programme ended. One of the students from a previous Masters' level student project had been hired into a local comprehensive school and he advertised the possibility of organizing such projects. A teacher initiated cooperation and a Masters' level student project was again established. The teacher as the customer set the project aims: to develop a game based on a Finnish national epic to support children's literacy skills and reading interest, and to involve children in game development as much as possible. The teacher and the former Masters' student working in the school were part of the steering group. The work was integrated with Finnish language lessons and was part of normal schoolwork for the pupils.

Altogether, 20 9th graders (14–15 years) and 7 8th graders (13–14 years) from different classes from a comprehensive school took part in the study. The 9th graders were responsible for game design. They created the story for the game that the Master's level students implemented. The 9th graders evaluated the game and then invited seven 8th graders to test the final game, the 9th graders arranging the tests. Overall, the children acted as design partners and evaluators of the new game and as participatory designers when arranging the tests for the younger children.

Data of the project includes game development related data, project management data, results reports, and two teacher interviews.

4.4   Data Analysis

When analyzing the data, we went through the project documentation of all the three projects and collected and categorized information based on the analytic lens developed in Sect. 3. The focus was on locating evidence on the activities and roles of the teachers in the projects. First an analysis was carried out on each project separately, after which the data was combined to form an overall understanding. The data was abstracted to a table form for synthesis and comparison. During this phase, the data was also extensively discussed to ensure that we agreed with the interpretations.

5 Empirical Insights

In Fig. 1, teachers' activities as intermediaries are summarized.

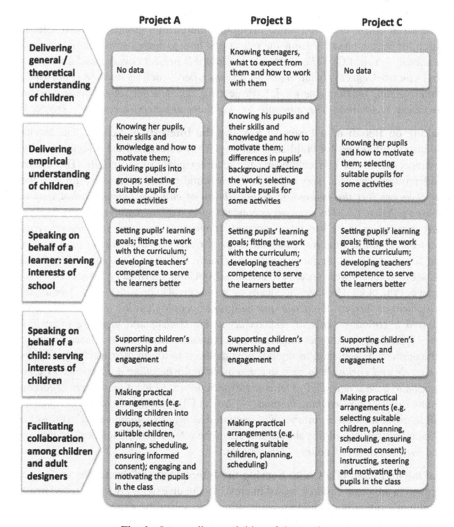

Fig. 1. Intermediary activities of the teachers

Delivering General Understanding of Children. The teachers contributed to the design process through 'knowing children' and through delivering this understanding to the design process. Teachers have a general understanding of children – their development and education related issues – based on their teacher education and experience. In Finland, the qualifications required from teachers are defined in the legislation. All teachers in general education hold a Master's degree and have pedagogical training. This provides a very useful basis for considering which kind of tasks suit children and their development. As an example, a teacher advises about working with teenagers: *"When teenagers are involved, (...) anything can happen. Most likely they behave well, but you can get any kind of feedback"* (Project C).

Delivering Empirical Understanding of Children. Teachers also know their pupils as individuals. This may also be very valuable information for the design process. Teachers can utilize this, e.g., when dividing children into groups or when selecting children for certain tasks: *"I know the pupils and how to make certain pupils work and get excited."* (Project C) *"The class selected into this project is very good ability-wise, so they can work effectively during those lessons where teaching must be condensed so that there is time for the game work."* (Project A) *"The teacher selects the test persons to avoid e.g. a situation where people are laughing at others' creations"* (Project C).

Speaking on Behalf of a Learner: Serving the Interests of School. The teachers acted also as advocates for children's learning. They considered the design work from the perspective of the curriculum and the learning goals of the pupils. The teachers considered these goals as very valuable for the children and tried to ensure they were met: *"Teacher has the pedagogic responsibility of children learning what they are supposed to learn. (...) The challenges concern specifically scheduling. In the final year of the curriculum there are many different language, literature, and media related issues that should be integrated into the project. Otherwise it would not be possible to spend so many lessons on dealing with one classic."* (Project C) Some of the learning goals set by teachers were specific to certain school subjects (history, project B; Finnish language, Project C). However, the learning goals can also be wider, e.g.: *"about game development as well as about working with other people than the teacher only, group work and negotiation skills as well as about the content and meaning of multi-literacies."* (Project A) Another important observation is that this was a learning process for the teachers as well, e.g. as regards new methods to use in their teaching: *"I joined this eagerly and curiously to gain new perspective for handling a classic (...) I expect the pupils to gain a new kind of learning experience (...) I want to actively experiment with and develop new teaching methods."* (Project C) *"I would like to learn as much as possible about multidisciplinary collaboration and project management."* (Project B). At the end of the day, all this should still serve the interests of the learner: *"it has to be useful for the pupils, of course"* (Project B).

Speaking on Behalf of a Child: Serving the Interests of Children. The teachers can be argued to advocate children's own interests too, to an extent. Project A relied heavily on children's interests as children were allowed to select the game theme, whereas in other projects it was defined by the teachers. Children's participation and ownership as regards the project and its outcome were nevertheless considered important: *"[It is important that] children feel that the game was made by themselves."* (Project C) *"It has* *been positive to see the excitement of the pupils (...) For many, traditional Finnish language lessons are not so interesting, so it has been great to see how excited they have been about this."* (Project A) In Project B the teacher also highlighted how important it is to advertise the results to other pupils: *"It would be important to let all try out the first version [of the game] to make the pupils' contribution visible. All [other] pupils could be informed about this project."* The teachers wanted the children to feel personally 'rewarded' in the projects. However, from the perspective of critical tradition, children need to be empowered to combat their oppressors and the organization and management goals. Our projects did not include any evidence of the teachers speaking on behalf of children in this critical sense, however.

Facilitating Collaboration Among Children and Adult Designers. The teachers also were a useful resource during the actual design sessions: they know how to motivate, inspire, and handle children and how to make things happen in the classroom: *"Teacher does a lot of pre-work with children so that everything happens smoothly and efficiently when [designers] enter the school and work with children (...) We decided together with [a former Master's student] that we hide the coloring pens in a closet as some pupils concentrated on coloring and not on what they were expected to. Some pupils were like: 'what, can't I color', but we were tough."* (Project C) *"The teacher mainly supported [working], walking among the pupils. (...) The interest was attempted to be aroused after the break with 'spies', according to [the teacher's] advice. One person was selected from every group to ['spy'] the outcomes of the other groups."* (Project A) The teachers were also active in ensuring that informed consent was gained from the parents. Teachers were also involved in selecting children for some activities: *"Pupils were selected with the help of the teacher. The project group asked for eager pupils as testers"* (Project A).

In Fig. 2, teachers' roles in the design process are summarized.

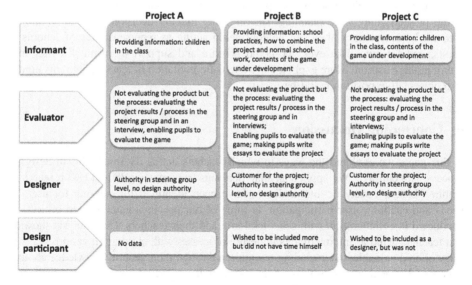

Fig. 2. Intermediary roles of the teachers

Acting as an Informant. The teachers clearly acted as informants in the projects, offering information about children for the design team: general information about the particular age group as well as specific information about their pupils. Moreover, they offered information for the basis of the design work, i.e. what they wanted the developed games to make children learn, i.e. contents of the national epic, or history. They also gave designers a lot of information of good working practices with school and how to plan the collaboration projects.

Acting as an Evaluator. Moreover, the teachers acted as evaluators of the process. They were interviewed during the project and they were also members of the steering groups of these projects, through which they were inevitably evaluating the progress and the outcome of the projects. Teachers also have a lot of expertise related to evaluating learning and that definitely could have been utilized more in the projects. Two of the teachers actually asked children to write essays related to their game development experiences after the projects had ended, thereby inviting children to reflect on and evaluate their learning. We could have invited the teachers to evaluate the developed games and to plan the evaluation of the process in collaboration with us, so that their valuable expertise would have been utilized better.

Acting as a Design Participant. The teachers did not act as design participants in the game design process. We did not even consider this option; however, the teacher in Project C specifically pointed out that she would have liked to take part in the design work: *"Would it be possible to include the teacher [in game development], my fingers were itching to make speech bubbles."* The teacher in Project B also mentioned his wish to take part and understand the game development process better. This could be taken into account in our future projects better as well.

Acting as a Designer. The teachers obviously were not in an authoritative designer position, as they were not involved in game design at all. On the other hand, they had a lot of authority and decision-making power as customers and steering group members in the projects: they were planning, steering, and making decisions in collaboration with us. In this position they can be considered acting as representatives of schools, pupils, and learning. However, we could prepare and support them much better in acting in this position. More explicit and systematic invitation of teachers into this kind of representative position could be useful.

6 Concluding Discussion

In this paper we explored the ways in which teachers act as intermediaries in design process with children. We applied an analytical lens from existing IS and HCI research, within which a variety of intermediaries have been identified for catering for users' needs and enabling user participation, to three of our previous game design projects, conducted in collaboration with schoolchildren and their teachers. Our analysis shows that teachers acted as intermediaries in design processes with children in various ways. They offered valuable understanding of children through their general knowledge about child development as well as through their knowledge of their class. They also acted as advocates of pupils and their learning. They especially considered children's learning goals and the project fit with the curriculum and also developed their own skills and knowledge to be able to serve the children and their learning even better. On some occasions they also seemed to act as advocates of children's interests more generally, e.g. when they highlighted how important it is for children to feel ownership of the outcome and celebrated children's interest and engagement in the design work. However, the teachers did not act as children's advocates in the sense of critical tradition, which would have necessitated advocating the empowerment of children to combat the organization and management goals, i.e., the school and learning goals in this case. Then again, the teachers acted as valuable facilitators in the design process: they made many practical arrangements and motivated, encouraged, steered, and instructed children during the design work. Overall, the teachers acted as informants and evaluators in the design process, but they did not act as design partners or authoritative designers in actual game design. However, they were active decision-makers as regards the goals and workings of the projects on a more general level.

We contribute to the existing literature addressing the position and contribution of teachers in IT design with children through offering a systematic and nuanced examination of teachers' roles and activities that was inspired by the IS and HCI literature on intermediaries in IT design. This study gives names to the issues that have been reported also previously but that have not been treated explicitly or systematically.

Overall, we maintain that we should try to take better advantage of the skills and competencies of teachers when organizing our design projects. Teachers can be considered as valuable intermediaries in IT design with children as they, e.g.:

- Have developmental knowledge of children: what is difficult/easy/suitable for children at particular age/stage of development [9]
- Have intimate knowledge of their pupils: of their background, homes, life situations, preferences, skills, and knowledge [21]
- Have knowledge of how to work with children (e.g. encourage, motivate, steer, instruct) [19, 20, 22, 23, 26, 28]
- Can fit design work with meaningful learning goals and the curriculum [4, 6, 7]
- Are experts in the evaluation of learning and can thus help in defining project goals and metrics for evaluating the achievement of those [20, 23, 29, 32]
- Want children's best; learning-wise but also more generally related to helping children to grow into better persons

However, we acknowledge that teachers' participation in IT design with children can also be criticized. Teachers may hamper the design process as they, e.g.:

- May make children conform to hierarchies and usual ways of working in the school context, hindering children's creativity and design contribution [3–5, 9]
- Do not necessarily know much about IT and design [22, 27, 28] and thus may misunderstand the project aims and guide the project towards wrong direction

In our projects the teachers carried out the activities and adopted the roles without any explicit assignment or request. On the other hand, many of them are quite natural for teachers to adopt: to offer understanding of children to designers, to speak on behalf of children's learning in the project, and to facilitate cooperation among users and designers in the classroom. However, the teachers were not experts in IT design and they would not have been able to plan the activities and roles in advance, but those just emerged ad hoc, in situ. We did not plan for them either, but appreciated them after the fact. It seems that teachers are quite well equipped for acting as intermediaries in IT design with children; however, the work would surely have benefitted from a more explicit and systematic approach to it. Moreover, empowering children to combat their oppressors was not something that the teachers advocated; rather, they advocated the management and organization goals in the sense of the school and the curriculum. Some other intermediaries may be needed to take care of children's empowerment in the critical sense, if that is considered as significant in a design project.

The intermediaries 'representing the user' in industry have been criticized for lacking power to make design decisions [10, 11], i.e. they mainly occupy weak informant and evaluator positions. The teachers actually occupied very powerful positions as steering group members, shaping the project goals and workings according to their agendas and interests. Hence, the teachers had their own interests and agendas, too; they were not merely representing the children. Due to this, children are the ones who actually should gain more decision-making power in design projects, to develop their agency and to empower them to have a say in issues concerning their life, instead of teachers, who already occupy quite a powerful position in school and in relation to pupils. Hence, empowering teachers is not our main goal. However, we hope that by empowering teachers and by giving them new tools and understanding for their central purpose, i.e., being useful to the pupils and serving children's learning, we also empower children a bit.

Moreover, as some teachers were eager to join in as game designers, we should in the future consider inviting them as participants into the design process. However, we might have limited time and resources to teach teachers what we expect from adults working as design partners with children. Thus, we need to consider very carefully what kind of tasks and task assignments we use and how we explain to the teachers how this kind of design work is different to normal schoolwork.

We observe many similarities between the work of teachers and the other inter-mediaries discussed in the literature [13–15, 18, 22, 30, 31]. Our results may bear relevance for other design contexts, too. For example in the case of health IT, in addition to designers and users, there may be e.g. healthcare professionals, relatives and friends, social workers and educationists available and needed to carry out the activities and adopt the roles the teachers did in our projects. We suggest that both researchers and practitioners reflect on our results in their design contexts and consider whether they can utilize them when planning and implementing their projects. Awareness and use of these concepts may help in formalizing the intermediary position and making conscious choices between different possibilities.

Future research is definitely needed to understand and appreciate the variety of intermediaries and their contribution in IT design. This study was based on three small-scale projects with many limitations and specifics. One clear limitation is that the children's voices were not really heard in this study. In the future, studies scrutinizing teachers' role in IT design with children should be carried out from the children's perspective. In addition, in this study a set of teachers' roles and activities were identified, but likely even more variety could be identified in other settings.

Nevertheless, we think that we succeeded in illustrating interesting versatility in the teachers' intermediary position in IT design with children.

Acknowledgements. We thank the teachers, pupils, Master's level students and LUKUINTO programme representatives for participating in this study. Especially we thank Tonja Molin-Juustila for her contribution.

References

1. Bødker, S., Buur, J.: The design collaboratorium – a place for usability design. ACM Trans. Comput.-Hum. Interact. **9**(2), 152–169 (2002)
2. Cooper, C., Bowers, J.: Representing the users: notes on the disciplinary rhetoric of human-computer interaction. In: Thomas, P. (ed.) The Social and Interactional Dimensions of Human-Computer Interfaces, pp. 48–66. Cambridge University Press, Cambridge (1995)
3. Druin, A.: Cooperative inquiry: developing new technologies for children with children. In: Proceedings of CHI, pp. 592–599 (1999)
4. Druin, A.: The role of children in the design of new technology. Behav. Inf. Technol. **21**(1), 1–25 (2002)
5. Druin, A., Bederson, B., Boltman, A., Miura, A., Knotts-Callahan, D., Platt, M.: Children as our technology design partners. In: Druin, A. (ed.) The Design of Children's Technology, pp. 51–72. Kaufmann, San Francisco (1998)
6. Druin, A., Bederson, B., Hourcade, J., Sherman, L., Revelle, G., Platner, M., Weng, S.: Designing a digital library for young children: an intergenerational partnership. In: Proceedings of ACM/IEEE Joint Conference on Digital Libraries, pp. 398–405 (2001)
7. Garzotto, F.: Broadening children's involvement as design partners: from technology to "experience". In: Proceedings of IDC, pp. 186–193 (2008)
8. Greenbaum, J., Kyng, M. (eds.): Design at Work. Cooperative Design of Computer Systems. Lawrence Erlbaum Associates, New Jersey (1991)
9. Guha, M., Druin, A., Fails, J.: Cooperative inquiry revisited: reflections of the past and guidelines for the future of intergenerational co-design. Int. J. Child Comput. Interact. **1**(1), 14–23 (2013)
10. Gulliksen, J., Boivie, I., Göransson, B.: Usability professionals – current practices and future development. Interact. Comput. **18**(4), 568–600 (2006)
11. Iivari, N.: Understanding the work of an HCI practitioner. In: Proceedings of NordiCHI, pp. 185–194 (2006)
12. Iivari, N.: Culturally compatible usability work - an interpretive case study on the relationship between usability work and its cultural context in software product development organizations. J. Organ. End User Comput. **22**(3), 40–65 (2010)
13. Iivari, N.: Usability specialists as boundary spanners – an appraisal of usability specialists' work in multiparty distributed open source software development effort. In: Kotzé, P., Marsden, G., Lindgaard, G., Wesson, J., Winckler, M. (eds.) INTERACT 2013, Part II. LNCS, vol. 8118, pp. 571–588. Springer, Heidelberg (2013)
14. Iivari, N., Karasti, H., Molin-Juustila, T., Salmela, S., Syrjänen, A.L., Halkola, E.: Mediation between design and use – revisiting five empirical studies. Hum. IT J. Inf. Technol. Stud. Hum. Sci. **10**(2), 81–126 (2009)

15. Karasti, H.: Increasing sensitivity towards everyday work practice in system design. Acta Universitatis Ouluensis, Scientiae Rerum Naturalium A 362. Oulu University Press, Oulu (2001)

16. Kyng, M.: Bridging the gap between politics and techniques: on the next practices of participatory design. Scand. J. Inf. Syst. 22(1), 49–68 (2010)

17. Mambrey, P., Mark, G., Pankoke-Babatz, U.: User advocacy in participatory design: designers' experiences with a new communication channel. Comput. Support. Coop. Work 7 (3–4), 291–313 (1998)

18. Markus, M., Mao, Y.: User participation in development and implementation: updating an old tired concept for today's IS contexts. J. Assoc. Inf. Syst. 5(11–12), 514–544 (2004)

19. Mazzone, E., Iivari, N., Tikkanen, R., Read, J., Beale, R.: Considering context, content, management, and engagement in design activities with children. In: Proceedings of IDC, pp. 108–117 (2010)

20. Mazzone, E., Read, J., Beale, R.: Design with and for disaffected teenagers. In: Proceedings of NordiCHI, pp. 290–297 (2008)

21. Molin-Juustila, T., Kinnula, M., Iivari, N., Kuure, L., Halkola, E.: Multiple voices in ICT design with children – a nexus analytical enquiry. Behav. Inf. Technol. 34(11), 1079–1091 (2015)

22. Pardo, S., Vetere, F., Howard, S.: Broadening stakeholder involvement in UCD: designers' perspectives on child-centred design. In: Proceedings of OzCHI, pp. 1–9 (2005)

23. Pardo, S., Vetere, F., Howard, S.: Teachers' involvement in usability testing with children. In: Proceedings of IDC, pp. 89–92 (2006)

24. Read, R., Bekker, M.: The nature of child computer interaction. In: Proceedings of BHCI, pp. 163–170 (2011)

25. Read, J., Gregory, P., MacFarlane, S., McManus, B., Gray, P., Patel, R.: An investigation of participatory design with children-informant, balanced and facilitated design. In: Proceedings of IDC, pp. 53–64 (2002)

26. Read, J., MacFarlane, S.: Using the fun toolkit and other survey methods to gather opinions in child computer interaction. In: Proceedings of IDC, pp. 81–88 (2006)

27. Robertson, J.: Experiences of designing with children and teachers in the StoryStation project. In: Proceedings of IDC, pp. 29–41 (2002)

28. Rode, J., Stringer, M., Toye, E., Simpson, A., Blackwell, A.: Curriculum-focused design. In: Proceedings of IDC, pp. 119–126 (2003)

29. Scaife, M., Rogers, Y., Aldrich, F., Davies, M.: Designing for or designing with? Informant design for interactive learning environments. In: Proceedings of CHI, pp. 343–350 (1997)

30. Simonsen, J., Robertson, T. (eds.): Routledge International Handbook of Participatory Design. Routledge, New York (2013)

31. Tuovila, S., Iivari, N.: Bridge builders in IT artifact development. In: Proceedings of ECIS, pp. 819–830 (2007)

32. Virvou, M., Tsiriga, V.: Involving effectively teachers & students in the life cycle of an intelligent tutoring system. Educ. Technol. Soc. 3(3), 511–521 (2000)

33. Yarosh, S., Radu, Y., Hunter, S., Rosenbaum, E.: Examining values: an analysis of nine years of IDC research. In: Proceedings of IDC, pp. 136–144 (2011)

Sound Bubbles for Productive Office Work

Martin Ljungdahl Eriksson[(✉)] and Lena Pareto

Media and Design, University West, 461 32 Trollhättan, Sweden
{Martin.Ljungdahl-Eriksson,Lena.Pareto}@hv.se

Abstract. A growing number of organizations are moving towards more open and collaborative workplaces. In these offices workers share a common open space, often with flexible seating based on activities, so called activity-based offices. Most problems in these workplaces are related to sound. Thus, the question of how to design suitable acoustic environments, supporting both collaborative and individual work, has emerged. Noise-reduction approaches do not suffice. In this study we explored the possibility of adding context-sensitive, activity-based sound environments to enhance the office workplace. For this purpose, we developed the "sound bubble," a prototype for individual work, sonically immersing the listener and generating a sensation of an encapsulating sonic environment. A total of 43 test subjects participated in an experience-based test using the sound bubble prototype while conducting self-selected, ordinary work tasks in their office landscape. Their behaviors during the test were observed and documented. All participants took a post-experience questionnaire about experiences working in the sound bubble, and two subjects were interviewed. The responses show that the sound bubble can enhance auditory work conditions for individual work that demands concentration.

Keywords: Acoustic design · Affordance · Ambient sound environments · Open plan offices · Sonic interactive design · Design-based research · Sonic immersion

1 Introduction

Developments in information and communication technology have led to major changes in the work environment in recent decades. A growing number of organizations are moving from traditional fixed open-plan offices to flex or activity-based offices. In the latter there are no personal workplaces, instead there are shared workplaces for different purposes for employees to choose from based on the current activity [1]. This flexibility is meant to support concentrated individual work as well as collaborative work in the same work environment. Sound is a problem in such offices. Even normal, unavoidable levels of low frequency noise from fans, ventilation or office machines affect our work capacity negatively [2]. Such noise is perceived as disturbing and annoying, and can cause physiological stress for noise-sensitive people facing high workloads. High-frequency noise also affects human productivity negatively [3]. A poor acoustic environment creates stress, which in turn leads to higher noise sensitivity [4], and thus

© Springer International Publishing Switzerland 2016
M. Gellerstedt et al. (Eds.): SCIS 2016, LNBIP 259, pp. 29–42, 2016.
DOI: 10.1007/978-3-319-43597-8_3

even minor noise disturbances may become problematic over time. Open plan offices are ranked lowest regarding health and productivity in a study comparing different office types [5], and it is primarily our ability to stay focused that is affected, not our health in short-term perspective.

The main source of noise interference in office environments is overhearing co-workers talk [1, 6]. However, talk is not just a problem in open landscapes; it also constitutes the ground for knowledge sharing and ease of direct communication between employees.

Previous research has primarily focused on reducing undesired noise by physical installations or understanding the effect of noise on work conditions. But it is not sufficient to consider the static relation between physical environment and noise alone; new innovative approaches must take into consideration the dynamic time-space interaction between people and their surrounding environment [7]. Moreover, sound perception is generally emotionally conditioned and perceived on an individual basis. For example, attitudes toward the workplace and relations with colleagues are aspects affecting the perceptions of sounds, as follows: A general positive attitude towards the work environment results in greater tolerance for the acoustic environment [8]; sounds derived from things we like are considered less disturbing [8]; sounds that we understand and find useful disturb us less [9]; constant noise disturbs us less than sudden noises [3, 9]; and the type of work we perform also affects our sensitivity to sounds. These aspects are not addressed by static physical noise reduction solutions. Therefore, noise interference in open office spaces is a significant problem that requires new approaches and solutions.

1.1   Research Question

In this study we explore the possibility of improving the sound environment by adding digital sounds to the acoustic environment. Our approach is to design ambient, context-sensitive sound environments to enhance work conditions in the office workplace. In earlier work in a laboratory setting [10] we found that context-sensitive sound environments have potential to enhance an ambient environment by immersing the listener and generating a sensation of an encapsulating sound bubble. In this study we take the design process one step further and evaluate prototypes in an office context. The design goal is to create local sound environments that are perceived as ambient, pleasant background noise which help office workers stay focused and concentrate on their work tasks.

The overall research question is as follows:
Does the sound bubble enhance work conditions in an open plan office space?

Particularly, we pose the following sub-questions:

(1) *How is the sound bubble used?*
(2) *How do users perceive the sound bubble?*

2   Research Approach

The overall approach is grounded in design-based research [11]; a systematic but flexible methodology aimed to improve practices through iterative design interventions. This approach, common in information systems research, is combined with the emerging field *acoustic design* [12]. Acoustic design concerns *adding qualitative sound* and altering the sound environments as opposed to the traditional architecture method of noise reduction, which involves removing undesired sound. The approach is new within acoustic environment research regarding solving noise problems. Aligned with the design approach to sound, there is an emergent trend within music research to talk about music in terms of user and using music for specific purposes rather than as a more passive listener [13]. Other methodological influences are contextual design [2], which as ecological psychology emphasizes the importance of context, and sonic interaction design (SID), which is an emerging field that interweaves auditory display, interaction design, ubiquitous computing and interactive arts [14]. SID research is based on knowledge of everyday sound perception, acoustic ecology, and also sound and music computing [14]. One aim in SID research is to identify unconventional ways to use sound in the interaction between users and artefacts, services or environments [15].

Hence, our approach is based on theories and methods from different research traditions where technological development, architecture and workplace studies are combined in a design thinking influenced by the fields of acoustic design, IT design, and sonic interaction design. It is aligned with the ideas and methods of *research through design* [16], where an active process of ideating, iterating, and critiquing potential design solutions is used in order to create the right thing. We use methods from informatics and workplace research with early user involvement, prototyping and iterative development in authentic settings focusing on a clear utility effect. Field studies are unusual in sound research where research normally is conducted in specialized sound laboratories. Hence, we are applying information system methodology in new domains.

3   Sound Design Theory

The conceptual sound design is based on acoustic design and sonic interactive design. The ambient sound environment system we propose is based on Pierre Schaeffer's Musique Concrète theory [17]. There, sound perception is categorized into four different "Listening Modes": *hearing, listening, present* and *understanding*. *Hearing* is the most elementary perceptual level, which means that we passively take in sounds that we do not try to listen to or understand. *Listening* involves situations where we direct our aural attention to someone or something in order to identify the event. *Present* involves processing and selection of sounds to choose what interests us. *Understanding* involves semantics where the sound is interpreted as a sign or code that represents something meaningful to us. The theory is relevant since our aim is to design a sound environment which helps the user to stay in hearing mode as much as possible, that is, subconsciously hear what is going on in the surrounding without diverting into listening to irrelevant talk and events. Gaver [18] describes the concept of "everyday listening" referring to situations when surrounding sounds are perceived as events blurred into a larger context and do not pay attention to the sounds themselves. In everyday listening mode we are aware on a more subconscious level of the origin of a sound. We often unconsciously shift between these listening modes.

When we are exposed to music we explore, select and focus our attention depending on the nature and attributes of the music. Music also causes actions and interactions with the surrounding environment on the behavioral side. Musical listening in this sense may not be clearly distinguishable from everyday listening, and is indeed rooted in the latter [19]. In order to encompass the perceptual impact and all these behaviors, the concept of *music users* has recently been proposed in music research [13, 20]. They argue that it is desirable not to speak of listeners or performers, as these encompass only some of the potential ways of dealing with music. Users in general should be regarded as a broad category of subjects that deal with music by means of one or more of these behaviors. A common use of music is as an atmosphere-enriching sonic additive. Music can effect individual and social actions: alter our mood and sharpen our attentional focus [21]. Music can also get us into different conditions of action-readiness required for various activities. The concept of user signals that music is used as a tool to support different activities.

In this paper we expand the notion of users to sound environments such as the sound bubble. It is reasonable to view a modified sound environment as a phenomenon with users (rather than listeners) since the environment is designed to generate a particular effect on the user. We also adopt the concept of affordance, used in music theory as well as in interaction design. An affordance is an attribute of an event or object, relative to an organism, which represents its potential for action [22, 23]. Musical affordance [19] specifies the different sorts of things we can do with music. In interaction design it usually refers to properties of visual and interactive elements, but can be applied to auditory elements as well.

A sound environment creates the conditions for different types of hearing modes and causes actions and interactions based on which sound components occupy the sound environment. A user will therefore react to the sound environment and act according to what possibilities the environment affords. Affordances are perceived through the pick-up of structured information, which may be accessible through any modality. As affordances are functions of the connection between an organism and its environment, they are not static; rather they affect each other mutually. Perceivers in an environment search out information which is already part of the environment and which affords perceptual significance to them [13].

4 The Sound Design

Our idea is to digitally manipulate the environment's existing ambient sounds in terms of space and time, by adding sounds from other contexts and merging these with the existing environment. As a first attempt, we have created two sound concepts; one for individual, concentrated work and one for collaborative, creative work. The sound designs are dynamic modulations, which means that they are functions taking the sound characteristics of the environment as input via microphones and from this generate new sounds which are transmitted and blended with the existing sound via speakers. For individual sound environments the speakers must be located near the head of the user to create a sound environment local enough to only affect one user. For collaborative settings, the speakers are placed in the designated collaborative space.

The sound environments are intended to invoke *hearing mode* only, which means they must be ambient enough not to attract too much attention, yet strong enough to have the intended effect. This can be achieved by composing the sounds as legato as possible. Legato means that the temporal structure in the sound is limited and the spectral variations are few because tones are played smoothly and interwoven with as little silence as possible between. In [24], it was shown that a legato sound was perceived as a continuous stream of audio and affected cognitive ability less than music with distinct temporal and spectral variations.

In Gibson's terminology, we want to design ambience with affordance to create calmness and concentration or creativity for its users. In a study [25] where ease of learning different sound types was investigated, the authors found that abstract sounds were learned with far greater difficulty than both speech and representational sounds. Therefore, the sound components should be abstract enough so that most people do not recognize them as something familiar or become irritated or bored because of a recognizable melody. Thus, music is not an option to achieve our goals.

The first design concept for individual work was generated to create a sound atmosphere that is perceived as spatially confining and soothing, and should help the user direct attention inward. The main purpose of the concentrated individual sound was to mask attention away from surrounding talk and noise. A way to achieve that is to camouflage undesired talk, and create what [26] describes as a "sonic micro milieu" that takes precedence over a distant or secondary perceptive field.

The second sound design concept, for collaboration, was designed to create sounds that gave the impression of space, with sound textures arising from random locations in the sound image including some unexpected elements meant to simulate the idea of opening up the senses, being open to the unexpected, and thereby stimulate creativity. The main purpose of the creative collaboration sound was to induce a sensation of movement and space.

5 Study Method and Material

In order to test the sound design concepts we constructed two prototypes able to play and alter the sounds. We identified suitable locations in the office for the prototypes and conducted a pilot test to assure that the study design was reasonable. Due to the explorative nature and novel approach in the field test, a thorough pilot test seemed necessary to detect any problems in the study design or prototypes before conducting the main study.

5.1 Sound Environments

Five sound environments were developed: two sound environments to support individual, concentrated work (S1 and S2), and two for facilitation of creative work (S3 and S4). The fifth sound environment (S5) was a recording of office background noise in an empty office. S5 served as a static ambient background sound related to the physical room, rather than the activity, yet noticeable as a distinct sound material within the local surrounding environment. It was the closest we could get to a "placebo" in medical experimental settings, since no transmission at all from the speakers was too apparent to serve as a neutral, control case. The five sound environments had a length of 15 min each and seamlessly looped when played. For the collaborative setting prototype we used four speakers and for the individual setting prototype two speakers were enough. All five sound designs were used in both prototypes, in order to explore if the activity type affected how the sounds were used and perceived.

5.2   Prototypes

The first prototype (Fig. 1) consisted of an office chair on which two speakers were attached, about 5–8 cm from each ear depending on how the user moved their head, at the headrest on two rods directed forward. A user could to some extent alter the preferred listening position because the speakers could be moved horizontally. A laptop was connected to the speakers. The laptop controlled audio playback and logged which sounds were played and for how long. The sound environment interface (Fig. 2) consisted of five sound-selection buttons and a slider to adjust amplitude level. The buttons were labelled A–E, and were assigned to the sounds S1–S5.

The users could not mute the sound completely since the purpose was to investigate how added sound in an office landscape is perceived. The prototype setup also contained a microphone that registered amplitude changes, which affected how the sounds were processed in the laptop. We assumed that an increased amplitude level registered by the microphone most likely originated from activities, e.g. people moving in the immediate environment or conversations. Such amplitude changes in the immediate environment affected the tempo and the panning of the sound in the speakers. If the amplitude increased it led to a reduced stereo width, making the sound bubble more compact and encapsulating. An increase of amplitude also generated a temporal acceleration in playback speed. The threshold for tempo and stereo width changes was set to 40 db, which is the sound pressure level of satisfactory speech intelligibility according to the Swedish Work Environment Authority, and just below the normal sound pressure level in offices [27].

Fig. 1. Prototype

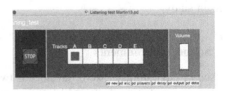

Fig. 2. The interface.

The second prototype consisted of four speakers attached to the ceiling with wires in the corners of a meeting room. A laptop and an external soundcard with the ability to route four channels, one for each speaker, were connected to the speakers. The interface was identical for both prototypes.

5.3   Field Test Location

The field test location was at an activity-based office at the IT department in a large manufacturing industry in West Sweden. The physical location for Prototype 1, the individual concentration setting, was a table with seating for ten people. Table occupants worked both individually and in groups. The table was located in front of three conference rooms that created a stream of passing people. The immediate environment thus became a natural gathering place for spontaneous meetings and conversations. The table was characterized by spontaneity as several group meetings could take place simultaneously and sometimes meetings would end up in new meetings among team members. The physical location for Prototype 2 was inside one of the meeting rooms behind the abovementioned table. It was a frequently used conference room with one large table and chairs for 10–15 people, and common equipment such as whiteboards and projectors.

5.4   Pilot Study

Prior to the field test, we conducted a pilot test for eight days where test persons performed self-selected work tasks while using the individual prototype. Which of the five sounds the participants played, how long they were played as well as what amplitude level the user chose was logged. After the test, the participants answered a questionnaire, with background questions about gender, age, and hearing ability as well as work-related and overall questions about the sounds and their experience of using the prototype.

Sixteen test subjects participated in the pilot test, with durations between 2.2 and 89 min. Experiences and responses were used to improve the study design. For example, the prototype interface was modified so that the sounds mapped to buttons A–E were randomly assigned for each participant, to control for the order of sounds affecting the perception and choice of sounds. We also decided to complement the log files and questionnaire with observations in order to better understand events in the environment that affected the users. Video recordings were not allowed, so a researcher observed all sessions and documented in a log time stamps together with events in the near environment and actions or reactions of the test person.

5.5   Field Study

The recruitment base for the field test was office staff not participating in the pilot test. Other employees were invited and enrolled on a voluntary basis. The participants were free to choose duration of prototype use, but were encouraged to work for at least

30 min. All participants were observed, and had the opportunity to read through the observation protocol to comment and clarify any misunderstandings.

Two participants were recruited to use the prototype for an entire working day, and these sessions were followed up with semi-structured interviews. Questions included how they felt during the day, if they perceived the sounds differently during the day, why they chose the sounds and suggestions for improvement of the prototype or the sound design.

The test subjects for the collaborative setting were recruited in a similar manner, but all meeting delegates had to accept having the sound environment running during the meeting. They were encouraged to use the prototype for the entire meeting, preferably at least 30 min. All meeting participants were asked to fill out the questionnaire. Observation in the meeting room was not allowed due to meeting confidentialities.

6 Results

There were 43 participants, 12 females and 31 males, testing the prototype for individual work. The gender ratio reflects the office staff. Participants' age ranged from 24 to 58 with a mean of 38.7. One person reported having not fully functional hearing. Participants reported doing the following types of work tasks during the tests: *technical development* such as requirements analysis or programming of the intranet (14 participants); *administration* such as budget planning (5); *communication* such as IT support or email conversations (8 participants); or a *combination of several tasks* (16 participants). The test session duration ranged from 24 min to 5 h and 59 min. All participants filled out the post-test questionnaire.

There were 38 participants in six groups testing the prototype for collaborative work during the study. Only one group with seven test subjects actually completed the questionnaire, all of whom were negative about the experience.

The remaining results are therefore derived from the test with the individual sound bubble prototype.

6.1 Answering the RQ: How is the Sound Bubble Used?

The question is addressed in four data sources: (1) the log files that recorded duration and changes of sounds played for each test session; (2) the survey question regarding preferred sound; (3) the survey question asking for rationale for choosing sounds; and (4) interview excerpts of sound environment usage.

How much the sounds were played in total by all participants was evenly distributed: sounds S2, S4 and S5 were played about 23 % of the time, S3 a bit less and S1 the least. The result of preferred sound question showed that S2 was the most popular, followed by S3 and S5. Fewer participants preferred the sounds S4 and S1. Playing time and preference did not always coincide, but participants were asked to play all sounds so duration was not expected to fully reflect preference. Details are found in Table 1:

Table 1. Amount played and preferences of sounds S1 to S5

Usage	Intention				
	Designed for concentration		Designed for creativity		Office sound
Sound	S1	S2	S3	S4	S5
Amount played	11.3 %	**23.9 %**	18.6 %	**24.1 %**	**22.2 %**
Preferred by	5.3 %	**31.6 %**	**26.3 %**	10.5 %	**26.3 %**

The third data source was a question about how sounds were selected. Five response categories were identified during analysis: that the sound was the most pleasant, supported concentration, blocked out surrounding sounds, was the least disturbing, or the participant did not provide a reason. See Table 2 for distribution of responses.

Table 2. Distribution of responses in sound selection rationale categories

Most pleasant	Helped concentrate	Blocked sounds	Do not know	Least disturbing
52.2 %	12.5 %	10 %	7.5 %	17.5 %

The rationale given by the majority was that the sound was the most pleasant, and typical responses included:

"Because they were quite pleasant and I listen a lot to instrumental music so I liked them very much."

"I tried them all, and most of the sounds were fine except the one with a constant noise (5). But 2, 4 and 3 were best."

"I chose 5 because it was more natural and sometimes at work you don't need musical sounds."

About 25 % responded that the sound bubble helped them concentrate or blocked sounds from the surroundings, and responses were for instance:

"To concentrate on work so sounds from outside can be eliminated."

"They made me disconnect from the surrounding noise, made me calm and focused."

Lastly, sounds were chosen because they were least disturbing:

"Thought it was the calmest, the least disturbing."

Finally, the interviews revealed the following descriptions related to usage by test persons *TP1* and *TP2*:

"I would use it when sitting for long periods with the same task, when I need to concentrate. I see this as a means to concentrate. I have no difficulties concentrating, but it has contributed a little to the focus you need to really get into a good work flow." (TP1)

"I would use the sound bubble for individual work demanding focus." (TP2)

6.2   Answering the RQ: How Do Users Perceive the Sound Bubble?

The question is addressed in two data sources: the questionnaire and the interviews. Responses to the question "How did you perceive the sounds?" were categorized in three groups according to appreciation of the sounds: (1) most or all sounds were pleasant and soothing; (2) some sounds were pleasant and some disturbing or neutral; and (3) some or most sounds were disturbing. The pleasant category resulted in 50 %, with 24 % in the middle and 26 % in the disturbing category. In the positive category, sounds were describes as: *varying, nice, pleasant, soothing, encapsulating, refreshing, calming*, and *good*. In the middle category participants replied:

> *"The musical sounds were better for work than the 'nature' sounds. Maybe because I found the white noise more distracting."*

> *"Sound 5 was pleasant, the others I didn't like at all. They disturbed me."*

In the disturbing category responses included:

> *"1, 3, 4 and 5 were horrible, but 2 was okay."*

> *"Too much noise in the speakers. Would have been fun to test 'cleaner' sounds."*

There was no clear relation between length of use and sound bubble perception, but the participants using the sound bubble for a whole day admitted in the interviews that they occasionally wanted to take a break from the bubble, but the overall impressions were positive. One interviewee described the sounds as follows:

> *"There was not too much melody in them, and I didn't think about chords either. It was simply tones from a spectrum creating a 'sound carpet,' but I didn't feel a theme in the music. [...] The noise sounds made me think of nature, wind, sea and whales. The others gave me space sensations. A feeling of science fiction, somehow futuristic." (TP1)*

6.3   The Overall Research Question

The overall research question *"Does the sound bubble enhance work conditions in an open plan office space?"* was addressed in the questionnaire, the interview responses and the observations.

Participants were asked if the sound bubble changed their work conditions. A great majority, 74.4 %, responded better, 16.3 % responded the same and 9.3 % responded worse. In the better category, explanations to their choice were as follows:

> *"Because I heard a pleasant sound (and not speech sounds) I focused on that and not the surrounding environment. However, it was possible to hear things in the surrounding environment if I chose to focus on that."*

> *"The task I did called for total disturbance-free environment. The sound I picked worked in two ways for me: (1) Devoid from other sounds/distractions from other people in the area. (2) The sound created a kind of hypothetical serene environment that was like a peaceful environment."*

> *"Better concentration, less disturbance."*

> *"I felt like I was sitting in my favorite environment for working. For example Sound D was exactly the kind of sound that I would like to hear while working. Made me less stressed."*

"Still I prefer using headphones even if it's nice to be able to be a part of the office landscape in a better way with this type of sound installation."

Among the 16.3 % participants who did not think the sound bubble changed the conditions, responses included:

"I'm not disturbed by working in loud noise."

"Could concentrate quickly, but got slight headache after a while. Maybe because of the can-like sound. Perhaps the speakers are to blame more than the sounds?"

Two of the four participants that considered the sound bubble worse responded as follows:

"You hear voices etc. anyway, so it becomes yet another sound image to listen to."

"The sound was too monotonous. After a while it was also annoying."

The interview responses support that the sound bubble enhanced the working conditions for the test persons, as evidenced from the following citations:

"Feel alert now, usually I'm rather dead other days when going [home] to the bus."

"It becomes a little easier to lose yourself into the job. It provides some form of positive screening." (TP1)

"I usually get tired during the day, but it feels like I've been working efficiently all day. Normally I'm disturbed when people go home, now I haven't noticed it."

"What I listened to mostly was relaxing, one might say that it brought me back when thoughts flew away elsewhere." (TP2)

TP1 compared the sound bubbles with headphones:

"It has somewhat the same effect as headphones. [...] But it is more transparent than headphones. The advantage is that people are not as afraid to disturb you, like when you have headphones. You don't need to bother stopping Spotify and take them off. Here you leave the bubble simply by moving your head."

The many hours of observations confirmed what the test persons described in the interviews, that it was easier to concentrate on the work task and not get disturbed by surrounding activities and noises from others. Below is an example excerpt from the observation log:

Time	Environment	Test person (Tp)
10.10	A person approaches the test location and starts talking with a person at the table. They both walk away to find a cord	Tp does not react, but looks around after half a minute and takes a sip of coffee. Then continues with the work task
10.12	Two persons pass in front of Tp while talking. Two other persons open a door behind Tp with 5 s between and walks behind him. Swedish language	Tp does not react, continues writing

7 Discussion

We can conclude that Prototype 2 did not function as planned and the collaborative test thereby failed. The chosen meeting room showed to be unsuitable for the test due to frequent videoconferences; a situation when adding more sound is not appropriate. The original plan was to install the collaboration prototype in the open office area, but we failed to make the sound bubble local enough with the available equipment not to disturb people nearby. The sounds were designed for collaboration in an open space, and a closed room has different acoustic conditions and did not generate the intended effect. Also, the additional challenge with videoconferencing was not foreseen. Responses from the collaboration test revealed that the sounds interfered and that the group could not agree on which sound to choose. Altogether, we cannot say anything conclusive about the collaborative sound environment.

However, we found support that the sound bubble can enhance auditory work conditions for individual work requiring concentration. Most participants considered the sound bubble advantageous compared to the usual acoustic environment in their office. Reasons included that the sound bubble provided aesthetic qualities to the sound environment that became more pleasant; it supported attention focus by masking unwanted sounds but still allowed picking up information from the environment. Supposedly, the sound bubble helped users to be in hearing mode.

Several subjects reported that they frequently used music in headphones while working. However, they also admitted that using headphones signalled "unavailable to talk to" and generated a social barrier towards colleagues, which can jeopardize the main advantage of an open office. The sound bubble can thus serve as an attractive alternative providing a semi-transparent membrane that is noticed but can be ignored by its user and which is invisible to others.

There was no clear finding regarding preferred sounds. The three most popular sounds were one designed for concentration, one for collaboration, and the "placebo." We do not have a clear understanding of why yet, so this calls for further investigations. One explanation is related to the limitations of the prototype. The premise for the collaboration was a movement of the sounds between the speakers in an appreciable manner that created a sense of random motion and space. Such effect was not possible to achieve in the simple two-speaker prototype, resulting in all sounds becoming rather monotonous and similar. Moreover, the sounds in the prototype were only 15-min-long loops, which become repetitious.

Yet the results suggest that the sound bubble supported an effective "everyday listening": the continuous perception process that discriminate between sounds to be noticed and to be ignored. The sound bubble seems to establish a sonic micro milieu, which means that our design concept gave rise to affordance for calmness and concentration for its users.

We do not know how the sounds are perceived over a longer period of time, and if the effect of the sound bubble will diminish over time. Long, continuous exposure may be tiresome and disturbing. Test sessions were short since subjects were busy with meetings or other appointments. At least one subject quit the test early due to an uncomfortable chair. The prototype construction was problematic due to location fixation and immobility. Half of those who responded that work conditions remained the same with the prototype blamed the location and requested the possibility to work in a standing position. Better prototypes and further tests in various places must be conducted to shed light on this issue.

8 Conclusion and Future Work

Since the study design failed for the collaborative test, we cannot draw conclusions as to whether the sound environment is suitable in a collaborative work situation, nor if the preference of sound design is related to type of activity.

However, we can conclude that 3/4 of the users considered the sound bubble enhancing the auditory environment for individual work that demanded concentration. The sound bubble was perceived as an aesthetic additive enhancing the acoustic environment. It was used as a semi-transparent filter towards the surrounding environment helping users to concentrate while still being aware and open to activities nearby.

Future work includes prototype constructions and further experiment with sound environments for collaborative settings, and exploring ways to personalize the sound bubble for the individual setting.

References

1. Jahncke, H.: Cognitive performance and restoration in open-plan office noise. Doctoral thesis/Luleå University of Technology, Luleå (2012)
2. Bengtsson, J.: Low frequency noise during work—effects on performance and annoyance. Doctoral thesis, Sahlgrenska Academy, University of Gothenburg, Gothenburg (2003)
3. Nassiri, P., Monazam, M., Fouladi Dehaghi, B., et al.: The effect of noise on human performance: a clinical trial. Int. J. Occup. Environ. Med. **4**, 87–95 (2013)
4. Sjödin, F., Kjellberg, A., Knutsson, A., Landström, U., Lindberg, L.: Noise exposure and auditory effects on preschool personnel. Noise Health **14**(57), 72–82 (2012)
5. Seddigh, A., Berntsson, E., Bodin Danielsson, C., Westerlund, H.: Concentration requirements modify the effects of office type on health and productivity. J. Environ. Psychol. **38**, 167–174 (2014)
6. Hellström, B.: Om Kontorslandskapens Akustik & Arkitektur - vad örat hör men ögat inte ser. Arkus, Stockholm (2012)
7. Hellström, B., Johansson, B., Zalyaletdinov, P.: Redesign of one atmosphere–what do you want to hear? In: Creating an Atmosphere, Grenoble, France, 10–12 September 2008
8. Västfjäll, D.: Influences of current mood and noise sensitivity on judgments of noise annoyance. J. Psychol. Interdisc. Appl. **136**, 357–370 (2002)
9. Kjellberg, A., Landström, U., Tesarz, M., Söderberg, L., Åkerlund, E.: The effects of non-physical noise characteristics, ongoing task and noise sensitivity on annoyance and distraction due to noise at work. J. Environ. Psychol. **16**, 123–136 (1996)
10. Eriksson, M.L., Pareto, L.: Designing Activity-Based and Context-Sensitive Ambient Sound Environments in Open-Plan Offices, vol. 6, no. 7 (2015). http://aisel.aisnet.org/iris2015/7
11. Wang, F., Hannafin, M.J.: Design-based research and technology-enhanced learning environments. Educ. Technol. Res. Dev. **53**(4), 5–23 (2005)

12. Hellström, B.: Theories and methods adaptable to acoustic and architectural design of railway stations. In: Twelfth International Congress on Sound and Vibration, Lisbon, pp. 11–14 (2005)
13. Reybrouck, M.: Musical sense-making and the concept of affordance: an ecosemiotic and experiential approach. Biosemiotics 5(3), 391–409 (2012)
14. Beyer, H., Holzblatt, K.: Contextual Design: Defining Customer-Centered Systems. Morgan Kauffman, San Francisco (1998)
15. Hermann, T., Andy, H.: The Sonification Handbook. Logos Verlag, Berlin (2011)
16. Zimmerman, J., Forlizzi, J., Evenson, S.: Research through design as a method for interaction design research in HCI. In: Proceedings of the SIGCHI Conference on Human Factors in Computing Systems, pp. 493–502. ACM, April 2007
17. Chion, M.: Guide des objets sonores. Buchet/Chastel, Paris (1983)
18. Gaver, W.W.: What in the world do we hear? An ecological approach to auditory event perception. Ecol. Psychol. 5(1), 1–29 (1993)
19. Windsor, W.L., de Bézenac, C.: Music and affordances. Musicae scientiae (2012). doi:1029864911435734
20. Krueger, J.W.: Affordances and the musically extended mind. Front. Psychol. 4, 1003 (2014)
21. Sridharan, D., Levitin, D.J., Chafe, C.H., Berger, J., Menon, V.: Neural dynamics of event segmentation in music: converging evidence for dissociable ventral and dorsal networks. Neuron 55, 521–532 (2007)
22. Gibson, J.: The theory of affordances. In: Shaw, R., Bransford, J. (eds.) Perceiving, Acting and Knowing: Toward an Ecological Psychology, pp. 67–82. Lawrence Erlbaum, Hillsdale (1977)
23. Gibson, J.: The Ecological Approach to Visual Perception. Houghton Mifflin Company, Boston (1979)
24. Schlittmeier, S.J., Hellbrück, J.: Background music as noise abatement in open-plan offices: a laboratory study on performance effects and subjective preferences. Appl. Cogn. Psychol. 23(5), 684–697 (2009)
25. Smith, S.E., Stephan, K.L., Parker, S.P.: Auditory warnings in the military cockpit: a preliminary evaluation of potential sound types (No. DSTO-TR-1615). Defence Science and Technology Organisation Edinburgh (Australia) Air Operations Div. (2004)
26. Augoyard, J.-F.: Sonic Experience. A Guide to Everyday Sounds. McGill-Queen's University Press, Montreal (2006)
27. Venetjoki, N., Kaarlela-Tuomaala, A., Keskinen, E., Hongisto, V.: The effect of speech and speech intelligibility on task performance. Ergonomics 49(11), 1068–1091 (2006)

Extending e-Health Infrastructures with Lightweight IT

Egil Øvrelid[(⊠)] and Bendik Bygstad

Department of Informatics, University of Oslo,
Gaustadalléen 23 B, Oslo, Norway
{egilov, bendikby}@ifi.uio.no

Abstract. Our interest in this paper is to understand the interplay between large technological programs and smaller innovation projects, i.e. how a small project may enter and change the larger structure. In our e-health context we conceptualise this as the interplay between heavyweight and lightweight IT. Our research questions are, how does an innovation initiative develop within an established information infrastructure, and how can we overcome the barriers for interplay between heavyweight and lightweight technologies? Our empirical evidence is a case study in the health care sector in Norway, where we investigated a mega-program called Digital Renewal, and a small lightweight initiative called Medicloud. The theoretical lens was actor-network theory and we offer two insights. First, we identify a set of barriers for fruitful interplay between heavyweight and lightweight IT. Second, we show that these barriers may be overcome by a careful combination of technical and organisational solutions, in order to stabilise a new network as a part of the larger information infrastructure.

Keywords: Heavyweight and lightweight IT · Information infrastructures · eHealth innovation

1 Introduction

Our interest in this paper is to understand the interplay between large technological programs and smaller innovation projects, and how it develops over time.

Public sector IT mega-programs with political and societal prestige are usually a response to perceived problems, such as poor services or high costs. Much attention is given to the coordination and control of these programs, because they are high-risk initiatives. In spite of several spectacular failures [1–3] many programs are relatively successful in building large information infrastructures. When successful, they tend to gain momentum, focus on consolidation and become irreversible just by size. Over time this often becomes a barrier to innovation, because (i) large-scale programs do not satisfy all user and organisational needs and (ii) new technologies continuously challenge the established thinking of the programs.

What does it take to change the trajectory of large programs? In his work on scientific programs and paradigms, Lakatos [4] argued that programs tend to continue in spite of experienced problems, as long as there are no clear alternatives present. Such

© Springer International Publishing Switzerland 2016
M. Gellerstedt et al. (Eds.): SCIS 2016, LNBIP 259, pp. 43–56, 2016.
DOI: 10.1007/978-3-319-43597-8_4

alternatives, in our context, usually emerge through a public discourse on information technologies, where a new *organizing vision* [5, 6] is presented.

In this research we investigate the relationship between a large e-health program and a small innovation initiative. The health sector is currently the target of large expectations to the contribution of IT solutions for better health care, and mega-programs are in work in most rich (and many poor) countries. Most of them include complex integration of various systems, and focus heavily on security and privacy.

In parallel, we have witnessed the arrival of new technologies, such as Internet-of-Things, and new ways of use, such as *consumerisation* and *bring-your-own-device* [7]. This development challenges the dominant knowledge regime of mega-programs in two ways; first, it allows professional users, together with vendors, to develop and implement IT solutions for special clinical needs, bypassing the programs and IT departments. Second, it has opened a new discourse on the relationship between *heavyweight* and *lightweight IT* [8, 9]. Heavyweight IT is defined as the established paradigm of software engineering, while lightweight IT is conceived a socio-technical knowledge regime driven by competent users' need for IT services, enabled by the consumerisation of digital technologies [8].

There are many unresolved issues regarding the interplay of lightweight and heavyweight IT. What we wish to investigate in this research is how a lightweight initiative unfolds and interacts with the mega-program and the established information infrastructure. The interplay between lightweight technologies and Enterprise IT, have some significant challenges [7, 9]. The extended digitalisation of organisational life gives what Tilson et al. [10] calls new paradoxical regimes of control that goes beyond the idea of hierarchical control [10]. This gives challenges theoretically as well as for IT governance and affects all levels of analysis [10]. Our research questions are:

- How does an innovation initiative develop within an established information infrastructure?
- How can we overcome the barriers for interplay between heavyweight and lightweight technologies?

We proceed by discussing heavyweight and lightweight IT, within the field of information infrastructures. To develop our argument we build on Actor-Network Theory to analyse two cases, one light- and one heavyweight initiative. The differences are highlighted during the negotiations; barriers against interplay arise and give new challenges to the participants and their respective organisations.

2 Related Research

2.1 Heavyweight and Lightweight IT

Developments of infrastructures in the health sector are often part of large programs, large-scale IT systems delivered by big and experienced vendors with complex and sophisticated organisation. These systems, usually IT silos of legacy systems, are often a major hindrance to organisational change and innovation [11]. The complexity of these systems increases as the number of interconnected links increases, making the

Table 1. Heavyweight and lightweight IT [8].

	Heavyweight IT	Lightweight IT
Profile	Back-end: supporting documentation of work	Front-end: supporting work processes
Systems	Transaction systems	Process support, apps, BI
Technology	Servers, databases, enterprise bus technology	Tablets, electronic whiteboards, mobile phones
IT architecture	Centralised or distributed	Meshworks
Owner	IT department	Users and vendors
Development culture	Systematics, quality, security	Innovation, experimentation
Problems	Increasing complexity, rising costs	Isolated gadgets, security
Discourse	Software engineering	Business, practice innovation

risk for unexpected incidents higher [12]. Integrations effort may mitigate some of these problems, but are also increasing complexity and costs.

The inherent inertia of these infrastructures is currently being challenged by a new type of technological regime called lightweight IT [8]. Lightweight IT is the new paradigm of mobile apps, sensors and bring-your-own-device, also called consumerisation or Internet-of-Things. It is typically cheap and easy to use technology, it can often be deployed without IT specialists and it tends to be mobile technology.

As illustrated in Table 1 the key aspect of lightweight IT is not only the cheap and available technology as such, but the fact that its deployment is frequently done by users or vendors, bypassing the IT departments. Bygstad claims that "Lightweight IT may be seen as complementary to heavyweight; it is well suited for the tasks that heavyweight IT has often failed to support, i.e. the simple and immediate needs of a user" [8: 3].

We believe it is fruitful to see this as two different knowledge regimes: heavyweight and lightweight IT. Heavyweight IT is becoming increasingly complex and specialised, while lightweight IT emerges as a new innovation arena, allowing non-specialist to experiment with cheap technology. Lightweight IT is defined as a socio-technical knowledge regime driven by competent users' need for IT services, enabled by the consumerisation of digital technologies [8]. While heavyweight IT is challenged by increasing complexity and rising costs, lightweight IT suffers from problems with security and governance [9]. There is currently no shared discourse between the two communities, as heavyweight IT is discussed in the software engineering community, while lightweight IT is an innovation discourse.

Several researchers have looked into the challenge of dealing with the new situation. Harris et al. [7] looks at the benefits and challenges related to IT Consumerisation tools brought into the workplace. Bygstad [8] identifies the generative potentials of interplay between heavy and light, while Willcocks et al. [9] suggest how interplay between lightweight and heavyweight should be designed. We aim to extend these insights by an in-depth investigation of the interplay between the two knowledge regimes.

2.2 Information Infrastructures

Infrastructure is used as a term to conceptualise interconnected system collectives. The past 20 years have witnessed research on digital infrastructures covering different settings such as health, telecom, finance, government, and manufacturing. Hanseth and Lyytinen [15] defined an information infrastructure as "a shared, open (and unbounded), heterogeneous and evolving socio-technical system (which we call installed base) consisting of a set of IT capabilities and their users, operations and design" [15: 4]. The heterogeneous mix of people and technologies are built on the installed base [13, 14]. As the installed base grows its development and growth become self-reinforcing, through cultivation [13]. Gateways, devices for enabling communication between parts of the infrastructure, are important tools to be used in such cultivation processes.

Infrastructures as emerging sociotechnical networks with a broad growth base with a multitude of actors on several levels have a certain dynamic which also create tensions. Tensions are over time "inscribed" into the networks and have obtained a certain closure, but new tensions may continually arise, and take the form of conflict.

The managing of infrastructural development then is about "the careful nurturance of infrastructural change, and attending to the tensions that emerge from it" [16: 28]. Tensions, can be seen as both barriers and resources to infrastructural development, and should be engaged constructively. Barriers can be both cultural or institutional dependencies which prevent adoption, as well as power relations which prevent action.

Resources can be equipment or personnel, or international organisational units, as well as financial and human capital. Both of them may be seen as constructive elements in the development. They are of particular importance to obtain "long-term properties of infrastructural fit, equity, and sustainability" [16: 29]. In our analysis we build on this duality of barriers and resources.

3 Theoretical and Methodical Lens

3.1 Actor Networks and Translation

Actor-network theory is known for the tight interplay between social and technical means. Human and non-humans are linked together in networks conditioned by actors pursuing interests. The stabilisation of interests is about alignment through negotiations [17]. ANT provides a language for describing how this translation takes place on a quite specific level, and looks at the role of discourse in establishing scientific facts [18]; technological systems [19]; and how discourse is used in order to seduce and displace actors into ones program [18].

The technology-in-the-making is conditioned by socio-technical negotiation between a whole range of actors, and outlines the "open-ended character of this process – the stumbling, the compromises, the way non-technical interests get dressed up in technical disguise…" [17: 71] This is in opposition to management processes dominated by top-down, rational, decision making. The alignment is not necessarily obtained through facts, solution or beliefs alone, "order is an effect of an achievement – it is not given a priori" [17: 72].

In his path-breaking paper on the domestication of the scallops and the fishermen of St. Brieuc Bay, Callon [20] looks at the "role played by science and technology in structuring power relationships", to understand "the emergence, development, and eventual closure of controversies" in the study of science and technology [20: 197]. Callons contribution to ANT is first that he demonstrates "the abandonment of all a-priori distinctions between the natural and the social" [20: 196], that is, he describes the interplay between technical and social actors in "equal" terms. Second he describes some of the challenges in obtaining network alignment through this interplay.

Callon demonstrates the establishment of networks through four moments of translation. The first, *problematisation*, has a double significance in that someone raises a problem, which involves a whole series of actors, while they at the same time have a way of framing the problem which positions them in the centre of the debate as an obligatory passage point: "we can help you; we have a solution to the problem." They are both trying to define the network and the links between the actors in the network by framing and addressing a common problem, but at the same time concrete enough to maintain the position in the centre. In addition, the problem is often so big that it cannot be solved by one or two individuals. It is a collective challenge. This leads us to the moment of *interessement*, which is about determining the solidity of the problematisation, or to redefine it in order to strengthen and stabilise the identity of the other actors. The rhetoric here is more like: "we have the same interest as you", and is about attaching the stakeholder's directly to the centre.

The moment of *enrolment* concerns the transformation of a question into a series of statements, which are more certain. Enrolment is achieved if interessement is successful. To describe enrolment is thus to describe the group of multilateral negotiations, trials of strength and tricks. This means that enrolment could turn into a battle between alternative stakeholders and where actors which threatens to cut the link between the central actors and the other actors has to be removed. The enrolment is also depending on some of the actors waiting to accept whatever conclusion drawn by the specialists.

The moment of *mobilisation* depends on the representatives being successful in their attempts to attract the actors, "will the masses follow their representatives"? [20: 214] This moment, thus, is about demonstrating the validity of the spokesmen's observations and the devices effectivity. The "mobilisation…has a definite physical reality which is materialised through a series of displacements" [20: 217]. The credibility of the earlier work is at stake.

In *Dissidence*, the fifth moment, the representatives are questioned, discussed, negotiated, rejected, etc., which again opens the network for intruders from competitive forces.

We use Callons framework in order to (1) describe the interaction between technological regimes of heavy and light through several moments in order to identify when and how tensions arise, and (2) use the moments in order to identify actual tensions, how, when and where they occur. After we have described our data collection and analysis, we look at two cases that can shed light on our interests.

4   Method

Our approach was a case study, conducted in the Health South-East Region in Norway. It covers 2.8 million people, representing more than 50 % of the Norwegian population. It consists of 11 hospitals, and is taken care of by a workforce of 77.000 employees, working on a total budget of over 8 billion euro [21].

We investigated a large e-health program called Digital Renewal and one lightweight initiative, Medicloud, and their interaction. Digital Renewal was a megaprogram of around 1 bn. Euro that aimed at standardising work processes and technologies in the Health South-East Region, running from 2013–18. Medicloud was a small initiative from within HospitalPartner (the IT department of the South-East Region) that emerged in 2014, aiming at supporting lightweight application, and connecting them to the established infrastructures of clinical systems.

We chose the two cases because they offered an opportunity to study in detail the emergence of a lightweight initiative, and its interaction with a large program. Information was gathered as a research activity with interviews and observations.

4.1   Data Collection

We interviewed top executives and IT managers, developers and architects, in Digital Renewal in the period 2013–16. In parallel we followed the evolution of Medicloud 2014–16 as well as conducting interviews, participating in conferences, seminars and workshops where both big vendors and smaller initiatives participated (Table 2).

Table 2.   Data collection

Year	Activity	Participants
2013–2016	Interviews	Executives, directors, developers and architects in the Digital Renewal program
2014–2016	Meetings	Medicloud, HospitalPartner, HealthSouthEast, Sunnaas hospital
2015–2016	Interviews	Medicloud live, or on email
2015	Conference	2 whole days, 4 sessions, discussions, conversations
2015	Workshops	Participants from 20 of the biggest health-IT vendors in Norway
2015–2016	Analysing documents	Written by Medicloud, HospitalPartner, HealthSouthEast authorities

4.2   Data Analysis

We conducted the following steps. First we established a chronology based on the evolution of Medicloud from 2013, as well as the emergent program of Digital Renewal from 2013. In step 2 we looked at the evolution of Medicloud and identified three periods where Medicloud moved from attracting interest to be an actor within the health conferences, and a possible actor in the innovation programs within the health sector. The findings were discussed with the informants. See Table 3.

Table 3. Data analysis

Step	Description	Output
1	Establishing a chronology 2013–16	Case description
2	Analyses of Medicloud evolution	Table 4
3	Analysing tensions between lightweight and heavyweight IT, and identifying barriers	Three barriers, Sect. 6.1
4	Proposing possible solution for overcoming barriers	Sect. 6.2

In step 3 we analysed the patterns of interaction between lightweight and heavyweight, and identified three barriers for interaction. In step 4 we proposed some possible solutions to overcoming the barriers.

5 The Case: Interplay Between Medicloud and Health South-East

We first present Digital Renewal, then the Medicloud initiative.

5.1 The Digital Renewal Program

Digital Renewal is an ambitious e-health program in Health South-East that aims at standardising the IT portfolio for all hospitals in the region, and integrating a large number of IT silo systems, including electronic medical records, patient administrative system, laboratory data and radiology [22]. It was established with a top-down governance regime, with four sub-programs, each with many projects. It has a time span of 7–8 years and a budget of around 1 bn. Euro.

Digital Renewals long-term work for consolidation of hospital IT systems, in order to enable communication between hospitals, systems and users, has been quite successful. The need to have long term and rational plans - giving both suppliers and the regional management predictability - and the demands to cope with the requirements of new systems, features and artefacts has, however, created some tensions. Clinical systems may take years to be implemented, because they need verification in accordance with a range of heavyweight principles like security, efficiency, economy, as well as planning, displacement of resources, etc. As a response to this, in 2014 some clinicians raised critical voices, claiming that the program was not paying enough attention to local clinical needs. In 2015 the Program Board decided that Digital Renewal had to take local needs into account. During 2015 an increasing interplay between the big program and smaller initiatives occurred, particularly thanks to Medicloud.

5.2 The Coming of Medicloud

The Digital Renewal strategy focused on standardisation and consolidation, not innovation. However, both within and outside the health region alternative initiatives

Table 4. Medicloud phases

Phase	Process moment (Callon 1986)	Description	Number of projects	Technology	Relation to digital renewal
P1 2013–14: Establishment and marketing	Problemati- sation and interessement	Attracting stakeholders, establish a common vision for innovation	0	None	Ignored
P2 early-mid 2015: Arena for innovation	Enrolment	Medicloud as a tool for innovative technology	9	None	Observed
P3 late 2015: Lightweight infrastructure	Mobilisation	Start of interplay, revealing tensions between knowledge regimes	10+	IBM Bluemix	Dialogue established

started to appear. Medicloud was established in 2013 as a small initiative within HospitalPartner, with one full time employee and people working in it part-time through projects.

Deploying the lens of ANT we describe the evolution of Medicloud in three periods. See Table 4. Phase 1 is about the establishment of an internal innovation project using workshops and seminars to attract stakeholders within health innovation. The goal in this period was to establish an arena for attracting vendors and clinicians working on innovation and technology, and to make available a technological environment. Through several workshops, relations towards smaller initiatives and big vendors were established, but no concrete pilot projects.

In the *second phase,* HospitalPartner funded the project, hired one more fulltime employee and gave access to 3–4 additional resources part time. The second phase saw a tighter collaboration between Health Sector innovations and Medicloud, as an arena for innovation and through the planning of a technological infrastructure to enable access to health information. Nine innovation initiatives within the Health Sector were collaborating with Medicloud, while Digital Renewal did not see the project as interesting in the first period; they gave it increasing attention in the second period when the debate within the South-East region included Medicloud as an innovation initiative.

In the *third phase* Medicloud was receiving increasing attention as an innovation arena. Before 2014 discourses around innovation was almost non-existent at the biggest Health-IT conference in Norway, Hels-IT. In 2015, innovation became the hottest issue in the same conference. Medicloud also arranged a popular two-day seminar at the conference with a lot of attendance, and entered later into strategic discussions on Medicloud's role as an innovation alibi in the Health South-East region. A group for light and heavyweight strategies was established in 2016 within Health South-East where the IT director and several other directors participate. Internal discussions on Medicloud's role in a new organisation model are ongoing. In this phase, several tensions that shed light on our challenges were emerging. Interplay is very important for Medicloud in that the innovation initiatives relying on them have to be provided with a range of heavyweight resources like access to valid information and security.

6 Analyses and Discussion

We return to our research questions:

- How does an innovation initiative develop within an established information infrastructure, as discourse and solution?
- How can we overcome the barriers for interplay between heavyweight and lightweight technologies?

To develop our argument we build on the insight that tensions may be seen as dualities; they are both barriers to solutions, but also reveal possibilities to overcome the barriers [16]. As shown in the case, the Medicloud initiative, with remarkably small resources, succeeded in setting innovation on the agenda, attracting the most important stakeholders in the Norwegian health sector, and enabled a possible establishment of a lightweight infrastructure within the regional system.

The first phases were characterised by using the innovation momentum to establish activities to attract as many stakeholders as possible, to make Medicloud known, and to be a specific arena for discourse around innovation. In the second phase (enrolment), which is about strengthening the ties by maintaining the interest and fight competition, nine initiatives collaborated with Medicloud. These initiatives gave Medicloud a respectable standing, demonstrating progress and increasing maturity.

However, during mobilisation tensions arose because of shortcomings in the lightweight infrastructure, and in the plan to expand it. The heavyweight actors raised critique towards Medicloud, requiring plans for how the development should take place, and a technological framework that enabled collaboration between Medicloud and Heavyweight technologies. The mobilisation thus rested on the ability to solve a set of barriers; otherwise the network will not be stabilised.

Tensions are as described in the literature part as both barriers and resources, and Table 5 below gives an overview of the findings related to tensions as barriers and resources.

Table 5. Tensions, barriers and resources

Tensions between heavyweight and lightweight IT	#1: Knowledge regime	#2: Scaling	#3: Security, privacy
Barriers to interplay	HW: Lightweight lacks Software Engineering professionality LW: Heavyweight is conservative and a hinder for innovation	Lightweight solutions difficult to industrialise	Lightweight communities prioritises usability before security/privacy
Resources for overcoming barriers	Opportunity - Innovation - Division of labour	New actors: (Such as Medicloud) Broker Middleware	Input to improve security/privacy solutions

6.1 Identifying Tensions and Barriers

As shown in Table 5 we identified three types of tensions relevant for our context; on knowledge regimes, scaling, and security/privacy.

Tension #1: Knowledge Regimes. Tensions between the two knowledge regimes were latent in the beginning, but surfaced in phase 3, when interactions became more direct. For example, in a large meeting in late 2015 between Medicloud and several heavyweight companies, (Microsoft, Apple, DIPS, Tieto and several others) Medicloud was presented as an arena for innovation, outside the heavyweight system of tenders, ordering, development and implementation. Medicloud was profiled as providing a technological platform, a playground, where the users can perform trial and error on medical data. The heavyweight vendors were not impressed:

HW1: "who is going to buy the Medicloud platform?"
HW2: "how are you going to industrialise innovation? What is the strategy besides teasing people?"
HW3: "what happens if all the pilot initiatives collapse because of the lack of a suitable technical environment"?
HW4: "What is Medicloud doing in order to move the attention from long-term order regime to a lighter which facilitates innovation and lightweight..."?

These tensions were also visible internally, in HospitalPartner and Digital Renewal. The Medicloud manager was at various occasions campaigning to "phase out the old model of production and replace it with a new one", where the clinicians and usability are in centre. He also expressed the desire to participate within a "bi-modal strategy" where heavy- and lightweight are separated into two platforms running independently of each other.

We interpret these tensions as a barrier between the two knowledge regimes, who found it hard to respect each other; the heavyweight community felt that the lightweight people lacked the required software engineering professionalism, while the lightweight proponents thought that the heavyweights were a hindrance for innovation. *Digital Renewal* consisted of long-term projects going on for years and where planning, ordering, implementation and training had to follow requirements of security and control. The Medicloud people said: "We would not like to be a part of Digital Renewal...the reason for this is the slow progress - we can do in two weeks what Digital Renewal need 4 years to do".

The heavyweight providers tend to see lightweight solutions as competition, and Medicloud's strategy to raise a new discourse on innovation that bypasses the heavyweight requirements was constantly countered by the heavyweight actors displacing the discourse back into heavyweight terrain.

Tension #2: Scaling. In the interactions between Medicloud and the lightweight projects we observed that the lightweight project managers went from enthusiasm over the potential of their solutions to frustrations over the obstacles of setting the solutions into production. One project manager said in a meeting with Medicloud:

"We have developed, in close co-operation with the clinicians, an excellent app solution for supporting an emergency unit. We were expecting that Medicloud could help us in setting it into production. But now you are telling us that we have to wait for a solution some time in the future, or going through the established bureaucracy?"

Medicloud acknowledged the problem, but could not promise a solution. "It takes time to provide a modern industrial production platform, and we need more money." While cloud solutions are readily available, they become easily stand-alone applications, without the necessary integration with basic medical registers.

We interpret this as a barrier for lightweight innovation. Lightweight project tend to make prototypes, aiming at getting feedback on the usability, and the continual modification of the prototype based on the interaction. The challenge is that projects may evaporate through the inability to provide long-term planning for the continuation of projects, including how the product finally will be industrialised. This shortcoming may also threaten some of the motivations within the spirit of innovation these initiatives rely on. The test and production routines of heavyweight IT are established to maintain stability for clinical solutions, and do not go well with lightweight entrepreneurship.

Tension #3: Security and Privacy. In large e-health infrastructures security and privacy are based on law and detailed regulations, and implemented with a number of technical and organisational mechanisms. For instance, in all applications that access patient information includes a filter for user identification and fine-granulated access and update rights.

The HospitalPartner managers and developers expressed concerns that these requirements were not treated sufficiently by the more entrepreneurial lightweight vendors. Also heavyweight actors like Microsoft, Apple, DIPS, and Cerner were challenging Medicloud's strategy for security and privacy. For instance, they argued, if they were to make APIs available for lightweight applications, they are required by law to ensure that access and information is compliant with regulations. Even more problematic, if lightweight app is designed to update clinical systems, the security requirements are heavy indeed.

There is no doubt that this constitutes a barrier for lightweight IT, because on the one hand the lightweight focus is on usability and feedback in interaction with the clinicians, making security a second priority. On the other hand, some of the success rests on the lightweight ability to provide trust amongst the users as they are dealing with very important privacy issues.

6.2   Overcoming Barriers

Our empirical evidence does not provide outright solutions for these barriers, but we use two sources to describe possible solutions. First, tensions are also resources; they give information, direction and suggestions. Second, we build on the existing literature [7–9] on communication and collaboration between heavy and light to carve out possible solutions.

#1. Overcoming Knowledge Regime Barriers. We observed that heavyweight concerns were sometimes mixed with acknowledgements of the limitations of the current heavyweight regime. A director within Health South-East Region commented:

> "In the Digital Renewal program there is a lot of central governance, and little freedom. There is a need to clean up the infrastructures, create order. There is a lot to do but not much time. These challenges are forcing us to rethink. We cannot own everything, command everything, and control everything. Medicloud is very good at teasing us, telling us to rethink our strategies".

This attitude may not be shared by the whole heavyweight community, but it opens up for some reflections on how the barriers may be overcome. First, the lightweight agenda of user-oriented innovation should be accepted as legitimate by the heavyweight community. It is a fact that many of the heavyweight systems do not support clinical processes sufficiently well [23, 24]. The opportunities offered by lightweight IT might help to improve this, not only by better usability of solutions, but also by establishing a culture for local innovation. Second, the increasing costs and complexity of heavyweight solutions are hardly sustainable over time, and there is a need to discuss the division of labour between heavyweight and lightweight IT [9]. A possible way forward is to think in terms of basic registers and their integration by heavyweight IT, and a user-oriented layer of lightweight non-intrusive systems on top, with local variations.

#2. Overcoming Barriers Related to Scaling. These barriers, as described above, relates to setting lightweight solution into production, and also enabling diffusion to a broader set of users.

Setting lightweight solutions into production, without invoking the heavyweight regime of SLAs, test regimes and toll-gates, requires new thinking. One possible solution is the "app store"; modelled on Apple`s platform for apps. An app store for the health sector is conceivable and easy to establish, and would be appreciated by the lightweight community and users. However, this does not solve the needs for integration with clinical systems. One way to solve these needs is to establish brokers (such as Medicloud) and necessary middleware between the inside and the outside of the heavyweight infrastructure. This would enable users on the outside to access the lightweight infrastructure, while the coupling between the infrastructures would secure that the two regimes interoperate in a loose manner. Obviously, there are many unsolved questions on how this can be implemented.

#3. Overcoming Barriers Related to Security and Privacy. Everyone working in or close to the health sector is informed about the sensitivity of information and thus the control regime needed for taking care of personality issues. There is no way that lightweight IT can take this lightly. While heavyweight IT has created extensive algorithms driven by distant servers, lightweight IT should look for simpler solutions.

One inspiration can be current mobile solutions, where vendors have innovated more pragmatic security solutions using fingerprints, chips or pins; this approach takes advantage of the cheap and available commercial solutions from the key innovation arenas. These are solutions that the users are comfortable with, and trust. The limitation of these solutions, however, is that many issues on security and privacy remain unresolved.

7 Conclusion

In this paper we investigated how information infrastructures are extended. Building on a case from e-health our aim was to understand the interaction of a heavyweight IT infrastructure and lightweight IT initiative, and the tensions of the interplay. We add to the existing literature with two contributions.

First, we extend information infrastructure theory by identifying three types of tensions relevant for the interplay with a larger structure, knowledge regime, scaling and security/privacy. These tensions are creating specific barriers for the integration of lightweight IT:

- *Knowledge regimes:* The heavyweight regime resists acknowledging the legitimacy of the rival regime.
- *Scaling*: Lightweight solutions are difficult to industrialise.
- *Security/privacy:* Lightweight communities prioritise usability before security/privacy.

Second, we discuss how these barriers may be overcome. There is a danger in that lightweight programs may be sucked into the bigger system, that they may become colonised by heavyweight regimes. Knowledge regime barriers can be overcome by accepting first the user orientation in lightweight initiatives, and second the need for division of labour between the two sides. Scaling barriers can be overcome by enabling use of digital diffusion of apps through app-stores and similar, and by establishing lightweight initiatives as brokers or middleware on the outside of the infrastructure.

Barriers related to security and privacy issues can be overcome by enabling the use of cheap and available commercial solutions, although these may have some limitations when used in the health sector.

References

1. Priemus, H., Flyvbjerg, B., van Wee, B. (eds.): Decision-Making on Mega-Projects: Cost-Benefit Analysis Planning and Innovation. Edward Elgar Publishing, Cheltenham (2008)
2. Currie, W.: Translating health IT policy into practice in the UK national health service. Scand. J. Inf. Syst. **26**(2), 1–24 (2014)
3. Sauer, C., Willcocks, L.P.: Unreasonable expectations – NHS IT, Greek choruses and the games institutions play around mega-programmes. J. Inf. Technol. **22**, 195–201 (2007)
4. Lakatos, I.: Criticism and the methodology of scientific research programmes. In: Proceedings of the Aristotelian Society, New Series, vol. 69, no. 1968–1969, pp. 149–186 (1969)
5. Swanson, E., Ramiller, N.C.: The organizing vision in information systems innovation. Organ. Sci. **8**(5), 458–474 (1997)
6. Ellingsen, G., Monteiro, E.: The organizing vision of integrated health information systems. Health Inform. J. **14**(3), 223–236 (2008)
7. Harris, J., Ives, B., Junglas, I.: IT consumerization: when gadgets turn into enterprise IT tools. MIS Q. Exec. **11**(3), 99–112 (2012)

8. Bygstad, B.: The coming of lightweight IT. In: Proceedings of European Conference of Information Systems (ECIS), Münster, Germany (2015)
9. Willcocks, L., Lacity, M., Craig, A.: The IT function and robotic process automation. In: The outsourcing Unit Working Research Paper Series, October 2015. http://eprints.lse.ac.uk/64519/1/OUWRPS_15_05_published.pdf
10. Tilson, D., Lyytinen, K., Sorensen, C.: Digital infrastructures: the missing IS research agenda. Inf. Syst. Res. 21(4), 748–759 (2010)
11. Bannister, F.: Dismantling the silos: extracting new value from IT investments in public administration. Inf. Syst. J. 11(1), 65–84 (2001)
12. Perrow, C.: Normal Accidents: Living with High Risk Technologies. Princeton University Press (1999)
13. Hanseth, O.: From system and tools to network and Infrastructure - towards a theory of ICT solutions and its design methodology implications (2002). http://heim.ifi.uio.no/~oleha/Publications/ib_ISR_3rd_resubm2.html
14. Hanseth, O., Monteiro, E.: Understanding information infrastructures, unpublished manuscript (2010). http://heim.ifi.uio.no/~oleha/Publications/bok.html
15. Hanseth, O., Lyytinen, K.: Design theory for dynamic complexity in information infrastructures: the case of building internet. J. Inf. Technol. 25(1), 1–19 (2010)
16. Edwards, P., Jackson, S., Bowker, G., Knobel, C.: Understanding infrastructure: dynamics, tensions and design. In: Report on a Workshop History and Theory of Infrastructure: Scientific Cyberinfrastructures (2007). http://deepblue.lib.umich.edu/bitstream/handle/2027.42/49353/UnderstandingInfrastructure2007.pdf?sequence=3&isAllowed=y
17. Monteiro, E.: Actor-network theory and information infrastructures. In: Ciborra, C., et al. (eds.) From Control to Drift – The Dynamics of Corporate Information Infrastructures, pp. 71–87. Oxford University Press, Oxford (2000)
18. Latour, B., Woolgar, S.: Laboratory Life: The Construction of Scientific Facts. Princeton University Press, Princeton (1986)
19. Monteiro, E., Hanseth, O.: Social shaping of information infrastructure: on being specific about the technology. In: Orlikowski, W.J., Walsham, G., Jones, M.R., DeGross, J.I. (eds.) Information Technology and Changes in Organizational Work, pp. 325–343. Chapman & Hall, Boca Raton (1995)
20. Callon, M.: Some elements of a sociology of translation: domestication of the scallops and the fishermen of St Brieuc Bay. In: Law, J. (ed.) Power, Action and Belief: A New Sociology of Knowledge, pp. 196–233. Routledge & Kegan Paul, London (1986)
21. Helse Sør Øst: Helse SørØst RHF – det regionale helseforetaket (2015). http://www.helse-sorost.no/om-oss/om-helseforetaket
22. Helse Sør Øst: Regional klinisk løsning (2015). http://www.helse-sorost.no/aktuelt_/digitalfornying_/tre-programmer_/Sider/regional-klinisk-dokumentasjon.aspx
23. Ash, J.S., Berg, M., Coiera, E.: Some unintended consequences of information technology in health care: the nature of patient care information systems-related errors. J. Am. Med. Inform. Assoc. 11, 104–1123 (2004)
24. Berg, M.: Patient care information systems and health care work: a sociotechnical approach. Int. J. Med. Inform. 55, 87–101 (1999)

The Ambivalent Characteristics of Connected, Digitised Products: Case Tesla Model S

Antti K. Lyyra[(✉)] and Kari M. Koskinen

Department of Management,
The London School of Economics and Political Science, London, UK
{a.k.lyyra, k.m.koskinen}@lse.ac.uk

Abstract. Connected, digitised products are assemblages that comprise digital and physical components and are linked to digital support infrastructures. Given that re-programmability of digital components allows a product designer to adopt a design philosophy that embraces incompleteness and continuous improvement, digitised (tangible) products may also become incomplete and open-ended if such a philosophy is embraced. This research uses Tesla Model S as a case study to explore the mutability of a passenger car over time. The results show that a type of a product that has traditionally been seen as stable may become open-ended, incomplete and mutable in terms of its specifications and functionality. This brings forward the relevance of complementary architectural frames and principles to conceptualise differing design cycles among physical and digital components in innovation and product management while also showing blurring boundaries of control between the owner and the manufacturer of a product.

Keywords: Connected · Digitised products · Hybrid materiality · Design cycles · Product lifecycle · Innovation management · Product management

1 Introduction

Innovation and product management practices strive to connect organisational capabilities to customer demands [12] over product lifecycles, ranging from design, manufacturing and maintenance to decommissioning and disposal.

Traditionally, production is perceived as a compilation of components to produce a final product [11]. That product is in turn perceived as a complete and fixed output that is sold to a customer. Whenever innovation occurs, it almost invariably leads to the design and introduction of a new model. Therefore, product design is seen as a clear and somewhat separable cycle, which is followed by production and eventually leading to the sales and transfer of ownership. After that, apart from a maintenance type of repair or service, products are not generally expected to improve in specifications or receive any new functionality.

The digitalisation of tangible products is challenging this view. While the physical components of products resist change, the digital components are more open-ended and readily changeable [5, 9, 17]. Therefore, the incorporation of digital components into physical tangible products blurs the boundaries of to what extent a product is perceived

© Springer International Publishing Switzerland 2016
M. Gellerstedt et al. (Eds.): SCIS 2016, LNBIP 259, pp. 57–69, 2016.
DOI: 10.1007/978-3-319-43597-8_5

as amenable to change, or according to which criteria a particular product could be seen as finished or complete. Moreover, added with connectivity to digital infrastructures and cloud-based support infrastructures, it is no longer clear where the boundaries and control of a product reside.

This study sets out to explore how such open-endedness of digitised tangible products might impact innovation and product management practices as well as customer experience using the Tesla Model S passenger car as a case study. The topic is approached by examining software releases that introduce changes to specifications and functionality of the car. This case is seen as an outlier in an industry that traditionally has focused its efforts on the design and production of well-engineered and complete products.

The results show that a product, which is traditionally seen as stable, can become open-ended and incomplete. The various specifications and functionalities are constantly changing, showing what it means in practice when a tangible product becomes increasingly digital, mutable, connected and dependent on its manufacturer throughout its lifetime. The results also empirically confirm the relevance of utilising complementary architectural design principles to conceptualise differing design cycles and levels of resistance to change among digital and physical components over the lifecycle of a product [7].

The paper is organised as follows. Section 2 discusses characteristics of hybrid materiality of digitised products and outlines potential impacts of this materiality in innovation and product management practice, after which Sect. 3 presents the research question to explore empirically how a product of hybrid materiality changes over time. Subsequently, Sect. 4 presents the case and summarises data collection and analysis procedures and methods. The results of the analysis are presented in Sect. 5, whereas Sect. 6 discusses the findings and their meaning together with limitations and possible avenues for future research. Sect. 7 concludes this paper.

2 Literature Review

The success of commercial enterprises commonly depends on their ability to introduce new products in a fashion that brings novelty and satisfaction to their customers. While product innovation has traditionally followed relatively predictable design cycles, increased use of digital components in tangible products is poised to alter the frequency of design iterations.

The material characteristics of physical and digital components in terms of their amenability to change have gathered interest among digital innovation researchers. Broadly speaking, the physical objects, components and artefacts are described as resistant to change; the digital objects, such as computer programs, are described as less resistant, something that can be separated from their physical carriers [13] and moulded from one form to another with relative ease [7, 17].

This lack of resistance in the digital domain is said to follow from the re-programmability of digital computers and homogenisation of data [13, 17]. The digital computer is a general purpose machine, which is able to process any set of stepwise instructions (software) as long as such a set is presented to a computer in an agreed and unambiguous format of binary numbers (bits). The notions of re-programmability and homogenisation of data imply that behaviour of the digital computer is readily changeable; it can be repurposed with minimal marginal cost and delay by supplying it with new sets of instructions [7]. As the functioning logic of a computer can be changed with relative ease, the digital materiality is often described as something that is malleable and amenable to change [9].

In contrast, the physical artefacts and objects typically lack ways for cost effective and instant collective changes. More tools, time and labour are needed to carry out modifications for each unit, increasing the marginal costs and making them more resistant to attempts of change and repurposing.

The concept of digitised (tangible) products has been used to describe products, which are assemblages of the digital and physical components [7], whereas the concept of hybrid materiality [2] has been used to describe the material characteristics of products that combine digital and mechanical components with asymmetric resistance to change.

Given the changeability of digital materiality, functionality and behaviour of digitised products can be redesigned and changed several times after their first introduction. By doing so, they can be made to better-match circumstances and environments, which might not have been even foreseen during the original design phase, yet pose no real problem as adaptations to this type of products can be made at any point during their lifecycle. As a result, similarly to software, digitised products can also be seen as unfinished, malleable and ontologically ambivalent [5, 9, 18].

Consequently, it appears that there is no urgent need to restrict the design and development of a digitised product to any particular point in time. Existing functionalities can be changed and new ones introduced continuously as long as they are in the reach of digital means and there is a connection to provide a product with a new set of software. While software can be easily changed, it is important to note that the logic embedded in software must conform with hardware as well as the aspects of the physical environment it seeks to model and manipulate. In that sense, digital and physical materiality are tightly connected as the physical restrains the digital; it can be argued that it places boundaries on what can or cannot be achieved by changing the digital [8].

The notion of abstract design patterns as a design principle has been proposed as a useful addition to conceptualise and manage the tensions that may emerge from the differing design cycles and levels of resistance among physical and digital components [7]. This forwards an idea of conceptualising design not simply as a hierarchy-of-parts, but rather as something which is combined with networks-of-patterns; well-defined and specified plans and components are complemented with generalisations, which are abstracted patterns that represent intended functions or purposes of components. Patterns are seen as comparable to placeholders for something that can be invented or improved later. The applicability of this principle is demonstrated in the case study of infotainment architecture design and development at a car manufacturer [7]. Although the authors of that study theorise that digitised products are amenable for change throughout their lifetimes, their empirical evidence does not reach beyond the design phase and is limited to the components and systems that revolve around an infotainment system.

The incomplete nature of a digitised product also begs the question on who decides when and how to change the functioning of a product. The incompleteness of a digitised product and its linking to a cloud based system have potential to shift some parts of control from the owner of a product to its manufacturer. Furthermore, the latter could introduce a change in specifications and functionalities of a product without seeking the approval of its owner. This deviates from the notion where the control of a product has resided almost entirely in the hands of its owner. In terms of seeing digitised products sharing characteristics with more traditional technological platforms, the tendency there has been for the platform owner to try to hold most of the control of the platform [3, 13].

As shown above, the digital and physical materiality differ in their capacity and resistance to change. Whereas the physical materiality is harder to change, the digital materiality portrays itself as open-ended that can changed repeatedly. While this ambivalent ontology of digitised products may provide a broad sphere of design and marketing choices for innovation and product management over a lifetime of a product, it also raises questions regarding consumer experience and where the ultimate control of a particular product actually resides. To explore the avenues of hybrid materiality and abstract design patterns, this study sets out to explore to what extent a product that is traditionally seen as stable can be changed through digital means after its production when it is already in use.

3   Research Question

To further investigate how this ambivalent ontology of digitised products might impact on innovation and product management strategies and practices, this study sets out to investigate the frequency and dimensions mutability of a passenger car once it has rolled out of the factory.

Typically, new car models are brought to market every four to seven years and supplemented with cosmetic facelift models about halfway through a model's lifecycle. A car is expected to stay much the same once it has been manufactured; oil, spark plugs and other consumables are changed and software updated in a service, but the specifications and functionalities are not expected to change. In other words, they are purchased as finished and complete products with their functionality fully specified and known.

This lifecycle model is being challenged. The recently established car maker Tesla sends out frequent software releases to change and improve functionality of the cars they have manufactured and sold while other car makers are planning to introduce the possibility of updating software of cars over the Internet connection. This introduces a novel time-based dimension to the configuration space of specifications and functionalities of digitised products.

To explore further the frequency of change and the functional domains that could benefit from the utilisation of abstract design patterns, we approached the topic through the following research question:

What are the characteristics of digitally-introduced change in a connected, digitised product?

The aim is to answer the question in three ways by surveying reported software releases with their respective functionality of the Tesla Model S car. First, the frequency of digitally introduced change will be established by surveying the quantity and quality of software releases. The physical changes and recalls are not in the focus of this analysis. Second, the contents of the software releases are examined and grouped in order to understand how specifications and functionalities of the car change over time. These groups demonstrate the scope of domains amenable to abstract design patters. Third, other relevant qualitative aspects of change are collected from the data and analysed. These include, among others, shortcomings found from the software, hardware-software conflicts and contractual and regulatory restrictions instantiated through software.

4 Case Selection

We focus on a particular model of Tesla, the Model S, in order to form a coherent understanding on what kind of changes can be and are made for a particular model through software updates. The customer deliveries of the Model S started in June 2012 and it has been on the market for more than three years now, going through several software releases and therefore providing longitudinal empirical evidence for this study. The Model S can be seen as a typical example of a passenger car in the sense that it is meant to be used in average road conditions and it is not meant for off-road activities or any other kind of special circumstances.

From a case study perspective, the Model S can be seen both as a representational and as an outlier case [15]. It is representational since it belongs to a rather common and well-established product category group of passenger cars. On the other hand, within this category it is also an outlier. What sets Tesla apart from the other car manufacturers is its heavy exploitation of open-endedness of connected, digital materiality. This happens not only in terms of the control functions of the car, such as adjusting the functioning of energy and power-train, but also in providing constant cloud-based software updates that can change specifications and functionality of the car in various ways. Much of the hardware of the model has been designed to offer maximum flexibility for software updates. As an example, the control panel of the car is a 17 inch touchscreen with no physical buttons, which enables it to be not only completely editable in relation to what it shows, but also in how it works.

It is expected that the case provides a useful empirical starting position to discuss further the potential implications of digitalisation to innovation and product management practices and consumer experience. Although much of mutability of a digitised product is enabled by the ambivalent characteristics of a digitised product, it is important to note that mutability does not automatically follow from any digital materiality embedded in a product. It should rather be seen as a design strategy or decision that is enabled by the hybrid materiality of digitised products. To prove the point, most of the modern cars are seen as stable products although they contain and exploit a large amount of software, yet they are not constantly in the making and are not generally expected to change over their lifetime.

4.1   Data, Method and Analysis

To update cars, Tesla delivers software releases in a phased manner; once an update is available, a car displays a notification on the screen with an option to install it immediately or to schedule the installation for a later time. Tesla's software release procedure contains major, minor and maintenance type of releases. A software version can be identified either by a release number or a software build number, both of which are shown at the time of update. Typically, major releases are issued with release notes whereas minor releases occasionally lack them. Maintenance releases seem to be left unspecified. Given that the authors did not have direct contact with Tesla, and the company does not make software release histories and their specific contents publicly available, the empirical evidence was gathered and combined from release notes that were available on the Internet, the Wiki and discussion sections of Tesla Motors Club[1] and Tesla Motors[2] and Teslarati[3] websites. All the data was collected online, following the example of other studies that have been able to show how online content can function as a valuable source of data for research [3, 14]. The evidence was arranged by listing software releases with their respective release and software build version numbers and dates and then matching respective releases with changed functionalities for further analysis.

The analysis started by surveying the frequency of software releases and calculating the average amount of days between releases. After establishing the frequency of releases, the qualitative data analysis was performed using the methods of thematic analysis [1]. The coding process started by creating categories based on the open coding of a subset of data. Subsequently, the analysis continued by examining changes delivered to cars through software releases over a period of time. The changes were assigned to categories according to their functional features. The evidence was also analysed according to the notions of restrictions and quality. Restrictions were mostly subject to two different factors: geographical location and configuration of a car. Quality refers to notions of improvement and decline in quality that are related to shortcomings in software and to the corrections of such shortcomings.

The data was coded by the two authors individually in order to guarantee the overall quality and inter-coder agreement. The agreement between coders was approximately 90 percent, and where the authors did not agree, discussion followed as to why not. The disagreements on the coding were mainly due to functionalities that affected different functional areas of the car and it was not clear which one of the functional areas prevailed over the others.

5   The Results of the Analysis

This section presents the results of the analysis. To begin, the frequency of software releases demonstrates the rate of mutability of a digitised product. This is followed by outlining the domains of functionalities and specifications that are amenable to the

---

[1] http://www.teslamotorsclub.com.

[2] http://www.teslamotors.com.

[3] http://www.teslarati.com.

open-ended principles of abstract design patterns. Finally, restrictive and qualitative aspects of software changes are brought forward before closing remarks.

5.1 The Frequency of Change

Tesla has provided the Model S with five branches of major release over the past three and half years (Table 1). The first branch I(*) was released when the first Model S was delivered to a customer on 22 June 2012, whereas the current major release 7 was first pushed to cars on 16 October 2015. The time between moving from one major branch to the next one varied from 161 to 431 days. During the lifecycles of major branches, each of them received 1 to 10 minor releases and numerous maintenance releases. In total, over this period of time, Tesla has issued 117 software releases for the Model S, approximate one every 11.49 days.

Table 1. Software releases with their respective frequency

Major release branch	I (*)	4	5	6	7	All
Releases in branch	1.7.36 1.9.11 1.9.17 1.13.16 1.15.8 1.15.14	4.0 4.1 4.2 4.3 4.4 4.5	5.0 5.5 5.6 5.8 5.9 5.10 5.11 5.12 5.14	6.0 6.1 6.2	7.0 7.1	All
Lifetime in days (approx.)	161	232	431	375	133	**1344**
First release	22 Jun 2012 (**)	30 Nov 2012	18 Jul 2013	11 Sep 2014	16 Oct 2015	22 Jun 2012
Latest release	30 Nov 2012	20 Jul 2013	22 Sep 2014	21 Sep 2015	26 Feb 2016 (***)	26 Feb 2016 (***)
Total number of software builds	6	19	32	45	15	**117**
Number of major releases	1	1	1	1	1	5
Number of minor releases	5	5	10	2	1	23
Number of maintenance releases	0	13	21	42	13	89
Average number of days between software releases	**26.83**	**12.21**	**13.47**	**8.33**	**8.87**	**11.49**

*The first major branch is referred to as I for initial.
**The first customer delivery of the Model S is used as the starting date.
***The latest release to this active branch is used as the end date.

5.2 Changes in Specifications and Functionalities

The analysis of the changes introduced by software releases established seven functional domains that were amenable to the open-ended principles of abstract design patterns, namely: information, entertainment, user interface design, energy and performance, ancillaries, connectivity and self-steering capabilities. The first three categories are often subsumed under a higher-level category of infotainment [7], however, we treat the three categories as separate for analytical purposes. It is also worth noting that these categories are not mutually exclusive; often a single feature or a change within a release could span across several categories.

The *information* category is comprised of changes to driving related map and navigation functionalities, as well as to personal time management and communication applications. The maps and navigation updates revolved around traffic information and functionalities, often with an aim to better localise, plan a route through and navigate to charging stations. The changes in time management and communication applications were related to functionalities to connect a driver's phone with a car's information systems using the Tesla mobile application.

The *entertainment* category includes changes that are geared towards entertainment, such as the introduction of the Spotify streaming service as well as enhancing the ability to browse a USB stick for media content. Improvements in radio buffering and reception and web browser performance and stability were considered to represent the categories of information and entertainment simultaneously.

The *user interface design* category was formed on the basis of updates in information and entertainment functions that were more of a visual than practical characteristic. Such changes include new voice commands, the introduction of "flat looks" and changes in font size and auto-brightness and search-box functionalities. Also, the changes to the behaviour of control buttons on the steering wheel are considered to be represented by this category.

The *energy and performance* category represents the chances and improvements in mileage, acceleration and top speed, the changes that revolve around battery management and the control of electric motors. Mileage maximising functionalities intend to minimise something that is often referred to as "end of range anxiety" (a fear of a car running out of battery), whereas acceleration and top speed are more geared towards maximising the driving experience.

The *ancillaries* category characterises changes to software that controls ancillary functions such as locks, door handles and windscreen wipers, introducing chances to their behaviour.

The *connectivity* category emerged to describe the changes that were introduced to improve a car's connectivity to telecommunications infrastructure and cloud-based services over 3G and Wi-Fi protocols.

The *self-steering* category contains updates that change the auto-steering capabilities and therefore alter the behaviour of a car. Such capabilities include traffic-aware cruise control, lane keeping with automatic steering, self-parking and automatic high/low beam headlights, which are a part of an autopilot convenience features package as well as collision warning systems, all of which allow a driver to shift some driving-related tasks to a car.

On average, each release led to the introduction or changing of 6.6 control setting items in the control panel, based on calculations from the release notes. Also, the analysis of functions showed that the emphasis of earlier releases were on the side of basic functionality and incremental enhancements, while the latter ones were more geared towards introducing new functionality.

5.3   The Restrictive and Qualitative Aspects of Change

The analysis revealed also that changes were not only about positive improvements. While generally aimed at improving and enhancing functionality, in some occasions bugs were also introduced. Wi-Fi issues, touch screen flashing, rebooting to overcome issues as well as unexpected shutdowns were reported. Also, while Tesla was investigating the causes of battery fires in late 2013, it removed active air suspension control to raise the ride-height and increase road clearance for precautionary and safety reasons. Once the investigation was closed and the protection of batteries improved by retrofitting stronger battery shields, the suspension control and lower ride-heights were reintroduced with a later software release.

Conflicts and interdependencies among hardware and software configurations were also encountered. To provide examples, the release of version 5.0 introduced GPS errors in certain cars, which prompted Tesla to replace hardware in the affected cars. Also, certain auto-steering capabilities are not available to the cars that lack appropriate hardware such as sensors. There were interdependencies among software-based configurations as well. If a certain software package was not purchased for a car, even if that car had the appropriate set of hardware installed, certain specifications and functions from a release were not available until that package was purchased for a car. Furthermore, Tesla provided mobile applications to remotely monitor and control a car only for iPhones and Android, leaving Windows Phone and BlackBerry users without a possibility to control their cars through mobile phones.

Another set of boundaries was found relating to geographical, contractual and regulatory reasons. The music streaming service Spotify was introduced only to certain geographical areas, whereas other areas were served by other music streaming services, and certain auto-steering functions are available only in certain countries. In Hong Kong, after Hong Kong's Transport Department requested a review of safety measures, Tesla temporarily disabled the Autosteer and Auto Lane Change functions on all Model S in Hong Kong with immediate effect.

The results show that the hybrid materiality of the car allows it to be changed frequently through digital means while simultaneously revealing functional domains that can be subjected to the open-ended principles of abstract design pattern philosophies. This multidimensional mutability characterises a product that is connected to centralised cloud-based infrastructures, incomplete and constantly in the making.

6   Discussion

The analysis of empirical evidence shows that a type of product that has traditionally been seen as relatively stable may become open-ended, incomplete and mutable within several functional and qualitative dimensions, depending on a particular configuration of hardware, software and connectivity. This demonstrates the applicability of digital theories in product-based domains and shows that the notion of abstract design patterns could be applied to conceptualise a wide range of mutability of digitised products throughout their lifecycles. The implications of mutability are envisaged to have impact on innovation and product management practices and consumer experience while boundaries of control are shifting.

To begin, the analysis confirms our initial, literature-driven conception, which shows that digitised products that consist of hybrid materiality may become ambivalent in their specifications and functionality. Given that much of that continuous change is enabled by the re-programmability of digital computers and digitalisation, connectivity, platforms and cloud-based infrastructures as general phenomena, it is envisaged that theories of digitalisation and digital innovation could gain more relevance outside typical domains of information systems research community. This supports the argument that digital innovation should be considered as a fundamental and powerful concept in the information systems curriculum [4] and shows that the lessons from digital innovation could contribute to innovation and product management research [16].

The mutability that is enabled by the digital materiality, however, is constrained by the physical materiality that sets boundaries on what functionalities and specifications can and cannot be modified through the means of releasing computer software. This tension among materialities was demonstrated in the study that examined differing design and development cycles among physical and digital components during the design phase of an infotainment systems of a passenger car [7]. Consequently, they introduced the notion of architectural frames and proposed the combination of types of frames, hierarchy-of-parts and network-of-patterns as a complementary ways to frame and conceptualise the rigidity of physical materiality and the open-endedness of digital materiality. The results of this study demonstrate empirically that the above-mentioned dynamics are not only pertinent to the design phase but may continue be exploited over the entire lifecycle of a digitised product. Also, abstract and mutable design patterns can be exploited along many dimensions of specifications and functionalities, ranging from infotainment to auto-steering capabilities, which are supported by cloud-based digital infrastructures and connectivity. The results imply a potentially increasing emphasis on developing digital-physical architectural frames that support changes in specification and functionality of a digitised product throughout its entire lifetime.

Utilising the complementary concept of architectural frames to make sense of an entire lifecycle from design to decommission suggests novel avenues and challenges for innovation and product management practices. On one hand, companies would have a larger spectrum of choice in their product and marketing decisions. To lower the upfront costs of product design, a company could decide to enter the market with a product that is good enough to get traction and subsequently improve and maintain it until decommissioning, should a need emerge either from the customer or the environment [5]. On the other hand, marketing messages could be tailored to emphasise the promise of continuous innovation and improvement instead of fine-tuned and complete products. This can give choices to consumers as well. They could choose to purchase a complete product that is fully known at the point of purchase, or, alternatively, to subscribe to a stream of improvements as well as an occasional decline, to release notes and the learning of new features, specifications, and settings. In order to bring market needs and organisational capabilities together [12], innovation and product managers and strategists should plan for mutability of a product throughout its lifecycle by reflecting upon the configuration of architectural frames [7], innovation [6] and cloud-based infrastructures that are required to support it [13].

While opening the spectrum of choice, the mutability of a connected, digitised product also blurs the limits of control between product owners and manufacturers. After the purchase it has traditionally been a matter for the owner to decide how the product he or she owns is going to change. With connected and digitised products, this aspect may no longer be valid. Since the manufacturer can alter a product, it also retains a significant portion of control over the specifications and functionalities of a product. This might not be much of a problem as long the software releases are seen as improvements. However, as products get more complex and their parts more inter-connected, the verdict on whether a particular software release is considered as an improvement or a deterioration becomes more difficult to make. The increased inter-connectedness among the functions of a car also means that an update in one area is likely to affect the functioning of other areas as well. A software release may not only enable new functionality, but also change the way the already existing functionality works, which might not always be received positively by the owners, but instead with more mixed reviews. Furthermore, as software release cycles become potentially shorter, it also raises the question as to how much change an average user is willing to accept. These constant changes place the user in a continuous learning mode, which can affect the overall satisfaction with a product. Therefore, the connected, digitised products have the capacity to change the relationship between manufacturers and owners, and not necessarily to the liking of the latter.

This issue in the area of control resonates with other issues relating to the control aspects of the digital, such as platform ownership [3] and the regulating power of code [10]. However, the connected, digitised products offer a slightly different research domain on control, as the key theme is the shifting power balance between manu-facturers and customers. In the case of Tesla, it seems that it is expected by the manufacturer that the users simply agree with and adapt to the updates. Further research is needed to explain the implications that this shift in control entails for customer relations, but also in other areas such as product ownership and the tuning processes that take place between the users and the manufacturers of connected, digitised products, also during the creation of the actual physical components of the product.

Overall, understanding the changes that are brought about by the connected, digitised products is of interest not only to practitioners but also to many scholars working in fields related to the topic. Even though this paper sheds further light on the questions at hand, it is admitted that generalisations based on a single case study are not very straightforward to make. Additional data and research is therefore needed not only to understand the implications connected, digitised products have in other industries and to their organisational strategies, but also to explore and theorise further on the hybrid materiality of digitised products as a whole. What remains clear is that the area provides several fruitful avenues for digital innovation and management researchers to test and enhance their theories and take them to new contexts and domains of application.

7 Conclusion

This paper provides an example of how innovation and product management philosophies of incompleteness and continuous improvement can be appropriated and exploited by an industry that has traditionally aimed at completely designed and finished products. The enabling factors behind the phenomena are the hybrid materiality of digitised products and the lifecycle-long connection between a product, its user and its manufacturer. Not cutting this digital cord between the product and its manufacturer has important implications to various areas of innovation and product management, ranging from product design to managing customer relations. More research is needed to better understand the effects that connected, digitised products can have in different industries and to various stakeholders. The authors of this work hope that it provides some indication on what are the factors future research could pay attention to.

Acknowledgements. This research was supported by research student grants that were made available by the Emil Aaltonen foundation and the KAUTE foundation (the Finnish Science Foundation for Economics and Technology).

References

1. Attride-Stirling, J.: Thematic networks: an analytic tool for qualitative research. Qual. Res. **1**(3), 385–405 (2001)
2. Barrett, M., et al.: Reconfiguring boundary relations: robotic innovations in pharmacy work. Organ. Sci. **23**(5), 1448–1466 (2012)
3. Eaton, B., et al.: Distributed tuning of boundary resources: the case of Apple's iOS service system. MIS Q. **39**(1), 217–243 (2015)
4. Fichman, R.G., et al.: Digital innovation as a fundamental and powerful concept in the information systems curriculum. MIS Q. **38**(2), 329–353 (2014)
5. Garud, R., Jain, S., Tuertscher, P.: Incomplete by design and designing for incompleteness. Organ. Stud. **29**(3), 351–371 (2008)
6. Henderson, R.M., Clark, K.B.: Architectural innovation: the reconfiguration of existing product technologies and the failure of established firms. Adm. Sci. Q. **35**(1), 9–30 (1990)
7. Henfridsson, O., et al.: Managing technological change in the digital age: the role of architectural frames. J. Inf. Technol. **29**(1), 27–43 (2014)
8. Jarrahi, M.H.: Digital and physical materiality of information technologies: the case of fitbit activity tracking devices. Presented at the 2015 48th Hawaii International Conference on System Sciences (HICSS) (2015)
9. Kallinikos, J., et al.: The ambivalent ontology of digital artifacts. MIS Q. **37**(2), 357–370 (2013)
10. Lessig, L.: Code - Version 2.0. Basic Books, New York (2006)
11. Muffatto, M.: Introducing a platform strategy in product development. Int. J. Prod. Econ. **60–61**, 145–153 (1999)
12. Teece, D.J., et al.: Dynamic capabilities and strategic management. Strat. Manag. J. **18**(7), 509–533 (1997)
13. Tilson, D., et al.: Research commentary—digital infrastructures: the missing IS research agenda. Inf. Syst. Res. **21**(4), 748–759 (2010)

14. Vaast, E., et al.: Talking about technology: the emergence of a new actor category through new media. MIS Q. **37**(4), 1069–1092 (2013)
15. Yin, R.K.: Case Study Research: Design and Methods, 4th edn. Sage, London (2009)
16. Yoo, Y.: The tables have turned: how can the information systems field contribute to technology and innovation management research? J. Assoc. Inf. Syst. **14**(5), 227–236 (2012)
17. Yoo, Y., et al.: Organizing for innovation in the digitized world. Organ. Sci. **23**(5), 1398–1408 (2012)
18. Zittrain, J.: The Future of the Internet-And How to Stop It. Yale University Press, London (2008)

Net Up Your Innovation Value

Jan Pries-Heje and Magnus Rotvit Perlt Hansen[(✉)]

Institute of People and Technology, Roskilde University, Roskilde, Denmark
{janph, magnuha}@ruc.dk

Abstract. Value from ICT Innovation may come from the building of social capital through relational coordination. Hence, for innovation-based companies, combining social capital and economic capital value through the creation and maintenance of business relationships and networking to obtain value plays a central role for their growth and survival. In this paper we design and evaluate a so-called "network nexus" prototype as an ICT value assessment tool for facilitators of innovation-oriented networks. To determine whether a business network is structured for providing value to its members, the facilitator scores the network based on a survey. The scoring of the nexus gives an indication of what to improve to increase value. Evaluation of the nexus resulted in the identification of six types of networks each with their own potential for value. We conclude that design challenges for ICT assessment tools of business network groups can be overcome but needs to be rooted in their context.

Keywords: Network groups · Innovation · Value · Nexus · Design science research

1 Introduction

Innovation and the value that follows from being innovative is becoming increasingly important for new entrepreneurial firms worldwide. Innovation has been framed as creating a product that is perceived as completely new or it may be to open up new market segments for groups of consumers or users, and one can distinguish between sustaining and disruptive innovation [1]. Sustaining innovations are usually developed and introduced to the market by industry leaders. The knowledge required for sustainable innovation comprehends existing knowledge either from inside or from outside e.g. on customer needs and problems, markets or technology. In order to do so it has been suggested that firms that share knowledge between each other are more innovative and gain more economic value than those that do not [2]. This is because networked firms can get a head start on new market opportunities [3] and being better at facilitating tacit knowledge through new communities of practice that translate into value quickly [4]. As such, focusing on what brings value-related innovation is central for firms that want to grow [5]. So-called brokered (henceforth known as facilitated) networks seem to have certain advantages in small and medium entrepreneurial firms [6]. Facilitation may include initiating a network, inviting people to the network, setting up meetings, running the meetings well, and documenting the results of meetings in the network.

© Springer International Publishing Switzerland 2016
M. Gellerstedt et al. (Eds.): SCIS 2016, LNBIP 259, pp. 70–85, 2016.
DOI: 10.1007/978-3-319-43597-8_6

In the IS literature, ICT tools to support network facilitation such as technological hubs have been proposed to play an important role in mediating the network, yet often with a focus on pure technological mediation through social media [7]. There is, however, the problem that much of the discussion on value and innovation focuses solely on monetary and economic value, e.g. by improving business cases or creating more detailed cost-benefit analyses through emerging value chains [8]. Innovation and value creation in interpersonal network groups between companies need to consider other forms of value that can be layered and are socially constructed and provide value over long durations of time [9]. However, it is not known how to properly design ICT tools for use to handle the delicate balance of creating, supporting and managing emergent innovation-based knowledge through interaction [8, 10].

For each of these tasks there are numerous ways to do things and no right way. This means that the problem of facilitating an innovative network well is a true "wicked problem", meaning that it may be influenced by many diverse values and in many different ways by many decision makers or other stakeholders. Wicked problems can only be formulated in terms of an unbounded solution space, good or bad as opposed to objectively true or false [11]. We propose that to gain value from interpersonal and inter-organizational innovation networks and make the network group work well, the network needs to be facilitated well.

We pursue the research problem of *"how to design an ICT artifact prototype that helps assess value through innovation networks?"*

The paper is structured as follows. First we go through literature on value creation in social settings and marketing for use as the theoretical lens to identify types of value from business network groups. Second we describe our design science research method for designing a nexus ICT prototype that can assess said value. Then we describe the case setting for our study followed by how we constructed the first iteration of the prototype through literature on facilitation of groups and networks. From here we show the results of the evaluation of the prototype that provided additional information on business network types and the relation to value creation. Finally, we discuss further research and conclude on our study.

2 Previous Research on Value: A Theoretical Lens on Necessities of Facilitating Business Network Groups

Value is a tricky thing to define from a theoretical as well as practical point of view. The classical way of defining value (and also dominant one in classic IS and marketing literature) is quantifying it through economic value [12]. In an organizational context this would ultimately translate into added revenue. However, this is just one way of conforming value as seen through the eyes of Bourdieu [13], who distinguishes between three forms of value, denoted as "capital": Economic, Cultural and Social. Social capital is "the aggregate of the actual or potential resources which are linked to possession of a durable network of more or less institutionalized relationships of mutual acquaintance and recognition." [13, p. 249]. Continuing this thought, Robert Putnam defines social capital as "[…] the collective value of all 'social networks' and the inclinations that arise from these networks to do things for each other." [14, p. 19].

Hence the relationships that make up social capital of an innovation network can also be perceived as value from building a durable network or relationships of mutual recognition. A more generic definition of social capital was given by Adler and Kwon [15]. They say that social capital as a construct can be defined as "the goodwill available to individuals or groups. Its source lies in the structure and content of the actor's social relations. Its effects flow from the information, influence, and solidarity it makes available to the actor" [15, p. 17]. This leads us to think that access to information can be seen as social capital value as well. Based on research on social capital, Gittell focuses on the relational coordination of work through relations based on the ability to cooperate through common goals, shared knowledge and mutual respect [16]. New value is created through communicating between multiple disciplines and functions with the aim of integrating the assignment [17].

Within the IS and ICT literature, the theoretical concept of value as anything other than economic or product-based logic has been rare, and with good reason. In their review of value in communities, Pigg and Crank [18] found that it was still difficult to show that ICT increased social capital in any notorious way. However, this has not refrained scholars to use the concept as explanatory for how ICT tools have impacted organizational relationships [19]. As such, we argue that we need to take a pragmatic view on how value can be perceived through innovation networks for it to be translated and facilitated through the dynamics of innovation networks.

Many business network groups rely on outside agents responsible for coordinating and facilitating formal products of the business network group [5]. According to O'Donnell et al. [20] these networks have the characteristic of working on an informal, personal level where the individuals of the network are viewed as the main actors that focus on exploring social, communicative and commercial interests. A business network group will thus hold both structural dimensions as well as procedural and interactive dimensions [21]. As such, value creation of business networks can be viewed as both a process and one or more products. In newer marketing theory, the perception of value as 'co-creation' between customers and companies providing products [22]. Rather than managing numbers and efficiencies, managers are now supposed to manage the customers' experiences involved in acquiring the products. Vargo et al. [23] expand on this by distinguishing between two types of logics: goods-dominant logic (GDL) vs. service-dominant logic (SDL). Rather than focusing on quantifiable quality and use of products (GDL), the creators of these products must acknowledge that value is further determined in the services, processes and experiences that these products provide (SDL). We argue that business networks groups can be viewed similarly, with the exception that the distinction between service provider and customer being not as clear cut as in marketing since the network both produces/ constructs value and consumes it with the aid of an external facilitator. This fits well with the systemic point of view of how to facilitate project groups where the performance of the group is correlated to contextual (decided outside of the group), structural and procedural aspects [24].

With the knowledge that value through socially constructed social, intellectual and economic capital through coordination, communication and problem solving, we see an area of non-knowledge between how to design ICT tools that can assess (and potentially support) these types of value. Examples of designing for this can be found in the

IS literature from e.g. Smart et al. [25] with rules for initiating innovation networks, though to our knowledge no guidelines have so far been given to support the facilitation process of the network post-initiation. We will use the above-mentioned concepts for assessing empirically what kinds of value network groups can provide.

3 Research Method

Our approach to solving our wicked research problem is a Design Science Research (DSR) approach. DSR is focused on understanding man-made designs of reality and is thus an alternative to both the social and natural sciences. As a result, DSR understands reality through creating and testing artifacts that serve human purposes and solves human problems [26, 27].

One of the benefits of DSR is that one can abstract designed solutions into design theory structured around solving classes of design problems [28]. This type of theory usually is framed by providing a design method for making meta-designs that frame design parameters for predictable outcomes dependent on the design theory detail. Many DSR scholars have provided different meta-designs for methods based on solving different solution designs [29, 30]. However, for specifically solving wicked design problems, we have chosen the Design Theory Nexus developed by Pries-Heje and Baskerville [31] and published in a special issue on DSR in MIS Quarterly. The Design Theory Nexus contains a five-step method for constructing nexus-artifacts:

1. Survey existing literature for approaches available in the given problem area.
2. Analyze alternative approaches. Identify conditions for the best approach for each.
3. Construct an artifact indicating whether the conditions identified can be found in the problem area.
4. Design and develop a decision-making process for evaluation of present conditions.
5. Integrate approaches, conditions, and the decision-making process into a tool (an artifact) that can evaluate if the wicked problem has been dealt with.

We have applied this five-step nexus-artifact developing a process and a prototype of an artifact that answers our stated research problem.

The first two of the Nexus were performed as a literature review of approaches and aspects of facilitation, and conditions to describe network groups (in this paper Sect. 5). From the literature the initial conditions of the nexus were interpreted as attributes and dimensions inspired by the qualitative research method by Strauss and Corbin [32]. They note that concepts consist of attributes (e.g. a person's attributes of "height" and "weight") and that attributes then contain two or more dimensions often set on a continuum (e.g. the person can be either tall or short, or thin or obese). We denoted these attributes and dimensions as central to understand the basic conditions of the situation, as described by Pries-Heje and Baskerville [31].

The third and fourth Nexus-steps was developing the prototype artifact based on network member interviews to further refine the attributes and dimensions. Two 2-h. focus group interviews with 4–5 people were held in April 2015 with the two authors as facilitators. Focus group members were selected based on their professional and network experience. The first focus group had much experience with networks and knew each other because they had previously been members of the same network group. The second focus group consisted of members primarily with little professional experience and working as a minor enterprise with only 1–3 employees. The purpose of the focus groups was for members to openly discuss characteristics of their own network groups and how this affected participation and value. This gained perceptual measurability behind it that could identify the conditions (through a set of questions to be answered) and evaluate which conditions were present (a value based on the answers). The next step, evaluation, was crucial. One can distinguish between formative (ongoing evaluation prior to construction) and summative evaluations (after artifact construction) [33].

The fifth Nexus-step was the integration of knowledge and construction of the final iteration of the nexus artifact based on learning points from the evaluation with facilitators. The purpose of the facilitator interviews was to evaluate the process and artifact design based on their own experiences with facilitation and how such a tool could add value and improve their own facilitation practices. As such, step 5 was performed as a summative evaluation through qualitative interviews with facilitators of chosen networks. It became clear that additional conditions needed to be identified and this spawned the different network types (see Sect. 6). Hence, six additional 1-h. semi-structured interviews were held with five facilitators in May 2015.

All 14 interviews were recorded, listened through and rewritten into 'thick' summaries. We employed coding tactics that focused on the conditions of the nexus that were found from the literature as well as finding contradictions and variables related to each other [34]. Codes were reviewed by both authors to ensure inter-coder reliability. Examples of initial high-level codes from the focus groups were part of the first iteration of evaluating attributes: "Facilitator roles", "Value types", "Composition", "Knowledge sharing" and "Trust". Codes were populated and revised into the seven attributes of the current nexus tool, e.g. the low-level code of "Moving away from the production-minded and into reflections on practice" would relate itself to reasons for joining networks and be a part of the high-level code of how the different network groups could provide "Value".

4   Case Setting

In order to answer our research question and applying the Nexus we found a case in the Northern part of Denmark. Company Forum Thy (Danish: "Thy Erhvervsforum", henceforth shortened CF Thy) in Northern Denmark is a network organization that aims to aid local entrepreneurs and companies in general with innovation at large. CF Thy have more than ten networks with over 265 small to medium businesses (SMEs) as members. Each network provides opportunities for members to increase their innovativeness through networking. Network topics range from e.g. larger maritime business networks aimed at the fishing industry to productivity networks where its members will learn more about how to use automated robots to increase productivity. The facilitators of these networks have to both apply for economic resources as well as facilitating networks to make sure they thrive. CF Thy wanted help finding a generic solution that could help them in assessing their network participants' needs through better communication, as well as to ensure that their networks were on the right track.

5 Constructing the Artifact Attributes from Literature

The core idea in constructing a Nexus is that you identify and apply a number of conditions followed by statements that are based on these conditions. In Table 1 the identified attributes can be found. We range the attributes into value dimensions from high (indicating that the attribute is difficult for the facilitator to manage) to low (indicating that the attribute is easier for the facilitator to manage).

Table 1. Table of literature identified to support the attributes of a network group. Note that some overlap exists between attributes and papers

Attribute	References
Size	Ghisi and Martinelli [5], Jack et al. [35], Mitchell [21], Zhao et al. [36]
Purpose and success criteria	Hannah and Walsh [37], Jack et al. [35], Möller et al. [12]
Member composition	Ghisi and Martinelli [5], Gruenfeld et al. [38], Klerkx et al. [39]
Knowledge level and type	Cook and Brown [40], Forehand [41], Nonaka et al. [42], Polayni [43], Sveiby [44]
Knowledge sharing and interaction	Brown and Duguid [16, 45], Connel and Voola [46], Jack et al. [35], Clegg and Porras [47], Tsoukas [48]
Facilitation and leadership	Hannah and Walsh [37], Kirkels and Duysters [49], Schwartz [24]
Activities	Connel and Voola [46], Cook and Brown [40], Jack et al. [35], Kolb and Kolb [50], Möller et al. [12], Schwartz [24]

5.1 Nexus Attribute of "Size"

Size of a business network is important for the development of the network and has been viewed as the sole measurable dependent variable for whether a network is thriving [36] and it is possible for the network group to expand without limit [5]. When facilitating a network group one must assume that the more participants involved, the more work needs to be done to facilitate the network well. To perform well, the network must meet and interact on a regular basis [21] and thus drop-outs of participants and cancellations must not be too high. Jack et al. [35] found that low attendance was not a problem for networks despite having a higher formal size, though this conclusion was based on network groups that had reached a high critical mass (in this instance 43 average monthly attending of a total size of 197 members) [35]. We still argue that low attendance can be a problem for the network group in general if the network has an initial low network size. We condense the two dimensions of this attribute to be from (a) large amount (>20 members) with corresponding high amount of cancellations to (b) small amount (<20 members) with corresponding few cancellations.

5.2 Nexus Attribute of "Purpose and Success Criteria"

Seeing as a network group is often facilitated by an outside facilitator, there exists a certain expectation of a level of formality [5] due to the strategic nature of a business network group [12]. Thus prior to forming or financing a network group an explicit purpose as well as economic success criteria is needed to varying degrees [35]. Despite the requirement of formal documents, the speed of which the purpose and success criteria emerge can vary [12]. The more explicit the purpose and success criteria of a network group, the easier it will be to finance [37]. We condense the two dimensions of this attribute to be (a) implicit purpose and success criteria with little common agreement, even conflict to (b) an explicitly written purpose and success criteria of the network group that is periodically updated and renegotiated.

5.3 Nexus Attribute of "Member Composition"

Composition makes up the variety of participants' backgrounds, competencies and experiences [5] as well as their originating type and line of business. Klerkx et al. [39] found support that even creating innovation within one line of business (the agricultural sector) it be difficult due to technological, social, economic and cultural divides. Gruenfeld et al. [38] also found support for this in terms of the difficulty of how to compose a network in order to solve desired tasks. We argue that the more heterogeneous composition of the network group, the more difficult it can be for a facilitator to pursue the intended purpose of the network group due to these divides and interests of the members. We condense the two dimensions of this attribute to be (a) diverse professional backgrounds and experiences to (b) uniform professional backgrounds and experiences.

5.4 Nexus Attribute of "Knowledge Level and Type"

The purpose of the network can be defined in terms of the knowledge level and type that is desired from the members. Nonaka et al. [42] (drawing on Polayni [43]) distinguish between two types of knowledge: tacit knowledge defined as technical skills that is rarely communicated but instead performed, and explicit knowledge conceptualized and shared among members in a social system. Nonaka et al. [42] have been criticized for over-simplifying the original concept, saying that tacit knowledge cannot be explained at all, only shown [52]. Cook and Brown [40] further proposes the distinction between explicit, individual knowledge and in groups to be that of individual, decontextualized 'concepts' and collective, contextualized 'stories'. Other scholars like Sveiby [44] proposed that all knowledge is equal and will lose value as it becomes decontextualized and processed over time, and that this shows that production of knowledge through innovating needs strong contextualization. This can be further emphasized by the taxonomy of knowledge types by Bloom [41]. The levels of knowledge go from remembering and retrieving information through understanding, applying, analyzing, evaluating up to the most difficult step: creating new knowledge. For business network groups, this means that innovating and creating new knowledge can be taxing on the facilitator and the activities needed during meetings. We condense the two dimensions of this attribute to be (a) low-level decontextualized knowledge that can be shared through concepts, shown or recalled from memory to (b) high-level contextualized knowledge that needs to be tested and evaluated in real-life settings.

5.5 Nexus Attribute of "Knowledge Sharing and Interaction"

Member interaction is central for any network group since a network group is a personal network and many participants join with the purpose of expanding their professional relationships. For knowledge sharing to work in a strategic alliance between members of different firms, a high level of trust is needed [46]. Trust has been defined as the belief that actions will be reciprocated in a beneficial way between one or more parties [46]. Trust is an essential motivation to share knowledge between the participants in order to gain value and occurs over time based on historical activities between participants [35]. As such, for knowledge sharing to take place, Brown and Duguid [16] point to the intersection and contradiction of two identities between being bound by the organizational purpose and the social practice of the network. Both identities inhibit sharing of knowledge depending on which identity is strongest. In addition, Tsoukas [48] point to the importance of members engaging in dialogue as a means for self-distancing and reflection on taken-for-granted everyday activities. We condense the two dimensions of this attribute to be (a) low level of trust and community identity with very little sharing of stories and experiences to (b) high level of trust and community identity with members engaging in dialogue to reach new understandings, insights and solutions to problems.

5.6 Nexus Attribute of "Facilitation and Leadership"

The facilitator of the network group is the one creating balance, direction but also adds asymmetry as they are required to at the very least make sure that the group process moves towards the intended purpose. Most business networks require either external facilitation (outside consultant or process facilitator) or internal (member having the task delegated to her or him, either permanently or from time to time). The facilitator is respected and sticks to the same role from meeting to meeting, typically as a process consultant [24]. Roles can also involve the expert consultant, the neutral coach, the expert trainer or the decision-capable leader. Certain groups require the network facilitator to be neutral [37], or keeps up to date with knowledge of the subject area, while others require the facilitator to be an expert and teach the subject area [49]. We condense the two dimensions of this attribute to be (a) facilitator requiring to change roles between network group meetings or during meetings and needing to act as an expert to (b) facilitator keeping the same role and acting mostly as process consultant.

5.7 Nexus Attribute of "Activities"

Performing common activities have been found to increase affection and trust between network participants [35, 46] and activities can range from being unpredictable and

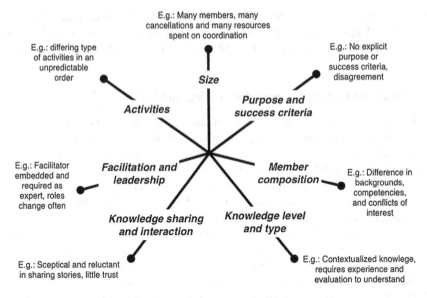

Fig. 1. Showing identified attributes of a network group to be considered in an ICT tool. Examples at the end of the lines are given of highest dimensional values of the attribute.

dissimilar from meeting to meeting while other meetings require fixed and predictable agendas [12]. Types of activities can be solving problems, making decisions, handling conflicts, sharing knowledge, experimenting or problem solving [24], all supporting either known or unknown goals through innovative capabilities [12]. As such, an agenda may consist of different actions yet still belong to the same type of activity. Activities should be selected to accommodate the desired knowledge level and type. According to Kolb and Kolb [50] learning is a process that involves different learning styles going from concrete experience, reflective observation, abstract hypotheses and active testing. The learning style that is needed to move from tacit knowledge to explicit knowledge would be focused on reflective observation and abstract hypotheses, while internalizing explicit knowledge into skills require active observation and testing concrete experience [40]. To create new knowledge, one must go from abstract hypotheses through testing and observation. We condense the two dimensions of this attribute to be (a) diverse requirements for different types of activities and varied meeting agendas with the aim of producing new knowledge, supporting accommodative learning from hypotheses to testing to observation to (b) stable and similar activities and meeting agendas that move from observation to testing in order to develop and assimilate new skills (Fig. 1).

6   Evaluation

Did the attribute-based nexus survey tool then actually assess value of network groups? No, was the outcome of the formative evaluation. Network group attributes could not be measured as absolutely good or bad for the network groups. Thus it was necessary to build an additional tool to assess network type to support the survey-based nexus. For example, it was clear that some of the facilitated network groups were business-focused and shared non-contextual knowledge relatively easy while other groups were focused on sharing personal or business-critical information and required building of trust through activities over time. As a result, the type of knowledge shared demanded significantly more attention to the activities and process of facilitation. With diverse network group types, this also had a strong impact on the assumption that the less work a facilitator do with a network group, the easier it is. For example, one facilitator did not notice that she spent time checking up on existing business knowledge, since she saw it as part of her job, while other facilitators deemed this completely irrelevant for their network. We identified 6 different network group types that had the potential of adding different kinds of value to the members. In the following we explain the network types and their most significant attributes and discuss the different kinds of value.

Type 1. The project network is typically formally composed with a very specific and formalized, measurable purpose in mind. The project network is specialist-driven and often also metrics-driven based on focused assimilation of learning and a business consultant or network facilitator will be the main driver of bringing designated members together that would seem to fit the purpose. Here relationship networking is used as the formal method for obtaining success in relation to the purpose. A project network often holds seminar-based activities that furthers the cause of the network, often with a knowledgeable facilitator acting like a project manager. Where other network groups span over years, a project network typically does not last for more than a year where at the end it will be evaluated and disbanded. A project network requires members with heterogeneous backgrounds and competencies and relatively small size (4–7 members). Central attributes: *Purpose and Composition*:

- Purpose: facilitator Four had a local food network turned into an "NGO" over time, which had been the main purpose all along. Now it is no longer considered as a business network.
- Composition: facilitator One noted how he was establishing a new network but had to refrain from using the word "network" because it contained associations of a never-ending duration of time. Rather, he was establishing a close, hand-picked group of people of 6 in various strategic positions with a well-known researcher to facilitate with a very clear deadline and purpose.

Provided Value. Economic value that often relies on learning from and adding to best processes and practices related to a specialized area of business. The value that the members gain from this network is translatable to the context of the member firm through organizational improvement and rethinking.

Type 2. The network sprout is an open network with the purpose of attracting as high a critical mass of members as possible through socializing (often 20–40 members but possibly more). Purpose and success criteria can be vague and the main purpose is to create new possible networks from those members who do participate. Many network groups start out as sprouts and will later develop into other types of networks groups. A facilitator of a network sprout is required to change roles as well as activities to hit a broad area of interest between the very heterogeneous membership compositions. Central attributes: *Size and Activities*:

- Size: facilitator Four told that she had previously experienced huge problems with too low attendance and her only way of solving the issue was to contact all members a couple of days in advance to make sure they remembered.
- Activities: facilitator Five noted that her own cluster networks were broad and required her to plan out very different activities and themes for each meeting and letting these be known to the members since the members participated in meetings based on the activities and content of the meeting.

Provided Value. Social value gained from introductory knowledge and relations based on common interests that can result in members finding alternative, focused groups. Value is not immediately measurable, being based primarily on how members will engage in new network relationships and gaining non-specific long-term effects.

Type 3. The skill-based network is a network with the purpose of learning how to use new tools or action-oriented knowledge between members, often centered on production-oriented, stable contexts. The progress can often be metrics-driven as it is simpler to count progress and learning that is implemented into the participants' working contexts. Often the members are from the same type or line of business and the purpose is very explicit with quantifiable evaluation criteria. The facilitator typically need easy access and is required to have a certain level of the subject area or at the very least keep up to date on a weekly basis. The critical mass for this network can be between 20–40 members. Central attributes: *Activities and Facilitation*:

- Activities: facilitator Two told that her members had called for more social activities because they were drowning in technical activities.
- Facilitation: facilitator Two felt obligated to keep up to date within the professional area. She also noted the she never differed her role, always being the planner, coordinator, pushing the process and rounding off the meetings at the end.

Provided Value. Economic value by increasing productivity through a metrics-driven approach by implementing new tools and optimizing work routines. The value gained here directly relates to the production environment and is translatable to existing business practices.

Type 4. The referral network has the purpose of exchanging customers between businesses to increase their value between them. Often smaller businesses and enterprises are part of the referral network and they embrace the dynamic and complex surroundings that make it important to explore for new business opportunities. Membership type is exclusive and heterogeneous to avoid cannibalizing customers or internal competition so only one business type is present. Purpose and evaluation criteria is based on both network and individual level (in terms of creating monetary value through new referrals). There is typically an internal facilitator present selected among the members themselves for a given time period. Meeting agendas are structured and predictable and only in breaks or prior or after meetings can the members socialize. The size is typically between 20–25 members. Central attributes: *Member composition and Size*:

- Member composition: in Focus Group Two one of the members gained access only because another member had left and they needed more fresh blood with an engineering background.
- Size: in Focus Group Two one of the participants noted that her referral network had a maximum amount of 25 people in order to cover all types and lines of businesses exclusively and create overview for the members.

Provided Value. Metrics-driven economic value from number of referrals and potential customers gained between each participant. Social capital is the direct mediator to increase the economic value and has both a short-term and long-term effect, e.g. through gaining a new client or gaining "dormant" relationships that can be used in the future.

Type 5. The exchange of experience network is characterized by participants being interested in socializing to exchange experiences with each other and learn from. The members are very much in control of what they want to focus on themselves and require a high level of trust and motivation to be successful. The purpose of the network is vague and easily risks being implicit and changed through the course of the network. It is up to the facilitator to make sure this does not happen and by stabilizing it. The role of the facilitator will typically be as a coach, coordinator and meeting facilitator. The size of the network is small (4–12 members) in order to further trust and business critical knowledge shared, and it is very much up to the members themselves to decide who they invite. Activities will often revolve visiting each other's' businesses. Central attributes: *Knowledge Sharing and interaction, and Facilitation.*

- Knowledge sharing and interaction: facilitator One noted that one member, who was a CEO, had begun a new project of reinvigorating the business culture. He had only been able to do this by asking, reflecting and getting help from the other members.
- Facilitation: in Focus Group Two participants referred to a bad experience with a facilitator where his role was very unclear and it was difficult to establish any trust in his actions because he kept profiling himself as an expert without focusing on the members of the network group. They did not attend the next network meeting.

Provided Value. Social and reflective value based on trust and collective problem solving by gaining insight into other people's current experiences and solutions. Value is gained through relational coordination of pursuing common goals, problem sharing and solving. Will rarely translate into short-term value but is based on the members' reflections on their practices over time.

Type 6. The innovation network is closely related to a project network, specifically regarding member composition and size. However, the innovation network does not necessarily have a set timeframe or specific measureable success criteria as innovation is focused on finding new knowledge. Often based on an urgent need and the purpose can be to increase new market segments, new products or enterprise collaborations as a result of dynamically changing surroundings that need adaptation. The member composition is also heterogeneous and specialist-driven and facilitator can have (though is not required to) have professional knowledge of the subject area. Size is typically 4–12 people with a stronger focus on trust and motivation than the project network in order to think creatively. Central attributes: *Knowledge level and type, and Activities:*

- Knowledge level and type: at Focus Group Two a participant explained a successful collaboration with multiple accountants that developed a new IT system with a new accounting standard that independent accountants could lease instead of creating their own individual standards themselves.
- Activities: facilitator Three experienced that the members of his innovation network group would overrule the agenda with new ideas and this was considered fine since they had to be creative and find new, creative solutions.

Provided Value. Economic value through market leadership or competitive advantages by re-engineering existing products or services. Value is gained through drastic change, though often only realized at the end of the lifecycle of the network group due to the structure of delivering a promised (but unknown) innovation product.

7 Conclusion and Discussion

We have now developed and evaluated a network nexus prototype; a tool that can be used to improve facilitation of innovative networks by assessing the value of the network based on its attributes and its type.

We used the five-step approach for designing a nexus given by Pries-Heje and Baskerville [31] and designed a nexus with seven attributes and questions for each. The scoring of the answers point in directions of where the network can be improved to better comply with the type of value that is required of the specific network type. Value types were derived from prior research on social relationships through social and economic capital [13, 16] and value from products, services and customer experiences [22, 23].

The summative evaluation of the nexus showed that it is possible to take a nexus-based approach to designing something as complex as assessment tools of social relationships and their value where both network members and facilitators were positive towards the tools and its intended usage. In addition, the evaluation brought forward some additional design challenges. First of all, designing an assessment tool for social relationships based on quantifiable dimensions requires a large amount of contextual assessment alongside. This was shown in the evaluation by the additional need for a support tool to assess different business network groups alongside the survey-based nexus to better compare. Second, the results can and should not be taken as an objective truth since it is perception-based on subjective judgement of the network group. The evaluation showed that the different attributes/dimensions of the specific network change over time and were socially constructed through the facilitation. For example, some of the structures and processes were still beneficiary for pursuing different sub-types of value. As such, we recommend to use the results of the tool along with dialogue with the network group members in order to better be capable of steering the network group in the desired direction. Third, the prototype strongly needs further testing in other scenarios and contexts for refining the attributes, questions and calculation mechanisms. Since it should currently be taken as a constructive dialogue tool, the exact calculation algorithm is of lesser importance but certainly requires more focused research further on.

Finally, while previous literature has shown that ICT cannot be said to add to value creation through the social capital concept [18], we have shown that it can in fact be used in designing an ICT value assessment tool.

References

1. Christensen, C.M., Overdorf, M.: Meeting the challenge of disruptive change. Harvard Bus. Rev. **78**(2), 66–77 (2000)
2. Kim, Y., Vonortas, N.S.: Cooperation in the formative years: evidence from small enterprises in Europe. Eur. Manag. J. **32**(5), 795–805 (2014)
3. Schoonjans, B., Van Cauwenberge, P., Vander Bauwhede, H.: Formal business networking and SME growth. Small Bus. Econ. **41**(1), 169–181 (2011)
4. Carlile, P.R.: A pragmatic view of knowledge and boundaries: boundary objects in new product development. Organ. Sci. **13**(4), 442–455 (2002)
5. Ghisi, F.A., Martinelli, D.P.: Systemic view of interorganisational relationships: an analysis of business networks. Syst. Pract. Act. Res. **19**(5), 461–473 (2006)
6. McNaughton, R.B., Bell, J.: Competing from the periphery: export development through hard business network programmes. Ir. Mark. Rev. **14**, 43–54 (2001)
7. Cantù, C., Ylimäki, J., Sirén, C.A., Nickell, D.: The role of knowledge intermediaries in co-managed innovations. J. Bus. Ind. Mark. **30**(8), 951–961 (2015)
8. Bragge, J., Tuunanen, T., Virtanen, V., Svahn, S.: Designing a repeatable collaboration method for setting up emerging value systems for new technology fields. JITTA: J. Inf. Technol. Theor. Appl. **12**(3), 27 (2011)
9. Holmlund, M., Törnroos, J.: What are relationships in business networks? Manag. Decis. **35**(4), 304–309 (1997)
10. Busquets, J.: Orchestrating smart business network dynamics for innovation. Eur. J. Inf. Syst. **19**(4), 481–493 (2010)
11. Rittel, H.W.J., Webber, M.M.: Dilemmas in a general theory of planning. Policy Sci. **4**(2), 155–169 (1973)
12. Möller, K., Rajala, A., Svahn, S.: Strategic business nets—their type and management. J. Bus. Res. **58**(9), 1274–1284 (2005)
13. Bourdieu, P. (ed.): Ökonomisches Kapital, Kulturelles Kapital Soziales Kapital. Otto Schartz & Co, Goettingen (1983)
14. Putnam, R.: Bowling Alone: The Collapse and Revival of American Community. Simon and Schuster, New York (2000)
15. Adler, P.S., Kwon, S.: Social capital: prospects for a new concept. Acad. Manag. Rev. **27**(1), 17–40 (2002)
16. Gittell, J.H., Seidner, R., Wimbush, J.: A social capital model of high performance work systems. Industry Studies Working Paper, University of Pittsburgh, no. 19 (2007)
17. Gittell, J.H.: Transforming Relationships for High Performance in Health Services: A Relational Model of Organizational Change (2015). http://rcrc.brandeis.edu/roundtable-webinars/video.html

18. Pigg, K.E., Crank, L.D.: Building community social capital: the potential and promise of information and communications technologies. J. Commun. Inform. **1**(1) (2004)
19. Widén-Wulff, G., Ginman, M.: Explaining knowledge sharing in organizations through the dimensions of social capital. J. Inf. Sci. **30**(5), 448–458 (2004)
20. O'Donnell, A., Gilmore, A., Cummins, D., Carson, D.: The network construct in entrepreneurship research: a review and critique. Manag. Decis. **39**(9), 749–760 (2001)
21. Mitchell, J.C.: Social networks. Annu. Rev. Anthropol. **3**, 279–299 (1974)
22. Prahalad, C.K., Ramaswamy, V.: Co-creating unique value with customers. Strat. Leadersh. **32**(3), 4–9 (2004)
23. Vargo, S.L., Maglio, P.P., Akaka, M.A.: On value and value co-creation: a service systems and service logic perspective. Eur. Manag. J. **26**(3), 145–152 (2008)
24. Schwarz, R.: The Skilled Facilitator: A Comprehensive Resource for Consultants, Facilitators, Managers, Trainers, and Coaches. Wiley, London (2002)
25. Smart, P., Bessant, J., Gupta, A.: Towards technological rules for designing innovation networks: a dynamic capabilities view. Int. J. Oper. Prod. Manag. **27**(10), 1069–1092 (2007)
26. March, S.T., Smith, G.: Design and natural science research on information technology. Decis. Support Syst. **15**(4), 251–266 (1995)
27. Simon, H.A.: The Science of the Artificial, 3rd edn. MIT Press, Cambridge (1996)
28. Walls, J.G., Widmeyer, G.R., El Sawy, O.A.: Building an information system design theory for vigilant EIS. Inf. Syst. Res. **3**(1), 36–59 (1992)
29. Hevner, A.R., March, S.T., Park, J., Ram, S.: Design science in information systems research. MIS Q. **28**(1), 75–105 (2004)
30. Peffers, K., Tuunanen, T., Rothenberger, M.A., Chatterjee, S.: A design science research methodology for information systems research. J. Manag. Inf. Syst. **24**(3), 45–77 (2008)
31. Pries-Heje, J., Baskerville, R.: The design theory nexus. MIS Q. **32**(4), 731–755 (2008)
32. Strauss, A.L., Corbin, J.: Basics of Qualitative Research. Sage, Newbury Park (1990)
33. Venable, J., Pries-Heje, J., Baskerville, R.: FEDS: a framework for evaluation in design science research. Eur. J. Inf. Syst. **25**(1), 77–89 (2014)
34. Miles, M.B., Huberman, A.M.: Qualitative Data Analysis: An Expanded Sourcebook. Sage Publications, Beverly Hills (1994)
35. Jack, S., Moult, S., Anderson, A.R., Dodd, S.: An entrepreneurial network evolving: patterns of change. Int. Small Bus. J. **28**(4), 315–337 (2010)
36. Zhao, X., Frese, M., Giardini, A.: Business owners' network size and business growth in China: the role of comprehensive social competency. Entrep. Reg. Dev. **22**(7–8), 675–705 (2010). 25(1), 77–89
37. Hanna, V., Walsh, K.: Small firm networks: a successful approach to innovation? R&D Manag. **32**, 201–207 (2002)
38. Gruenfeld, D.H., Mannix, E.A., Williams, K.Y., Neale, M.A.: Group composition and decision making: how member familiarity and information distribution affect process and performance. Organ. Behav. Hum. Decis. Process. **67**(1), 1–15 (1996)
39. Klerkx, L., Hall, A., Leeuwis, C.: Strengthening agricultural innovation capacity: are innovation brokers the answer? Int. J. Agric. Resour. Ecol. **8**(5/6), 409 (2009)
40. Cook, S.D.N., Brown, J.S.: Bridging epistemologies: the generative dance between organizational knowledge and organizational knowing. Organ. Sci. **10**(4), 381–400 (1999)
41. Forehand, M.: Bloom's taxonomy. Emerg. Perspect. Learn. Teach. Technol. 41–47 (2010)
42. Nonaka, L., Takeuchi, H., Umemoto, K.: A theory of organizational knowledge creation. Int. J. Technol. Manag. **11**(7–8), 833–845 (1996)
43. Polanyi, M.: The Tacit Dimension. Doubleday, New York (1966)
44. Sveiby, K.-E.: Transfer of knowledge and the information processing professions. Eur. Manag. J. **14**(4), 379–388 (1996)

45. Brown, J.S., Duguid, P.: Knowledge and organization: a social-practice perspective. Organ. Sci. **12**(2), 198–213 (2001)
46. Connell, J., Voola, R.: Strategic alliances and knowledge sharing: synergies or silos? J. Knowl. Manag. **11**(3), 52–66 (2007)
47. Clegg, S.: Trust as networking knowledge. In: Trust in the Workplace Conference, University of Newcastle (2000)
48. Tsoukas, H.: A dialogical approach to the creation of new knowledge in organizations. Organ. Sci. **20**(6), 941–957 (2009)
49. Kirkels, Y., Duysters, G.: Brokerage in SME networks. Res. Policy **39**(3), 375–385 (2010)
50. Kolb, A.Y., Kolb, D.A.: Learning styles and learning spaces: enhancing experiential learning in higher education. Acad. Manag. Learn. Educ. **4**(2), 193–212 (2005)

Sustaining Sustainability: Investigating the Long-Term Effects of a Sustainability Initiative

Fredrik Bengtsson[(⊠)] and Pär J. Ågerfalk

Department of Informatics and Media, Uppsala University,
Box 513, 751 20 Uppsala, Sweden
{fredrik.bengtsson,par.agerfalk}@im.uu.se

Abstract. This study investigates to what extent holistic sustainability values persist when a sustainability innovation initiative is transformed to standard mode of operation in a Swedish municipality through the lens of actor-network theory. The focus is on the effect of change in sustainability routines, inscribed in IT systems, when governance shifts from a dedicated initiative management to regular management. This longitudinal study shows that information systems can play a central role to enrol stakeholders in sustainable practices, but that sustainability outcomes are closely related to the view of sustainability inscribed in routines and supportive IT systems.

Keywords: Sustainable IS · Sustainability · Green IT · Green IS · Actor-network theory · ANT

1 Introduction

Sustainability is becoming increasingly important, especially in relation to climate change allegedly caused by the emission of greenhouse gases. The value of information systems research in pursuit of reaching sustainability goals is widely recognized [1, 2] and vindicated by a growing number of publications [3, 4]. Contributing to this discourse, the current study addresses the long-term effects of regional sustainability innovation initiatives by paying special attention to one such initiative in Sweden. During 2005–2010, three Swedish municipalities, in collaboration with the Swedish National Board of Housing, Building and Planning, The Swedish Transport Administration and the Swedish Association of Local Authorities and Regions conducted a set of projects jointly referred to as "The Good City" (TGC). The aim of TGC was to explore new ways of making cities more people friendly, focusing on city planning and development. Individual projects covered, amongst other things, transports of goods and people, city centre environment and traffic planning. Even though many of the projects referred to sustainability effects, no conclusive definition of sustainability was presented. Furthermore, sustainability effects were generally not the main focus or goal of the projects, but rather by-products. This bias was also evident in the TGC by the use of the term "environment", which usually referred to the living environment of the inhabitants rather than environment as habitat that is affected by environmental change and pollution.

© Springer International Publishing Switzerland 2016
M. Gellerstedt et al. (Eds.): SCIS 2016, LNBIP 259, pp. 86–99, 2016.
DOI: 10.1007/978-3-319-43597-8_7

In May 2008, Uppsala municipality launched an initiative called Pilotprojekt Hållbara Varutransporter (PHV), as part of TGC. The project aimed at reducing negative impact by transports on sustainability [5] via better logistic and transport solutions. In total, 93 workplaces were involved in PHV. During the project, a sustainability reporting system was introduced along with a web-based system to support new ordering routines. Drawing on a triple bottom line (TBL) perspective of sustainability [6], PHV had a clear vision about the centrality of sustainability outcomes. In line with the view presented at the 2005 World Summit on Social Development [7], a TBL perspective emphasizes three interconnected aspects of development: social, economic and environmental. Accordingly, a pre-existing sustainability reporting system, designed to support a TBL view of sustainability, was proposed to track and report sustainability performance based on data collection and reporting reflecting ecological as well as economic and social performance. This view was further accentuated because the project manager was a strong advocate of this view of sustainability. These factors paved the way for a view of transports and logistics as something that would become more efficient by striving for positive sustainability outcomes. This was in stark contrast to the opposing view that efficient transports have outcomes that may have positive sustainability impact, which can be seen as a form of greenwashing – i.e. communicating an environmental message to increase legitimacy to sustainable actions based on activities that are not primarily based on sustainable motivation [8]. In the beginning of 2009 it was decided that the changes tried during the project should stay in place and later be implemented throughout the municipality.

PHV ended in spring 2009 and the final report [5] stated that it had been a success with positive impact on the three measured dimensions: ecologic, economic and social sustainability. Academic studies of the initiative also showed that the organizational and sustainability goals set out in the project were reached [9, 10].

Prompted by the success of PHV, it was decided that the logistics and information systems scheme tried during the initiative should stay in place and be implemented in other areas of the municipality, most visible to the citizens by the project slogan printed on the delivery trucks run by the municipality depot at the time. The changes implemented during PHV were thus maintained at the participating and additional workplaces within the city centre. More rural areas of the municipality were subsequently included. PHV also featured in an article in the local newspaper [11] that highlighted the dramatic decrease in the number of transports and the positive effect this has had on the environment as well as the wellbeing and safety of the citizens; signed, most importantly, by the Chair of the Municipality Executive Committee. Today, many of the changes proposed and implemented during PHV are still in place. From that perspective, the initial claim of success proved to be true. However, the question remains whether PHV had a long-term effect in accordance with the overarching goal of a positive impact on all three dimensions of sustainability.

In an effort to answer this question, the purpose of the current paper is to investigate the long-term effects of a sustainability initiative in a municipality. The specific research question is, to what extent may holistic sustainability values persist when the results of a sustainability innovation initiative is transformed to standard mode of operation? This question is pursued by revisiting the original PHV study [9] and comparing the findings with the current (2015) state of affairs in the same municipality.

The paper proceeds as follows. In the following section, we introduce sustainability, focusing on sustainability in relation to information systems. We then introduce the research approach. Finally, the analysis is presented followed by findings and implications.

2   IS and Sustainability Performance of Organizations

At the time of the original study [9], the predominant focus within the sustainable information systems (SIS) discourse was on energy consumption caused by information technology (IT) and the underlying infrastructure such as data centres. The study found that 16 of 36 SIS publications in the premier academic information systems outlets focused on the environmental impact of IT rather than the economic and social aspects of sustainability, of which only nine clearly acknowledged a TBL perspective [9]. More comprehensive literature reviews have identified 98 [3] and 144 [4] relevant publications related to SIS. These also find a bias towards environmental issues that ignores the broader picture of sustainability. Clearly, the environmental impact of IT dominates the research on SIS [12].

Drawing on a TBL perspective, several frameworks for the study of information systems and sustainability have been suggested, including (a) an energy informatics framework with a focus on the ecological domain and resource reduction [13], (b) a resourced based sustainability framework focusing on business strategies of firms to achieve sustainability outcomes with sustained economic growth [14], and (c) a conceptual model focusing on the effect on the environment as intended impact caused by changed human behaviour in regards to the environment [15]. The latter model (c) recognizes the human aspect of sustainable development to a larger extent than (a) but is predominantly set on the environmental domain, lacking the societal and organizational perspective of the social and economic domains of sustainability. In the (b) framework, the social aspect is reduced to human capital for the human resource management to foster into more sustainability-conscious employees; both environmental and economic sustainable performance is achieved via technological solutions and resource management.

In contrast to the frameworks mentioned above, the Belief-Action-Outcome (BAO) framework acknowledges that beliefs within societal as well as organizational structures influence the behaviour of those structures [16]. BAO also recognizes that both societal structures and organizational structures influence individuals, thus pointing out that socially sustainable development can be understood as the interplay of actions taken by individuals influencing the behaviour of the social system and organizations. While (a), (b), and (c) describe changes required to reach sustainability goals, BAO explains how the involved parties can reach a state where such change is feasible. Even though BAO focuses on the environmental and economical dimensions, the social dimension of sustainability is seen as vital to understanding the complexity of sustainability performance.

Drawing on the holistic view expressed by a TBL perspective of sustainability and how the connectivity and influence among involved parties are constituent of sustainable actions as described by the BAO framework, we conclude that individual and organizational behaviour are key drivers of sustainable actions and subsequent sustainable change.

3   Research Approach

The original study [9] used actor-network theory (ANT) to analyse the PHV sustainability innovation initiative. To facilitate comparison, this paper uses the same analytic and visualization approach [17, 18] as the original study.

3.1   Actor-Network Theory

The BAO framework describes how social and organizational structures influence the beliefs of the individuals who, as a collective, re-enact and reinforce these structures. The framework suggests that these beliefs are translated into actions that impact behaviour of the social system and organizations. In a sense, beliefs propagate within a system to form actions that influence the systems and change beliefs. By acknowledging that individuals, social systems and organizations are actors [19], the web of beliefs, actions and outcomes form actor-networks that by negotiations translate beliefs into action, and thereby transform the configuration of the network itself [20].

Actor-network theory (ANT), developed by Callon and Latour [20–22], is a network theory that acknowledges that translation processes within a network can stem from both human and non-human entities. Allowing non-human agency to influence the network widens the network theory to encompass the complexity of socio-technical systems relevant to information systems research [18, 23–27].

In ANT, anything that takes part in the translation process is considered an actor [28]. Thus, human and non-human entities that take part in reconfiguring the network are considered actors. Examples of actors in an actor-network include employees, legal documents, standards, technical artefacts, software, IT systems, information systems, organizations and other actor-networks. The translation from one configuration of a network to a new configuration is driven by relations formed by negotiations and interactions aligning the interests of diverse actors to that of the primary actor stabilizing the network by translations and inscriptions.

Translation is a four-stage process by which an actor-network is created; different actors seek to align other actors to a network, often followed from the perspective of one actor [20]. An important aspect of this process is that it is on-going and never accomplished, the network need to be maintained by enrolling actors to the interests of the primary actor. Should this process fail to stabilize the actor-network the network will collapse. If the primary actor manages to mobilize the other actors to its goals the network passes an obligatory passage point and is viewed as stable and irreversible. As a consequence, the primary actor is no longer needed [29].

Inscription, in turn, is an actor's embodiment of interests in artefacts, such as technical objects, documents and embodied skills [29, 30]. Artefacts embody patterns of use, not only the intended use but all effects caused by the artefact in the actor-network [28]. Over time, as the network evolves, the inscription of an artefact may change.

3.2   Data Collection and Analysis

The methodology adopted for this work is an interpretive single-case study approach, which is suitable when exploring social practices [31]. The study is longitudinal in that it revisits the municipality to gain further insight into how the changes and system implementations during the initial pilot study have been translated into organizational routines.

The original study was conducted from December 2007 to January 2009 with analysis finished by November 2009 [9]. During this phase of the study, data was collected via surveys, interviews, observations and documents. In total 93 workplaces were involved in PHV, a survey was distributed to 60 of these, with a response rate of 25 %. The aim of the survey was to get an understanding of the logistics situation, how orders were placed, sustainability awareness and motivations for change within the workplace. Additionally, 39 interviews were conducted with stakeholders ranging from sustainability experts, external suppliers and representatives at municipality workplaces. Seven hours of participative observation at board meetings with stakeholders and at local workplaces was performed. Complementary sources of information were internal project reports, legal documents, presentations and minutes from stakeholder meetings [10].

During 2014–2015, documents were collected from the municipality web (www. uppsala.se), The Swedish Transport Administration (www.trafikverket.se) and trough Internet searches using Swedish keywords translating to "Uppsala" and "Uppsala municipality" in combination with "sustainability", "sustainable transports", "sustainable development", "environmental" and variations indicating content related to sustainability. Links and references within the identified sources were followed, in total covering 2245 pages. A brief summary of data sources is presented in Table 1.

Table 1. Summary of data collected 2014–2015 and used in this study.

Data source	Description	Page count
TGC documents	Final project reports of the TGC project as well as a subset of individual project reports	338
PHV documents	Final project report, complemented with publically available documents and presentations related to the PHV project and its continuation	236
Annual reports	Annual reports published by the municipality	782
Policy documents	Official reports and documents outlining environmental initiatives, declarations of intent towards environmental development	613
IT systems	Documents related to relevant IT systems	82
Press	Articles and releases related to the initiative and its continuation	9
Other	Related documents that don't fit in the other categories	185
Observations	Two hour demonstration of the Sustainability Portal	
Interviews	Five semi-structured interviews with respondents that hold strategic insight in the sustainability initiative, related activities and the current situation	

Additionally, five interviews with key informants [32] were conducted during 2014 to gain insight into what legacy the proposed changes, tried during PHV had had at the municipality. These interviews also provided additional context aiding in the interpretation of the written material. Purposeful sampling [33] was employed to select respondents. This is a suitable approach when one needs to identify people with specific knowledge of a phenomenon of interest and that are also willing and able to communicate experiences and opinions in an articulate, expressive, and reflective manner [34]. The respondents represented different key functions within the municipality related to sustainability issues at a strategic level or sustainability reporting responsibility, thus providing insight from different perspectives on the issue within the municipality. To preserve anonymity of the respondents we refrain from identifying the actual positions but provide an overview in Table 2.

Table 2. Overview of respondents.

Respondent	Role
R1	Coordinator, responsible for transports and goods logistics within the municipality
R2	Process manager, part of the steering committee of the original initiative and working with sustainability on a strategic and practical level within the municipality
R3	Head of department at a workplace that took part in PHV
R4	Process manager, responsible for coordination of data collection and sustainability reporting for the municipality
R5	Senior strategist, leading role of the TGC initiatives in Uppsala municipality

Sustainability initiatives within a municipality are a complex operation influenced by many different aspects and interests. Actor-network theory allows for human as well as non-human representations to influence configurations of the network around the implementation of sustainability adherence. Recognizing that technical artefacts, legislation, and internal and external parties can function as actants, all with potentially very different accountability in regards to TBL allows for a richer narrative. Since an actor-network can be treated as a single actor or a conglomerate of connected actor-networks, different actors are represented based on their influence in the studied case and not based on the strength of the underlying actor-network constituting that actor. Thus the focus falls on the translation process and the strength of inscriptions aimed at stabilizing the actor-network.

4   Analysis

The original sustainability initiative achieved a stable network of actors as depicted in Fig. 1. Routines and standards where put in place and inscribed in IT systems, predominantly to enforce procurement routines and sustainability reporting. Several actions served to ensure the enrolment of various actors that initially were reluctant to take part in the initiative [9, 10]. The hesitation from these actors was not caused by

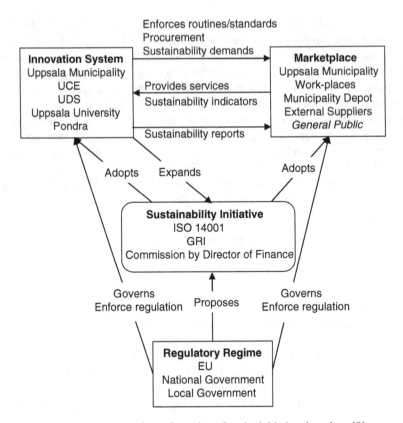

Fig. 1. Actor-network configuration after the initiative, based on [9].

unwillingness to be part of a project aimed at sustainability goals, but boiled down to a fear that participation in the project would result in a heavier workload and changes in well-established work routines. Evaluation of PHV showed that the goal of more sustainable practices in regards to the activities involved in procurements and transports within the municipality had been reached. Furthermore, the final report [5] stated that the initiative had reached the goal of having a positive impact on the environmental, economic and social dimension of sustainability.

After PHV had been handed over to maintenance, Uppsala University and Pondra had no longer any relation to the innovation system. Thus, the actor-network resembles the pre-initiative network. The innovation system now consisted of Uppsala Municipality, Uppsala Care & Education (UCE) and Uppsala Direct Services (UDS), UCE and UDS being divisions within the municipality. The marketplace and regulatory regime remained unchanged. Although PHV had ended, the supporting information system and the vision declared as an outcome of the initiative, "Coordination of goods transport for all activities carried out under the authority of the Municipality of Uppsala are expected to have positive economic, ecological and social effects" [5], had been incorporated into the municipality's general sustainability practices.

For the duration of PHV, the sustainability initiative was the obligatory passage point, enrolling the actors to realize the necessary changes in order to promote the desired sustainability effects. In regards to the sustainability effects, the sustainability initiative was replaced by the municipality's sustainability practices as the new obligatory passage point concerning these issues [9].

Throughout the original initiative monthly reports were generated via the Sustainability Portal to support continuous sustainability monitoring at the workplaces. This was an important tool to facilitate more reactive decision-making regarding sustainability impact caused at the workplaces. Detailed data collection to track the performance of the new transport scheme continued until 2012, when, according to R2, "the results were so good that no further monitoring was necessary to motivate its adoption throughout the municipality", which clearly enrolled upper management in adopting the transport scheme. In practice, this ended data collection to support a TBL perspective. Presently, data concerning energy and environmental impact (CO_2 and NO_X) are collected quarterly from the workplaces. These data are primarily used for yearly sustainability accounting reported in the municipality's annual report. Complementary to this, each workplace is responsible for a yearly sustainability audit reported via the Sustainability Portal to give a more detailed picture of the sustainability impact that includes economic and social aspects of sustainability, as well as ecological aspects. When this information is aggregated and the result is presented in the annual report, the information is further aggregated with external information to a level where it is impossible to discern between the sustainability impact of Uppsala municipality, as an organization, and the sustainability impact of the municipality as a collection of all its inhabitants, businesses and activities within its borders.

Although compiled by the municipality administration, each workplace has access to the final sustainability report should they request it. Where possible, the information is broken down by month. Nonetheless, sustainability reporting as a method for frequent feedback to support sustainability work is lost. However, instead of letting the information be available by default, an extra hurdle of asking for access has been created. This severely limits the sustainability performance of the overall municipal information system. As mentioned above, the most important outlet for the sustainability reporting conducted within the municipality is the annual report. Within this, very little information can be traced back to workplaces in the municipality since the information regarding sustainability is aggregated to reflect sustainability impact on a municipality level that primarily concerns the inhabitants of the municipality of Uppsala.

As already noted, the sustainability initiative was deemed a success and most of the actions taken to improve transports were seamlessly continued as established routines. However, one of the key changes that were tried during the initiative was to establish routines and inscribing them in the information system to increase the awareness of, and engagement in sustainability issues amongst employees. These changes were not implemented in the transition from sustainability initiative to established routines.

Directly after the sustainability initiative was ended in early spring 2009, but before the new accounting system was introduced, the actor network can be regarded as the one depicted in Fig. 1. Pondra and Uppsala University were no longer part of the innovation system, but no other issues had had time to be introduced to prompt any reconfiguration and the actor network was still stable. The changed routines and IT solutions put in place during the initiative continued to be in effect. At the workplaces, little had changed.

Later that same year, the new accounting system replaced the old and the integration with the Sustainability Portal was not implemented to accommodate the previous functionality. From the perspective of the involved workplaces this basically meant that the new routines regarding sustainability reporting was reverted back to the pre-initiative state, thus destabilizing the network. The parts of sustainability reporting that had been automated once again needed a human middleman to bridge the accounting system and the Sustainability Portal and they could no longer access regularly updated information about their sustainability performance.

However, procurement and delivery routines tried during the initiative had been firmly established. These routines were viewed as a positive change compared to the routines, or lack of routine, that they replaced as they were now "better structured and ordered, better forward planning in regards to procurement and logistics" (R3). With increased insight into the general performance of municipality logistics, "Overall, the workplaces are positive to the new logistics routines. They know when transports are due; they don't need a service man that receives the goods since they can plan for receiving goods and take care of it themselves." (R1)

As noted, comparing the current state (Fig. 2) with the state at the end of the initiative (Fig. 1), this level of analysis obfuscates the representation of the changes in

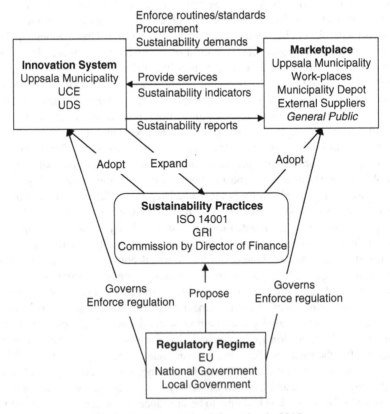

Fig. 2. Actor network configuration in 2015.

the information system. By zooming in and focusing at a lower organizational level, closer to workplaces that where directly affected in their day-to-day activities by the implemented changes, the change becomes more apparent. The involved parties are, in principle unchanged, but the underlying motivations enrolling the actors to achieve a stable network have changed.

Figure 3 depicts the initial relation between Innovation System and the Marketplace in the actor network at the time when PHV was ended in January 2009. Most notably, the adherence to a TBL perspective of sustainability is inscribed in the sustainability reporting systems' information requirements needed to compile reports with sufficient depth. The configuration of the actor network in 2015 is depicted in Fig. 4.

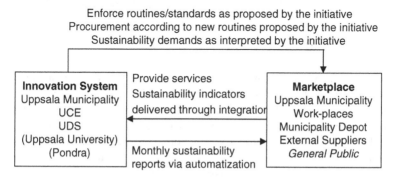

Fig. 3. Initial relation between Innovation System and the Marketplace.

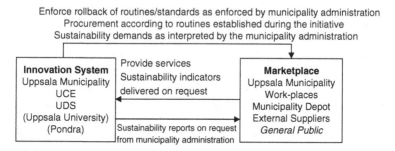

Fig. 4. Relation between Innovation System and the Marketplace in 2015.

It is apparent that the role of sustainability has changed compared to the intentions of the original initiative. The central role that sustainability had as an intrinsic goal has been transformed. It is now one of many metrics that should be collected from the workplaces in order for the municipality to live up to legislative demands. As a consequence, the TBL view of sustainability is phased-out and replaced by an emission view of sustainability where the focus is on CO_2 equivalents as the measure of sustainability performance as inscribed in the reporting systems. This can probably explain why there were no efforts made to re-integrate the system architecture tried during the initiative with the new accounting system.

The sustainability reporting system and the procurement system's integration with the accounting system during the initiative was designed to measure a broad set of sustainability parameters and support the workplaces with frequent feedback on sustainability performance. None of these features are necessary in order for the individual workplaces to perform their duties or deliver the required level of sustainability reporting, nor are the features necessary for the municipality in fulfilling their obligations in regards to sustainability reporting. The current situation is expressed as: "Sustainability issues are incorporated in working routines. Primarily through regulations from higher-ups, but when internal decisions are made we try to take sustainability into consideration. However, there are no specific support systems for this." (R3)

5 Discussion and Conclusion

The specific research question was, to what extent may holistic sustainability values persist when the results of a sustainability innovation initiative is transformed to standard mode of operation? Based on this study the short answer is 'very little'. The long answer, however, is more complex. It is evident from the original study, that sustainability when supported by IT can function as the primary driver to accomplish change that have a broad spectrum of positive effects in addition to sustainability outcomes that adhere to a TBL perspective.

However, this holistic view of sustainability will not persist when it is no longer supported by the extra efforts available during a dedicated initiative, nor translated into the supporting IT infrastructure. When operations return to normal those aspects of the initiative that are in line with the requirement and goals of the organization will survive, but more altruistic ideas will succumb.

In order to visualize and understand the effects of sustainability initiatives, a multi-level analysis is required. Employees, as part of their work assignments perform most of the activities that impact sustainability. To what degree they act sustainably, and in regards to what aspects of sustainability, is basically governed by requirements from higher management. The network formation after PHV is at an aggregated organizational level treating all participating workplaces as one actor. Using the same level of analysis to depict the current situation, it became obvious that it did not fully reflect the details necessary to understand the nature of what had actually changed after the initiative. By zooming in on the entities that actually take part in the actions that have sustainable impact, the factors that govern how a workplace relate and act on sustainable issues reveal the fundamental shift in how the work practices in relation to sustainability has changed. At this level of analysis it becomes apparent that introducing changes in sustainability practices that affects ecologic, economic and social sustainability is fully doable. It requires, however, management with a holistic view of sustainability who lets that view guide the actions taken to influence practice. Furthermore, it requires IT systems and routines that support those practices. When the support structure is removed and the workplaces that had been involved in the initiative no longer have a strong advocate for holistic sustainability practices, and the IT infrastructure supporting those practices are dismantled, the workplaces have no choice but to adapt. A central aspect of how sustainability is perceived within an organization is thus down to what is measured and how it is measured. This implies that activities that have a sustainability impact that is measured are important and little or no credit will be given for improving other aspects of sustainability. The latter could of course have other effects that are measured against other goals than sustainability.

Although there are limitations to statistical generalizability of findings based on a single case study, important analytical conclusions can still be drawn [35]. Our findings suggest that to promote operations that account for ecological, economic and social sustainability, management need to (a) actively support a holistic view of sustainability, (b) let this be reflected in required data collection and (c) instigate systems that ensure reporting of this information. Furthermore, the result of sustainable performance measures should be reported back to the workplace that provides the information in a format that is usable for formulating local actions. This requires regular data collection, analysis and feedback. Thus, it is possible to implement changes based on a holistic view of sustainability without hampering efficiency. The majority of the published work on sustainable information systems is biased towards technology impact and resource reduction rather than the use of technology as driver for social and organizational change towards more sustainable behaviour. Somewhat paradoxically, we find the same bias in this study even though a specific aim of the studied initiative, as well as our own understanding of sustainability, emphasized the importance of a holistic view. It seems, however, that a holistic view of sustainability can be inscribed in the individual and organizational behaviour that constitutes and continuously re-enacts the organizational and societal structures that frame everyday practices. In order for a holistic view of sustainability to be established and maintained, such a view needs to be reflected in the way sustainability is measured and supported by the reporting infrastructure through its information systems.

References

1. Butler, T.: Compliance with institutional imperatives on environmental sustainability: Building theory on the role of green IS. J. Strateg. Inf. Syst. **20**, 6–26 (2011)
2. Loock, C.M., Staake, T., Thiesse, F.: Motivating energy-efficient behavior with green IS: an investigation of goal setting and the role of defaults. MIS Q. **37**, 1313–1332 (2013)
3. Tushi, B.T., Sedera, D., Recker, J.: Green IT segment analysis: an academic literature review. In: Proceedings of the Twentieth Americas Conference on Information Systems (AMCIS 2014), pp. 1–15 (2014)
4. Esfahani, M.D., Rahman, A.A., Zakaria, N.H.: The status quo and the prospect of green IT and green IS: a systematic literature review. JSCDSS **2**, 18–34 (2014)
5. PHV: Utredningen Effektiv Handel – Logistik; Rapport: Pilotprojektet Hållbara Varu-transporter. Uppsala, Sweden (2009)
6. Elkington, J.: Cannibals with Forks. Capstone Publishing Limited, Oxford (1997)
7. United Nations General Assembly: World Summit Outcome, Resolution A/60/1, adopted by the General Assembly on 15 September 2005
8. Seele, P., Gatti, L.: Greenwashing revisited: in search of a typology and accusation-based definition incorporating legitimacy strategies. Bus. Strat. Env. (2015)

9. Bengtsson, F., Ågerfalk, P.: Information technology as a change actant in sustainability innovation: insights from Uppsala. J. Strateg. Inf. Syst. **20**, 96–112 (2011)

10. Iveroth, E., Bengtsson, F.: Changing behavior towards sustainable practices using information technology. J. Environ. Manag. **139**, 59–68 (2014)

11. UNT: Sju veckotransporter blev bara en. Uppsala nya tidning 11 January 2010, Uppsala, Sweden (2010)

12. Chasin, F.: Sustainability: are we all talking about the same thing? State-of-the art and proposal for an integrative definition of sustainability in information systems. In: 2nd International Conference on ICT for Sustainability (ICT4S 2014) (2014)

13. Watson, R.T., Boudreau, M.C., Chen, A.J.: Information systems and environmentally sustainable development: energy informatics and new directions for the IS community. MIS Q. **34**, 23–38 (2010)

14. Dao, V., Langella, I., Carbo, J.: From green to sustainability: information technology and an integrated sustainability framework. J. Strateg. Inf. Syst. **20**, 63–79 (2011)

15. Elliot, S.: Transdisciplinary perspectives on environmental sustainability: a resource base and framework for it-enabled business transformation. MIS Q. **35**, 197–236 (2011)

16. Melville, N.P.: Information systems innovation for environmental sustainability. MIS Q. **31**, 1–21 (2010)

17. Lyytinen, K., King, J.L.: Around the cradle of the wireless revolution: the emergence and evolution of cellular telephony. Telecommun. Policy **26**, 97–100 (2002)

18. Yoo, Y., Lyytinen, K., Yang, H.: The role of standards in innovation and diffusion of broadband mobile services: the case of South Korea. J. Strateg. Inf. Syst. **14**, 323–353 (2005)

19. Callon, M., Latour, B.: Unscrewing the big Leviathan: how actors macro-structure reality and how sociologists help them to do so. In: Knorr-Cetina, K.D., Cicourel, A.V. (eds.) Advances in Social Theory and Methodology: Towards an Integration of Micro and Macro-Sociologies, pp. 277–303. Routledge and Kegan Paul, London (1981)

20. Callon, M.: Some elements of a sociology of translation: domestication of the scallops and fishermen of St. Brieuc Bay. In: Law, J. (ed.) Power, Action and Belief: A New Sociology of Knowledge?, vol. 32, pp. 196–233. Routledge, London (1986)

21. Latour, B.: The Pasteurization of France. Harvard University Press, Cambridge (1988)

22. Latour, B.: On recalling ANT. In: Law, J., Hassard, J. (eds.) Actor Network and After, pp. 15–25. Blackwell and the Sociological Review, Oxford (1999)

23. Orlikowski, W., Walsham, G., Jones, M., DeGross, J.I. (eds.): Information Technology and Changes in Organizational Work. Chapman and Hall, London (1996)

24. Hanseth, O., Monteiro, E.: Inscribing behavior in information infrastructure standards. AMIT **7**, 183–211 (1997)

25. Walsham, G.: Actor-network theory and IS research: current status and future prospects. In: Lee, A.S., Liebenau, J., DeGross, J.I. (eds.) Information Systems and Qualitative Research, pp. 466–480. Chapman and Hall, London (1997)

26. Gao, P.: Counter-networks in standardization: a perspective of developing countries. Inform. Syst. J. **17**, 391–420 (2007)

27. Hanseth, O., Jacucci, E., Grisot, M., Aanestad, M.: Reflexive standardization: side effects and complexity in standard making. MIS Q. **30**, 563–581 (2006)

28. Akrich, M., Latour, B.: A summary of a convenient vocabulary for the semiotics of human and nonhuman assemblies. In: Shaping Technology/Building Society, pp. 259–264 (1992)

29. Callon, M.: Techno-economic networks and irreversibility. In: Law, J. (ed.) A Sociology of Monsters: Essays on Power, Technology and Domination, pp. 132–161. Routledge, London (1991)

30. Latour, B.: Drawing things together. In: Lynch, M., Woolgar, S. (eds.) Representation in Scientific Practice, pp. 19–68. MIT Press, Cambridge (1990)
31. Walsham, G.: Interpretive case studies in IS research: nature and method. Eur. J. Inform. Syst. **4**, 74–81 (1995)
32. Marshall, M.N.: The key informant technique. Fam. Pract. **13**, 92–97 (1996)
33. Patton, M.Q.: Qualitative Research and Evaluation Methods, 3rd edn. Sage, Thousand Oaks (2002)
34. Pallinkas, L.A., Horwitz, S.M., Green, C.A., Hoagwood, K.E.: Purposeful sampling for qualitative data collection and analysis in mixed method implementation research. Adm. Policy Ment. Health **42**, 533–544 (2015)
35. Yin, R.K.: Case Study Research: Design and Methods, 5th edn. Sage Publications, Los Angeles (2013)

A Boundary Practice Perspective
on Co-creation of ICT Innovations

Lars-Olof Johansson[1]($\boxtimes$), Ulrika Lundh Snis[2], and Lars Svensson[2]

[1] Halmstad University, Box 823, 301 28 Halmstad, Sweden
lars-olof.johansson@hh.se
[2] University West, 461 86 Trollhättan, Sweden
{ulrika.snis,lars.svensson}@hv.se

Abstract. Research has shown that collaboration and co-creation among different groups of stakeholders add complexity and challenges to the innovation process. In this paper a study of co-creation in a multi-stakeholder innovation process is presented. The co-creation is explored and described from a boundary practice perspective. The empirical data presented in the study is based on a user-centric innovation project, Free2Ride, where researchers, developers and members of two equestrian clubs co-created a piece of ICT safety equipment consisting of a transmitter (on the horse) and a receiver (application on a smartphone) to be used by equestrian club members during their everyday riding activities. Three episodes were extracted from the empirical data and presented in the paper. From these episodes the researchers have identified four characteristics of the spanning of boundaries in co-creation from a boundary practice perspective. One of the contributions in the papers is a description of boundary practice-spanning. The research approach adopted in the study is the action case approach.

Keywords: Boundary practice · Co-creation · ICT innovation

1 Introduction

It has become widely acknowledged that ICT innovation processes benefit from the involvement of end users [1], vendors, clients [2] and other relevant stakeholders [3]. The main argument is that supplementary knowledge and multiple perspectives of the involved stakeholders have the potential of resulting in high quality innovations [4] and can even boost the innovation capability [1]. Eriksson et al. [1] claims that the involvement of stakeholders in the innovation process is

> "thereby leveraging on a larger mass of ideas, knowledge and experiences etc. and substantially boosting the innovation capability." (p. 1)

The idea that heterogeneity of participants (end users, vendors, clients and other relevant stakeholders) is an asset during systems development has roots in the field of participatory design [5] and in the Scandinavian tradition of information systems development [6]. Furthermore, user-driven innovation (e.g.); living lab approach [7] and open innovation [4] are all examples of theoretically informed approaches to the *innovation process* that share the fundamental principle of involving heterogeneous participants.

© Springer International Publishing Switzerland 2016
M. Gellerstedt et al. (Eds.): SCIS 2016, LNBIP 259, pp. 100–115, 2016.
DOI: 10.1007/978-3-319-43597-8_8

However, research also shows that collaboration and co-creation among different groups of stakeholders add complexity and challenges to the innovation process in terms of cultural, linguistic and epistemological *boundaries* between stakeholders [3]. The authors illustrate the challenges by stating:

> A key challenge in this development context is representing, negotiating and integrating the diverse knowledge, viewpoints and interests of these stakeholders, in order to create a shared understanding of the development work and outcome (p. 570).

Social, cultural, linguistic and epistemological boundaries have been addressed in the socio-cultural learning tradition [8]. Therefore it becomes natural to explore and understand the challenge with boundaries in co-creation with the boundary practice perspective [9]. A boundary practice is a practice that "provides an ongoing forum for mutual engagement" [9, p. 114] between different communities of practice (CoP). The purpose of the boundary practice is to maintain connections and interaction between several CoPs [10]. Hence, we regard the groups of stakeholders participating in the innovation process as different communities of practice. At the same time we consider a boundary practice as a social configuration of different CoPs taking action in a temporal project, such as a user-driven ICT innovation process.

In this paper, we report from an ICT innovation process, Free2Ride. Free2Ride was set up as a living lab process involving stakeholders in co-creation. The project aimed to develop a piece of ICT safety equipment to be used during horseback riding. In Free2Ride three different groups of stakeholders were involved: ICT developers, members from two equestrian clubs and a group of information systems researchers.

The aim is to understand and describe the characteristics of the boundary practice in order to span boundaries. The research question in the paper is: What are the characteristics of the boundaries from a boundary practice perspective?

The contribution of our research is insight into a co-creation process between CoPs regarded as a boundary practice. In many cases spanning or crossing boundaries is described based on a dyadic relationships, that is, involving two individuals [10]. This, when compared to a process of co-creation, often involves boundary spanning between different groups, e.g. a boundary practice spanning.

2   Co-creation in ICT Innovation

During the last decade, several "open" approaches have received attention within the research field, as opposed to more "closed" settings, in which companies internally manage all stages of the innovation process [2]. Among these open approaches we will mention (i) open innovation [4]; (ii) user driven innovation [11]; and (iii) living labs [1] as forms of various innovation processes. Together, they involve a multiplicity of stakeholders and information sources that are connected to the innovation process in different ways. Open innovation is described as inflows and outflows of knowledge to accelerate internal innovation in order to expand the markets for external use of innovation [2, 4, 12, 13]. A living lab approach is, according to [14], an ICT innovation process which is characterized by a user-centric approach. User influence and partner engagements are important parts of this approach, along with the importance of them always being performed in real-life contexts. The third approach, user-driven innovation [11, 15, 16], also has a focus on users, i.e., those who will benefit from using the product or service.

Relating the living lab approach [17] with previous research on the Scandinavian tradition of information systems development [18], as well as the participatory design research [19], shows a strong connection, namely, that they share the fundamental idea of empowering the users, co-creation among several partners, and the involvement of researchers in action-oriented projects.

From the approaches mentioned above we realise that they all encourage cross-sector collaboration, openness, empowerment of users, and detection of creative initiatives. In some sense the goal is to create and develop an innovation, and in some situations such an innovation is an ICT product. The main reason why we regard the Free2Ride project as an innovation process is that the activities in the process are intended to produce a new ICT product with regards to the needs of a customer group that will change the everyday practice of that group.

The main element of such an innovation process is the collaborative effort of co-creation. Relating to [20], co-creation is an active, creative and social process, based on collaboration between firms and end users. In co-creation, dialogue between stakeholders is often presented as a key challenge e.g. [21, 22]. From the perspective of the producing company, dialogue means listening to customers, but also interaction, communication, and engagement between two equally empowered problem solvers [23]. Dialogue then creates the capacity for stakeholder groups to suspend assumptions and enter into a genuine "thinking together" mode [24]. Consequently, dialogue can help organizations to understand the complex nature of the customers' social and cultural contexts [25].

From the related research we can identify challenges concerning the problem of handling collaboration and boundaries. There are boundaries between organizations, between departments within an organization and, of course, boundaries between an organization and their customers. [26] state: "Overall, innovation is about spanning or breaking the prevailing boundaries". The body of research provides substantial advice on conducting more such research, but we still do not know how communication and interaction within and between boundaries of stakeholder groups are handled and how they affect the progress of the innovation process in a boundary practice. In co-creation, members of different communities need to engage in collaboration in an inter-community practice which initially has no shared history, and where no sources of knowledge or cultural tools exist to be negotiated. In the next section we will introduce the key concepts that are central to our understanding of co-creation in a boundary practice.

3   A Boundary Practice Perspective

In order to clarify the boundary practice perspective we start by defining a practice and continue by characterizing a boundary practice. A practice is understood as a "recurrent, materially bounded and situated action engaged in by members of a community" [27, p. 256]. Members of a community share a concern (or a set of problems) and deepen their knowledge by interacting on an ongoing basis in a community of practice, i.e., a CoP [28]. Wenger [29] defines a CoP by three main characteristics: (i) it has an identity defined by an interest; (ii) members engage in joint activities, and (iii) they develop a shared repertoire of resources. CoPs consider activities such as learning and working as interrelated, compatible, intertwined and connected to innovating [30].

Wenger et al. [28] present three forms of membership in a CoP: core members, active members and peripheral members. Core members typically initiate different projects and function as leaders of the community. Furthermore, core members are engaged in the progress and development of the CoP. Active members are also involved in projects and engage actively, but in different negotiations. Active members seek advice from core members and lack the mandate to develop and change the CoP. The peripheral members are observers of the interaction in the community and do not contribute to the creation of meaning in the practice of the community. The status of a member changes over time; an active member can become a core member, a core member can become more peripheral, and of course other trajectories towards the core and periphery are constantly enacted as new members enter and exit the CoP. As pointed out by Wenger [9], any individual has to cope with her nexus of multi-membership, being for instance a parent, employee and equestrian instructor simultaneously and in different contexts.

3.1 Boundary Practices and Boundary Objects

The concept of boundary practices [9] is a practice that provides an ongoing forum for mutual engagement between different CoPs. The purpose of the boundary practice is to maintain connections between several CoPs [10]. The inter-community practice, such as a boundary practice, is important [31] because it helps to overcome some of the problems a community creates for itself [30].

The connection between the boundary practice and the CoP is by members acting as boundary spanners [32] or brokers, and their use of boundary objects (Fig. 1). Wenger [9], describes this as reification and participation. Participation is used to introduce elements from one practice into another by being a broker. Two different types of brokering are proposed by [33] in user-centric innovation processes: process

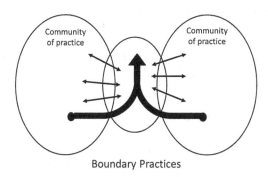

Fig. 1. Boundary practices according to Wenger [9]

brokering and product brokering. Product brokering is aimed at introducing elements useful for the product developed while process brokering is aimed at introducing elements useful in the process. Brokering [9] and boundary spanning-in-practice [32] are both concepts aiming at relating practices in one field to practices in another by negotiating the meaning and terms of the relationship.

The boundary spanning literature has been criticized for its focus on dyadic relationships, that is, boundary spanning involving two individuals [10], compared to organizational settings, which often involve boundary spanning between groups. The same authors also argue that there is a lack of understanding of how a boundary practice can achieve the purpose of connecting practices.

A boundary practice uses boundary objects (forms, documents, sketches, etc.) to interconnect CoPs. Such boundary objects are any objects that are relevant to the practices of multiple communities, but are used or viewed differently by each of them [30, 34, 35]. Levina and Vaast [32] distinguish the difference between designated boundary objects and boundary objects-in-use; where a boundary object-in-use has to be locally useful (incorporated into practices). A crucial quality of boundary objects that facilitate sharing and coordination is their interpretive flexibility [35], which allows for multiple interpretations by the multiple parties utilizing them [36]. This also makes boundary objects meaningful and commonly applied across communities.

3.2   Summary of the Boundary Practice Perspective

There are three concepts that are recurring during the description of the analytical lens: engagement, interaction and boundary objects. A boundary practice is dependent on mutual engagement by members from different CoPs in much the same way as co-creation is dependent on mutual engagement from involved stakeholders. Co-creation is described as a social process of interaction where dialogue is important when examining basic assumptions through interaction. The boundary practice maintains connections through the different types of members that interact with CoPs. Core members are engaged in the co-creation process by creating engagement and negotiating meaning.

The concept of boundary practice neatly frames the challenges of a co-creation project where members from different CoPs join together in a new setting. Through focusing on translational activities such as boundary spanning and the negotiations triggered by boundary objects we can begin to understand the central challenges of co-creation in practice. However, the nature of membership in a boundary practice (core, active or peripheral member) is not specified in the literature, and the question of how such different levels of membership are enacted in order for co-creation to be developed in practice is in our understanding not clear.

4   Applying the Action Case Method

The research presented in this paper is characterized as qualitative research with an underlying interpretative philosophy [37]. The main research approach applied in this paper is the action case approach [38, 39]. The authors place the action case method between action research and soft case study. One of the goals of action research is to make a change based on an intervention. In the same way the goal of a soft case study is to reach an understanding based on an interpretation. Therefore, the action case has support for interpretation and intervention, much in line with Mingers [40] multi-method approach. The intervention and interpretation was done in a cyclical and intertwined manner. There was a greater focus on intervention during the Free2Ride project (further described in Sect. 4.1), but interpretations were made. The focus on the more interpretive research was done after the project (further described in Sect. 4.2). In Free2Ride the researchers had a focus on the co-creation between the involved actors, which is an important aspect in the clinical perspective of Schein [41]. Schein [41] argues that the process should be client driven, i.e., the needs of the client are more important than the needs of the researcher. Thus, the focus should be on client's issues rather than involving the client in the researcher's issues.

4.1 Intervention – The Free2Ride Project

The Free2Ride project was initiated by researchers from Halmstad Living Lab (HLL), ICT developers (from Alpha Bluetooth Inc) and two equestrian clubs (Laholmsortens RF and Hylte RF) during the autumn of 2009. One of the main ideas behind the project was to develop an ICT prototype based on wireless technologies that matched the needs of members of the equestrian clubs through an open and explorative approach during the early stages of the project. The involved ICT developers belonged to a company with a background in wireless technologies, especially Bluetooth communication between embedded systems. Prior to Free2Ride the company addressed problems related to safety, security and communications within different sport activities such as climbing, sailing, football, and bicycling.

The Free2Ride project followed a structure of six phases conducted in an iterative manner according to the principles of a living lab [17]: *identifying needs and generating requirements; (re)design; developing conceptual prototypes; evaluating the design and prototypes (the design concept); developing the ICT demonstrator; and evaluating the ICT demonstrator.*

The first phase of Free2Ride was to come up with new ideas, which were generated by members of the two equestrian clubs. The three most urgent areas according to these ideas related to safety during outdoor horse riding, communication during competitions and indoor equestrian training activities. In order to identify the most urgent area, a survey was distributed and used during different horse shows (show jumping, dressage, etc.). The prioritized area, according to the survey, was safety during outdoor horse riding.

The second, third and fourth phases focused on creating and evaluating a design specification. It is notable that the design was focused on a solution involving two units: a transmitter and a receiver. The first unit (a transmitter) should be attached to the bridle of the horse (Fig. 2) and communicate through Bluetooth with an application in a smartphone (the second unit) which is carried by the horse rider (Fig. 2). There were some specific requirements for the transmitter having to do with weight, size, battery lifetime and being waterproof. After all, most horse riding is done outside regardless of weather conditions.

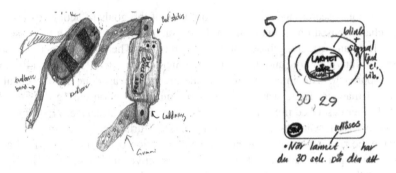

Fig. 2. The transmitter to the left, the interface in the application to the right

In the fifth phase, the development of the transmitter followed the design specification and standard models from ICT developers. The transmitter was also equipped with a microchip that communicates with a heart rate monitor for horses in order to develop add-on services within the application. During the fifth phase, the ICT developers reported in a continuous manner, and progress was available to the equestrian clubs on the Free2Ride website. The members of the equestrian clubs also had the opportunity to give feedback to the developers.

Prior to the final phase, four pairs of prototypes (IT demonstrator and application) were developed and tested in their natural environment at the equestrian clubs, according to the basic principles of a living lab. The test period lasted about four weeks. During this period a member of the equestrian club documented the testing on a blog, where the members of the involved communities of practice could comment on the test. A list of suggested changes to the application and the transmitter was compiled after the test period.

4.2   Interpretation – Data Gathering and Analysis

The Free2Ride project held 12 workshops with members of all three communities of practice (researchers, ICT developers and equestrian clubs as end users); five meetings between researchers and developers; four field studies at the equestrian clubs; on-line activities that lasted for three months; real life testing/evaluation of the ICT demonstrator; and follow-up interviews (six of them) after the project (see Table 1). The workshops were recorded and notes were taken at some of them, which were also documented by pictures. Field notes were also taken during the meetings and field studies. There were at least two researchers at every workshop or meeting that compared notes afterwards.

A typical workshop during Free2Ride lasted for three hours and consisted of the following activities: a progress report (what has happened in the project since the last workshop), presenting the activities and goals of the workshop (how? why? and what?), teamwork, presenting the results of the teamwork, summing up and discussing the future.

Table 1. Summary data collection

Data collection	Period	Descriptions
Field visits	During F2R	Understanding and documenting the activities that take place in the equestrian clubs
Meetings	During F2R	The meetings took place between the researchers and the ICT developer and were related to the progress of the project, such as deliverables, project documentation etc.
On-line activities	During F2R	Blogs, questionnaires, videos and news. All with the possibility to make comments were used during the evaluation
Workshops	During F2R After F2R	12 workshops where at least 15 people from two different communities of practice met and discussed needs and problems in relation to the project
Interviews	After F2R	Follow-up interviews focused primarily on questions related to expectations in contrast to the actual outcomes but also covered questions in order to clarify different issues revealed in the analysis

We made a literature survey to develop a conceptual understanding of co-creation practice. The survey was conducted in two areas, co-creation [21, 23, 25] and ICT innovation processes where heterogeneous actors were involved [1, 2, 11, 14]. This literature survey became our theoretical framework.

In order to analyze our empirical data we made a second literature survey on literature addressing boundary practices [9, 10, 28, 42, 43]. The specific concepts of core members, boundaries, boundary objects-in-use [32], dialogue [21, 23–25, 44] between members were used to describe what actually happened at the boundaries between communities of practice in a boundary practice.

We structured the empirical data in a timeline according to the different activities and within these activities we categorized the empirical data with the abovementioned concepts as main categories. From this categorization we selected three episodes that have two things in common: an impact on the outcome of the project and initiating a shared understanding of the co-created value.

5 The Three Episodes

The three selected episodes are referred to as the drawing episode Sect. 5.1 the interface episode Sect. 5.2 and the video episode Sect. 5.3.

5.1 The Drawing Episode

The drawing episode took place in a workshop aiming to specify the design of the Bluetooth sender. Before one of the workshops Rachel approached the researcher and said that she had made some drawings (Fig. 3) that she wanted to show the rest of us. The drawings were made during a break when she worked as a substitute art teacher.

Fig. 3. The transmitter on the bridle

Rachel dedicates her spare time to the equestrian club and activities related to horse riding (35-40 h/week). It all started when she was a kid and has continued ever since. She is an instructor for children (beginners and semi-beginners). Rachel is also involved in horse camp activities in the summertime at the equestrian club. The horse camp is not only about horse riding, show jumping, etc., but also includes other social activities. Rachel has two daughters (age 18 and 9) who are also members of the equestrian club. Rachel works as a substitute art teacher in the municipality where she lives.

The researchers scanned the drawings and the digitized drawings were inserted in the PowerPoint presentation that the researchers had prepared. During the start of the workshop, the presentation was given and Rachel presented her drawings, and indeed they triggered a discussion where all of the participants were engaged.

During Rachel's presentation a lot of questions and comments were raised. Some of the comments were rather general like "great drawings" and other comments were more specific, such as, "How should the ICT product be attached to the bridle?". Not all of the comments were addressed to Rachel; instead the participants started to discuss amongst themselves, pointing at the different drawings as reference. An open discussion and a free dialogue started regarding requirements for the transmitter general discussions about riding horses, and the needs of the horse riders in particular.

One of the discussions dealt with the placement of the transmitter on the bridle. The members of the equestrian clubs all agreed that the placement must not disturb the horse and should be viewable from the saddle. The discussion also addressed how to attach the transmitter to the bridle and how durable the straps that hold the transmitter should be. During the discussion it was decided to contact a saddler for advice on how to attach the transmitter to the bridle. During this dialogue there was not only consensus about the needs and requirements of the transmitter (and the straps) on the bridle but also consensus about how to proceed in the project.

5.2   The Interface Episode

Two weeks after the drawing episode the researchers and the ICT developers had a meeting at the workplace of the ICT developers. During that meeting a discussion was held concerning the structure and graphical interface of the smartphone application. During that meeting Chandler presented a "rough" sketch (Fig. 4) of the interface to the researchers and we discussed how we should use these sketches in the forthcoming workshop.

Fig. 4. The first drawing of the interface

Chandler has worked as an ICT developer since 2005. He has both a Bachelor's and a Master's degree in mechatronics engineering. He started his first job as product developer when he was writing his master's thesis. Chandler's competences are within embedded systems and wireless communication between embedded systems. He is highly experienced in Bluetooth, RFID and Linux. During the Free2Ride project Chandler started a new job as a system integrator and to an extent left the organization where he had been employed as a product developer. According to him it was a matter of phasing out ongoing projects.

It was decided that Chandler should improve and present these in the next workshop. Chandler had realized that it is difficult for someone without previous experience of using a smartphone to understand how the interface would look and how to use the functionality on the smartphone.

The fourth and fifth phases of the Free2Ride project took place at the following workshop, where we evaluated the design concept, developed the first version of a prototype and the sketch was presented. There were of course a lot of questions from those who were unfamiliar with the interface of a smartphone as well as comments made by those who were familiar with smartphones, directed either to Chandler or to the other participants in the workshop.

5.3   The Video Episode

During the last phase of the Free2Ride project, evaluating the ICT demonstrator, we used both a video and a blog to document the use of the smartphone application and the transmitter in the real life environment of equestrian club activities. One of the video cameras was taken care of by Phoebe, who promised to document the use of the transmitter and the smartphone-application during practice (Fig. 5). After a couple of weeks Phoebe contacted the researchers and said the she had made some recordings. The video was uploaded to the Free2Ride website and was commented upon by some of the other members of the equestrian clubs, but no comments were given by the ICT developers during the time between our workshops.

Fig. 5. End user testing the prototype

Phoebe dedicates most of her spare time to the equestrian club and horse riding, much in the same way as Rachel. Her time is spent on board meetings and management of the equestrian club. Phoebe is also involved in the association of equestrian clubs on a regional level. It would be fair to say that Phoebe is not only involved in the operational level of the equestrian club, but on a more strategic/tactical level.

A decision was made by the researchers to show the video at the last workshop of the project. During the presentation of the video a lot of comments were made by members of the equestrian clubs but also from the ICT-developers. The members of the equestrian clubs highlighted the condition of the practice (weather and a not a very cooperative horse). After the video a rather long discussion about the problem of false alarms started. It was decided that the ICT-prototype needed some further testing in a more controlled environment. At the end of the workshop, after the video, the participants became involved in constructing the first version of a "to-do list".

6 Deriving Characteristics of Boundary Practice-Spanning

Through the episodes presented in the previous section, we have identified a set of characteristics with the common denominator of enhancing value creation in the Free2Ride project.

In this section we will discuss the characteristics of the boundary practice and activities that are played out in the selected episodes, and by applying the boundary practice lens we arrive at a richer understanding of what makes the co-creation process work in practice.

Before we take a closer look on the characteristics of boundary practice we need to understand what kind of boundaries that has been spanned. The reported episodes demonstrate how boundaries can manifest themselves in a co-creation process as being social, cultural and epistemological [8], where riding and the wellbeing of the horses are at the center of members of the equestrian community, who perceive riding as a life-style, in contrast to developers, where horse riding initially is framed merely as an application area for innovation and novel artefacts. Another type of boundary is the linguistic boundary [3]. The members of the equestrian clubs have specific words (bridle etc.) that need to be translated (The drawing episode and video episode) in order to reach a shared understanding of their needs. Another example of overcoming a linguistic boundary is the interface episode where the developers used a sketch to initiate a dialogue about the smartphone application.

6.1 Core Members of CoPs Become Core Members of a Boundary Practice

When identifying the episodes and analysing field notes and workshop transcripts, two findings was identified: (1) all episodes were the result of an initiative occurring outside the pre-planned activities; and (2) each initiative was always taken by a core member of a particular community.

Rachel is very engaged in their equestrian club. She is highly involved in activities that make the everyday life of horse riders easier; she is also an instructor. Rachel has initiated different projects and functions (summer camp and communicating with the co-owners of horses at the club). Rachel fit the description of a core member very well [9]. Similarly, Chandler represents a key actor of the developers, through his central engagement in the project.

We believe that the fact that the episodes were initiated by core members of respective CoPs, is to some extent related to them having legitimacy and authority [28], and furthermore, by taking these initiatives they also claim a role as core members in the boundary practice that the project constitutes.

6.2 From Boundary Spanning-in-Practice to Boundary Practice-Spanning

Boundary spanning literature has been criticized for its focus on dyadic relationships, that is, boundary spanning involving two individuals [10]. The key episodes clearly demonstrate how boundary spanning between CoPs occurs and evolves in and around a boundary practice [9]. Boundary spanning-in-practice is aimed at relating practices in one field to practices in another by negotiating the meaning and terms of the relationship. Rachel, Chandler and Phoebe acted not only as boundary spanners-in-practice [32] but even more so as boundary practice-spanners.

6.3   A Boundary Object-in-Use Becomes a Tool for Dialogue in Boundary Practice-Spanning

A boundary object is described as objects (forms, documents, sketches, etc.) that interconnect CoPs [9, 28, 45] but are viewed differently by each of them [30, 34, 35]. In the episodes a objects (Video and drawings) was developed. These objects are considered to be designated boundary objects.

A designated boundary object is a boundary object that is not yet incorporated into a practice in a community [32]. In the three episodes a designated boundary object is presented at a workshop. During the preparation of the presentation, members of at least two CoPs are involved and during the presentation members from all three CoPs interacted in a dialogue which rather quickly leads to consensus among workshop participants. Our interpretation is that the designated boundary objects became boundary objects-in-use during the interaction. As Levina and Vaast [32] describe boundary objects-in-use, they must be locally useful and incorporated into practice. However, there is one aspect that needs to be highlighted; instead of being useful in a community it became useful in the dialogue within the boundary practice-spanning. The interpretative flexibility [34] that a boundary object has is an important attribute in the dialogue. Another important attribute of the boundary object is that it expresses a problem of interest in a CoP or within boundary practices. Furthermore, we saw the designated boundary objects serve as reifications of the discussions and reflections that the participants have engaged in within the timespan between pre-planned workshops (Wenger [9]).

6.4   Boundary Objects Are Catalysts for Decision-Making that Support the Progress of the Innovation Process

Senge [24] describes dialogue as genuinely thinking together, examining assumptions and gaining insights on a group level. In line with this, we observed that during the workshop dialogues the various members constantly engaged in negotiations which resulted in insights not only as individuals but also as a boundary practice. The workshop dialogues had the character of collective negotiation of meaning (Wenger [9]) that eventually led to a shared understanding: of the problem, the situation or the solution. The three episodes are examples where dialogue leads to consensus, which leads to a decision regarding the progress of the co-creation process. The drawing episode initiated a re-design that adapted to placing the artifact on the bridle. The interface episode moved the project into the concept evaluation phase, where participants jointly negotiated design details such as the size of the screen, interactional affordances and logical structure.

When deriving characteristics of boundary spanning-practice in the co-creation process it was noticed that in order to overcome the boundaries, core members take initiatives and become boundary practice-spanners. As a result, a mode of "thinking together" was settled, built on interaction, communication, and engagement that enhanced co-creation.

7 Conclusion

As outlined in the introduction, the aim was to understand and describe the characteristics of the boundary practice in order to span boundaries. The research question in the paper is: What are the characteristics of the boundaries from a boundary practice perspective?

In this study we started to explore the empirical findings from F2R in order to gain a deeper understanding of co-creation and boundary practices. In conclusion, we have derived four characteristics of the spanning of boundaries in co-creation from a boundary practice perspective:

- Core members of CoPs become core members of a boundary practice
- From boundary spanning-in-practice to boundary practice-spanning
- A boundary object-in-use becomes a tool for dialogue in a boundary practice
- Boundary objects are catalysts for decision-making that support the progress of the innovation process.

We have proposed four characteristics of the spanning of boundaries in co-creation from a boundary practice perspective for the information systems researchers interested in ICT innovation. This list is not exhaustive, instead the characteristics have emerged through the Free2Ride project. The proposed characteristics have not yet been tested or evaluated in any co-creation project, which makes it important to evaluate these characteristics in practice during innovation research which could lead to insights for the innovation researcher.

One contribution of our research is the description of boundary practice-spanning, as an example of non-dyadic boundary spanning. Another contribution is a description of how boundary objects-in-use become useful in a boundary practice as a tool for dialogue and decisions.

References

1. Eriksson, M., Niitamo, V.-P., Kulkki, S.: State-of-the-art in utilizing living labs approach to user-centric ICT innovation - a European approach (2005)
2. Chesbrough, H.W.: Open Innovation: The New Imperative for Creating and Profiting from Technology. Harvard Business School Press, Boston (2003)
3. Doolin, B., McLeod, L.: Sociomateriality and boundary objects in information systems development. Euro. J. Inf. Syst. **2012**(21), 570–586 (2012)
4. Chesbrough, H.: The era of open innovation. In: Mayle, D. (ed.) Managing Innovation and Change. Sage, Thousand Oaks (2006)

5. Greenbaum, J., Kyng, M. (eds.): Design at Work: Cooperative Design of Computer Systems. Lawrence Erlbaum Associates, Hilsdale (1991)
6. Loebbecke, C., Powell, P.: Furthering distributed participative design. Scand. J. Inf. Syst. **21**(1), 77–106 (2009)
7. Bergvall-Kåreborn, B., Ståhlbröst, A.: Living lab an open and user-centric design approach. In: Information and Communication Technologies, Society and Human Beings: Theory and Framework (2010)
8. Akkerman, S.F., Bakker, A.: Boundary crossing and boundary objects. Rev. Educ. Res. **81**(2), 132–169 (2011)
9. Wenger, E.: Communities of Practice: Learning, Meaning, and Identity. Cambridge University Press, Cambridge (1999)
10. Vashist, R., McKay, J., Marshall, P.: How well do we understand boundary practices? Empirical evidence from a practice of business analysts. In: ECIS 2011, Helsinki (2011)
11. Hippel, E.V.: Democratizing Innovation. MIT Press, Cambridge (2005)
12. Chesbrough, H.: Open Service Innovation. Wiley, New York (2011). Ed. by Mayle, D.
13. Chesbrough, H., Vanhaverbeke, W., West, J.: Open Innovation: Researching a New Paradigm. Oxford University Press, New York (2006)
14. Bergvall-Kåreborn, B., et al.: A milieu for innovation – defining living labs. In: ISPIM 2009, New York (2009)
15. Hippel, E.V.: Horizontal innovation networks–by and for users. In: Industrial and Corporate Change. Oxford University Press (2007)
16. Hippel, E.V.: Democratizing innovation: the evolving phenomenon of user innovation. J. für Betriebswirtschaft **55**(1), 63–78 (2005)
17. Ståhlbröst, A.: Forming future IT - the living lab way of user involvement. Department of Business Administration and Social Sciences, Luleå University of Technology, Luleå (2008)
18. Kyng, M.: Designing for cooperation: cooperating in design. Commun. ACM **34**(12), 30–34 (1991)
19. Kensing, F., Simonsen, J., Boedker, K.: MUST: a method for participatory design. Hum.-Comput. Interact. **13**, 167–198 (1998)
20. Piller, F., Ihl, C., Vossen, A.: A typology of customer co-creation in the innovation process. In: Hanekop, H., Wittke, V. (eds.) New Forms of Collaborate Production and Innovation: Economic, Social, Legal. Technical Characteristics and Conditions. Lichtenberg kolleg, Goettingen (2011)
21. Prahalad, C.K., Ramaswamy, V.: Co-creating unique value with customers. Strategy Leaders. **32**(3), 4–9 (2004)
22. Grover, V., Kohli, R.: Cocreating IT value: new capabilities and metrics for multifirm environments. MIS Q. **36**(1), 225–232 (2012)
23. Prahalad, C., Ramaswamy, V.: The co-creation connection. Strategy Bus. **27**, 50–61 (2002)
24. Senge, P.: The Fifth Discipline: The Art & Practice of the Learning Organization. Broadway Business, New York (1994)
25. Prahalad, C.K., Ramaswamy, V.: Co-creation experiences: the next practice in value creation. J. Interact. Mark. **18**(3), 5–14 (2004)
26. Avital, M., Lyytinen, K.: Track: Innovation Theory, Research and Practice in Information Systems (2010). http://www.ecis2011.fi/program/conference-tracks/innovation-theory-research-and-practice-in-information-systems/index.html. Cited 29 Nov 2010
27. Orlikowski, W.J.: Knowing in practice: enacting a collective capability in distributed organizing. Organ. Sci. **13**(3), 249–273 (2002)
28. Wenger, E., Mcdermott, R., Snyder, W.M.: Cultivating Communities of Practice. Harvard Business School Press, Boston (2002)
29. Wenger, E.: Communities of practice: a brief introduction (2006)

30. Brown, J.S., Duguid, P.: Organizational learning and communities-of-practice: toward a unified view of working, learning, and innovation. Organ. Sci. **2**(1), 40–57 (1991)
31. Cook, S.D.N., Brown, J.S.: Bridging epistemologies: the generative dance between organizational knowledge and organizational knowing. Organ. Sci. **10**(4), 381–400 (1999)
32. Levina, N., Vaast, E.: The emergence of boundary spanning competence: implications for implementation and use of information systems. MIS Q. **29**(2), 29 (2005)
33. Johansson, L.-O., Snis, U.L., Svensson, L.: Dynamics in an innovation boundary context: exploring a living lab process from a community of practice perspective. In: Molka-Danielsen, J. (ed.) Selected Papers of the 34th IRIS Seminar. Tapir Press, Molde (2011)
34. Star, S.: The structure of ill-structured solutions: boundary objects and heterogeneous distributed problem solving. In: Distributed Artificial Intelligence, vol. 2 (1990)
35. Star, S.L.: This is not a boundary object: reflections on the origin of a concept. Sci. Technol. Hum. Values **35**(5), 601–617 (2010)
36. Pawlowski, S., Robey, D.: Bridging user organizations: knowledge brokering and the work of information technology professionals. MIS Q. **28**(4), 645–672 (2004)
37. Myers, M.D.: Qualitative research in information systems. MIS Q. **21**(2), 241 (1997)
38. Braa, K., Vidgen, R.: Action case: exploring the middle kingdom in information system research methods. In: 3rd Decennial Conference on Computers in Context: Joining Forces in Design, Aarhus, Denmark (1995)
39. Vidgen, R.: Balancing interpretation and intervention in information system research: the action case approach. In: Lee, A.S., Liebenau, J., DeGross, J.I. (eds.) Information Systems and Qualitative Research. IFIP, pp. 524–541. Springer, Heidelberg (1997)
40. Mingers, J.: Combining is research methods: towards a pluralist methodology. Inf. Syst. Res. **12**(3), 240–259 (2001)
41. Schein, E.H.: The Clinical Perspective in Fieldwork. Qualitative Research Methods Series. SAGE Publications, Thousands Oaks (1987)
42. Vashist, R., McKay, J., Marshall, P.: The roles and practices of business analysts: a boundary practice perspective. In: Australasian Conference in Information Systems (ACIS 2010), Brisbane (2010)
43. Vashist, R., McKay, J., Marshall, P.: A framework to support the planning and implementation of work practice research: an example of using boundary practice lens on the work of business analysts. Syst. Signs Actions: Int. J. Commun. Inf. Technol. Work **5**(1), 30–66 (2011)
44. Senge, P., et al.: The Fifth Discipline Fieldbook. Random House, London (1994)
45. Lave, J., Wenger, E.: Situated Learning: Legitimate Peripheral Participation. Cambridge University Press, Cambridge (1991)

The Roles of Conference Papers in IS:
An Analysis of the Scandinavian Conference
on Information Systems

Arto Lanamäki[1(✉)] and John Stouby Persson[2]

[1] University of Oulu, PO Box 3000, 90014 Oulun Yliopisto, Finland
arto.lanamaki@oulu.fi
[2] Aalborg University, Selma Lagerløfs Vej 300, Aalborg 9220, Denmark
john@cs.aau.dk

Abstract. Information Systems (IS) research has both a journal-oriented publication culture and a rich plethora of conferences. It is unclear why IS researchers even bother with conference publishing given the high focus on journals. Against this backdrop, the purpose of this paper is to increase our understanding of conference papers in IS and the role they play for the authoring researchers. We present the first analysis of the papers published during the first six years (2010–2015) in the Scandinavian Conference on Information Systems (SCIS). We conducted interviews with ten SCIS authors. Following a framework adopted from Åkerlind [1], we identified how SCIS papers have the roles of fulfilling requirements, establishing oneself, developing personally, enabling change, and other roles. This article contributes to the reflection literature on the IS field by applying a practice lens to understand the role of conference papers in research.

Keywords: Reflective practice · Conference publishing · Scandinavian IS research

1 Introduction

In most scientific fields, journal articles are the preferred outlet for research, in contrast to any other types such as conference proceedings, books, or book chapters [2, 3]. Not just any journals, but a specified set of "elite" journals are emphasized in national publication rankings, in tenure and promotion, and in the policies of scholarly communities [4, 5]. In our field of Information Systems (IS), the Senior Scholars' Basket of Journals[1] has become the dominant standard [6].

Alvesson and Sandberg [7] claim that publishing solely in journals is typical for a "gap-spotting" mentality. This means that researchers seek consensus instead of challenging it, aim to maintain a narrow scope instead of spanning across knowledge boundaries, and contribute in small increments instead of aiming for the interesting and controversial. Further, they [7] argue that a healthy scholarly community requires different types of publication outlets. In fact, there is quite much evidence that strong

---

[1] https://aisnet.org/general/custom.asp?page=SeniorScholarBasket.

© Springer International Publishing Switzerland 2016
M. Gellerstedt et al. (Eds.): SCIS 2016, LNBIP 259, pp. 116–131, 2016.
DOI: 10.1007/978-3-319-43597-8_9

orientation in journals can weaken funding and research culture [8]. Thus, reflection on research practices in our IS field should not only attend to journal papers but also on papers in highly prevalent conferences.

There is no shortage of academic conferences in the IS field. If you have subscribed to the AIS World, or any similar mailing list, you are receiving daily "calls for papers" to conferences around to world. We have global conferences such as ICIS, continental conferences such as ECIS and AMCIS, and topic-related conference such as DESRIST, IFIP WG 8.6, and EGOV. Furthermore, we have regional conferences such as MCIS, ACIS, and SCIS, and national conferences such as Nokobit.

In the journal-centric publication culture of our field, this abundance of conferences may seem odd. For example, Recker [9, p. 119] recommended that "the best rule for any academic in Information Systems is that you need to publish in journals, not conferences". Recker sees one purpose for conferences: those offer a "stepping-stone in the research and publication process – not the end goal" (p. 119).

The valuation of different publication forums is not set in stone, but as any social practice it is under constant transformation. This is visible in the IS publication forums outline that Hardgrave and Walstrom provided in 1997 [10]. Other than MIS Quarterly is still considered as the best journal, and ICIS the best conference, the list looks rather different today. It is also worth acknowledging that the relationship between conference publishing and journal publishing varies between academic disciplines [11]. Harzing [12, p. 24] describes conference proceedings as

> "...a very common and respected outlet in some disciplines, such as Computer Science. However, in the Social Sciences they are seen as mere stepping stones to future publication in a peer-reviewed journal. The more prestigious conferences (such as the Academy of Management in the field of management) either do not publish proceedings or publish only short abstracted papers."

The role of conference publishing in our field should not be taken for granted, but instead be the focus of investigation and reflection. What we know about conference publishing – in our field and in general – comes from a large and varying set of sources. These include suggestions given in doctoral supervision, career advice in textbooks, scholarly conventions, expert opinion, and scholarly mythology. In fact, it is surprising how little research we have of the role of conferences in our research practice.

In this paper, we address this gap by conducting a case study of publications and authorship in the Scandinavian Conference on Information Systems (SCIS) during its first six years (2010–2015). We first extract the bibliometric data (author, countries, and universities) from the 61 articles published during these six years. Then we conducted 10 interviews with SCIS authors. In these interviews we attempted to understand practices regarding conference papers. The research question guiding this investigation was:

What are the roles of conference papers in IS research?

By answering this question, we provide the IS community with insights on the research practices in our field. While a majority of the papers that attempt to aid our collective reflection focus on research methods and topics, we focus on the practices of research dissemination in relation to conference papers. This is particular prudent given the high number of IS conference papers but limited discussion of their role in IS research practice.

2 Conference Papers in IS Research

Reflections on the nature of IS research is a recurring topic in our field [13–15]. However, the reflections based on literature reviews are commonly focused on the high ranked IS journals [6, 16–18]. In Table 1, we have identified 21 studies that provide an analysis of papers that are published as the proceedings for a particular IS conference. The table provides an overview of the studies that analyze each conference in relation to authors, citations, and content of the papers.

We identified 11 IS conferences that have been investigated by 21 studies. Interestingly, the leading global IS conference ICIS has only been studied in two papers, while examples of continental (ECIS) and regional (IRIS) conferences has been investigated five and four times. A popular focus of the studies is social network analysis, which has been conducted in six cases and covering all of the largest conferences. These studies also provide comparisons of the conferences' social networks. In addition to investigations of a particular IS conference, other research efforts have investigated multiple conferences, e.g. in a scientometric study of three major global, regional and national conferences [40, 41] and the frequency of research methods in five IS conferences [42].

The studies of IS conferences provide insights concerning where contributors come from and how they collaborate (Authors column in Table 1), what they most often reference (Citations column in Table 1), and the popular topics and methods of investigation (Content column in Table 1). However, these studies do not unfold why researchers target the conferences to publish their research. Furthermore, these studies focus on the data available in the conference proceedings without additional data collection from the authors. Drott [43] is one of very few investigations of the role of conference publishing as a scholarly practice. His study from 1995 challenged the evolutionary "stepping stone" view, and showed that in the field of information science only 13 % of conference papers are further improved towards journal articles. Instead, he offered a view of conference publications as self-improvement, as group contributions, and as final products. Conference publishing, as any social practice, is under constant transformation. Thus in order to understand the role of conference papers in contemporary IS research we investigate the proceedings of SCIS and collect additional data by interviewing authors.

3 Research Approach

In this section, we present the research approach to investigating IS conference papers with SCIS as the case. This research is an interpretive investigation into the role of conference papers in IS research practice, which are developed within a social context. Such an epistemological approach recognizes the socially constructed nature of the subjective phenomena pertaining to conference papers. Interpretive research is an accepted research paradigm in IS [44], and our study adheres to the interpretivist principles. [45].

We take a broad perspective of a case (as a group of people, organisation, process or information system) as outlined by Carroll and Swatman [46]. To understand the

Table 1. Studies of IS conferences

Conference	Studies	Authors	Citations	Content
ACIS - Australasian Conference on IS	1. Cheong and Corbitt [19] 2. Gable et al. [20]	1. Contributors, social network analysis 2. Acceptance rates, affiliation		2. Topics
AMCIS - Americas Conference on IS	1. Takeda et al. [21]	1. Social network analysis, single vs. multi authorship, Hirsch index		
ASAC IS - Administrative Sciences Association of Canada Conference, IS division	1. Serenko et al. [22]	1. Contributors, affiliation		1. Topics, methods
ECIS - European Conference on IS	1. Galliers and Whitley [23] 2. Galliers and Whitley [24] 3. Stein et al. [25] 4. Vidgren et al. [26] 5. Whitley and Galliers [27]	1. Country, affiliation, authors and institutions per paper, contributors 2. Country, affiliation, contributors 3. Country, affiliation 4. Social network analysis, contributers, panels network 5. Country	1. Most cited references, outlet ranking 2. Most cited references, popular social theory sources, country 3. Most cited references 5. Most cited references, outlet rankings, social theory texts	2. Topics 3. Methods, topics 5. Themes

(Continued)

Table 1. (*Continued*)

Conference	Studies	Authors	Citations	Content
ICIS - International Conference on IS	1. Chuan Chan et al. [28] 2. Xu and Chau [29]	1. Affiliation 2. Contributors, social network analysis, affiliation, keywords	1. Outlet rankings, most cited references	
IFIP WG 8.2 - IS and Organizations	1. Flynn and Gregory [30]	1. Gender, region		1. Empirical social theory: paradigm, data, methods, social focus, theory type, metacategory of IT
IFIP WG 8.6 - Transfer and Diffusion of IT	1. Dwivedi et al. [31] 2. Henriksen and Kautz [32]	1. Contributors, gender, occupation, affiliation, country	1. Most cited contributions, author citations	1. Keywords 2. Theoretical perspectives, process vs. factor orientation
IRIS – IS Research Seminar in Scandinavia	1. Molka-Danielsen et al. [33] 2. Nurminen [34] 3. Nurminen [35] 4. Trier and Molka-Danielsen [36]	1. Social network analysis, country, contributors 2, 3. Gender, affiliation, contributors 4. Social network analysis	2, 3. Most cited references	1. Keywords
MCIS - Mediterranean Conference on IS	1. Pouloudi et al. [37]	1. Country, industry sector, funding		1. Topics, paradigm, methods, unit of analysis
PACIS - Pacific Asia Conference on IS	1. Cheong and Corbitt [38]	1. Contributors, social network analysis		
PCIS - Portuguese IS Conference	1. Esteves and Ramos [39]	1. Gender, language	1. Most cited references	1. Keywords; topics, methods

SCIS case, we assess the first six years of the conference. We study which authors, universities, and countries have been represented in the conference (Sect. 4). We conducted 10 interviews to investigate how each SCIS paper relates to the greater picture in publication activities of each author (Sect. 5). The interviewed authors were selected to represent:

(1) the four Scandinavian countries and a country outside the region,
(2) different career stages: Ph.D. student (3), full professor (4), and 3 variations in between (lecturer, assistant professor, associate professor)
(3) single and multiple authors with both national and international collaboration,
(4) all the six conference years with at least two representatives.

We conducted laddering interviews [47] appropriate for studies of "personal constructs systems, its structures and hierarchical relationships" (p. 14). In seeking structure and pattern, we planned our interview guide according to the framework synthesized by Åkerlind [1]. In her framework (p. 25), she presented four categories and five dimensions (Table 2). Åkerlind [1] developed her framework by synthesizing a literature review and a phenomenographic study of research practice in Australia where the IS community is seen to have some commonalities with Scandinavia [48].

We used Åkerlind's framework (Table 2), to structure our analysis while also being open to alternative categories and interpretations. Thus, our analysis involved in Weick's [49] terms *disciplined imagination* aiming for a holistic understanding of the role of conference papers in the SCIS case. Our analysis was supported by *writing as a method of inquiry* [50] by approaching writing as a process to new insight and understanding, rather than just a final product.

Table 2. Key aspects of the range of variation in ways of experiencing being a researcher [1].

Dimensions	Categories			
	1. Fulfilling requirements	2. Establishing oneself	3. Developing personally	4. Enabling change
Researcher intentions	Fulfil academic role	Become well known	Solve a puzzle	Make a contribution
Research process	Identify and solve a problem	Discover something new	Investigate an interesting question	Address community issues
Anticipated outcomes	Concrete products	Academic standing	Personal understanding	Benefits to community
Object of study	Independent research questions, bounded by a field of study	Integrated research questions, related to a field of study	Integrated research questions, related to field and personal issues	Integrated research questions, related to field/ social issues
Underlying feelings	Anxiety to satisfaction	Frustration to joy	Interest and enthusiasm	Passionate engagement

4 The Scandinavian Conference on Information Systems

The Scandinavian Conference on Information Systems (SCIS) has been organized since 2010. The conference is held in conjunction with the Information Systems Research Conference in Scandinavia (IRIS) that has been organized annually since 1978. As such, IRIS is the oldest consecutive Information Systems conference in the world.

At the business meetings for IRIS 2009, the members formally decided to start another conference to be organized in conjunction with IRIS the next year and onwards. A major reason for the initiation of SCIS was to broaden the audience of IRIS. IRIS is a working seminar with participants discussing the papers in workgroups, maintaining an inclusive and constructive Scandinavian spirit. The primary audience of IRIS are doctoral students, who can get detailed feedback on their papers in an understanding and supportive environment.

The SCIS conference, was constructed as a more traditional conference with a rigorous peer review process that selects the best work upfront, rather than including the majority of submissions as in IRIS. SCIS has been envisioned as a high quality forum that publishes research with a particular view on the Scandinavian research community. The IRIS-SCIS combination was seen to attract mid-career researchers, who were also sought after as participants in the IRIS workgroups.

During the six first years of SCIS, a total of 61 articles have been published (See Table 3). These 61 total articles have been contributed by a total of 113 authors.

Table 3. The first 6 SCIS conferences

Year	Theme	Location	Editors	# papers
2010	Engaged Scandinavian IS research	Denmark	Kautz and Nielsen [51]	10
2011	ICT of Culture – Culture of ICT	Finland	Salmela and Sell [52]	10
2012	Designing the Interactive Society	Sweden	Keller et al. [53]	10
2013	Digital living	Norway	Aanestad and Bratteteig [54]	6
2014	Designing human technologies	Denmark	Commisso et al. [55]	9
2015	Designing for the user, with the user, and by the user	Finland	Oinas-Kukkonen et al. [56]	16

The SCIS author distribution is very even, with 102 authors being involved in just one article. Margunn Aanestad is the most actively published SCIS author with 3 articles. Ten researchers have authored two articles, who in alphabetical order are Pernille Bjørn, Tone Bratteteig, Bendik Bygstad, Judith Molka-Danielsen, Miria Grisot, Netta Iivari, Peter Axel Nielsen, Harri Oinas-Kukkonen, Polyxeni Vassilakopoulou, and Mika Yasuoka.

Finland and Denmark are so far the dominating SCIS-publishing countries. Finland takes the first place with 21 publications, followed by Denmark with 20. The difference between these two is very narrow, as Finland has provided an average of 3.5 papers each year, with a median of 2. In contrast, Denmark has produced an average of 3.33 papers each year, with a median of 3.5. Finland is strongly represented whenever IRIS/SCIS has been in Finland (5 papers in 2011, and 9 papers in 2015). In other years, Finland has been much less active, with the lowest in 2013 with just one paper. In contrast, Denmark has sustained a stable delivery of two to four papers every single year.

The third place goes to Norway with 16 papers. Their annual output average has been 2.66, with a median score of 2.5. That is, then, a higher median than Finland. Similar to Denmark, Norway sustain a flow of two to four papers each year.

These three countries – Finland, Denmark, and Norway – are by far in a class of their own. The true surprise is how under-represented Sweden is in SCIS. Sweden, as the most populous country in the Nordics, is largely absent in SCIS. Swedish authors have been involved in just three papers thus far. Sweden is even bypassed by USA and Japan, whose author involvement is present in four papers respectively. Of the five Nordic countries, Iceland has not participated in SCIS during this period.

In total, 11 different countries are represented in these publications. The Nordic countries are represented with slightly over 82 percent of all participants. There has been much variation in the "Nordicness" of SCIS, when taken a year-by-year analysis. In both 2011 and 2012, SCIS had full 100 % Nordic representativeness. In other years, there have been some articles from outside of the Nordics.

The two leading SCIS-publishing universities are University of Oslo and Aalborg University, both with eight publications. The third place goes to University of Oulu with seven papers, followed by University of Turku with five papers. Copenhagen Business School and Roskilde University share the fifth place with four papers each.

A total of 37 universities are represented during the six first years of SCIS. An interesting anomaly is the small number of Swedish institutions. Of the three Swedish SCIS-papers, two are from Luleå University of Technology, and one from Linköping.

5   The Roles of SCIS Papers in IS Research Practice

In this section, we present our analysis of the interviews with ten SCIS paper authors. We found different variations of each of the four categories proposed by Åkerlind [1] pertaining to the roles of a SCIS paper. In addition, we include the *other* category, which contains explanations that Åkerlind's framework did not capture. The different ways of understanding the roles of a SCIS paper are summarized in Table 4. The following five subsections describe each category using evidence from the interviews.

5.1   Fulfilling Requirements

The first category is *fulfilling requirements*. The view of research in this category, according to Åkerlind [1], is that it responds to "academic job expectations" (p. 24). In contrast to the next three categories, the requirements do not originate from the

Table 4. Ways of understanding the role of a SCIS paper

Fulfilling requirements	Establishing oneself	Developing personally	Enabling change	Other
(1) Fulfilling publication requirements as a doctoral student (2) Fulfilling funding requirements of a research project (3) Fulfilling require-ments of national publication rankings	(1) Establishing oneself in a network (2) Establishing oneself by face-time	(1) Ideational stimulation (2) Testing new research directions (3) Engaging with progressive research	(1) Scholarly boundary spanning (2) Identification within a tradition	(1) Creating synergies (2) Practical convenience (3) Achieving closure

researcher herself, but from external sources. When such requirements are met successfully, it may lead to "concrete outcomes, such as the solution of a problem or completion of a grant, doctorate, publication, etc." (p. 25). We identified three variations of this category: (1) fulfilling publication requirements as a doctoral student, (2) fulfilling funding requirements of a research project, and (3) fulfilling requirements of national publication rankings.

In relation to the first variation, all Ph.D. students we interviewed told that they include the SCIS publication in their doctoral thesis. For example, a Ph.D. student published a literature review in SCIS that was the first paper in her thesis trajectory. As such, it provides a launch for her thesis publications. Another doctoral student described how her SCIS paper fits in her doctoral work:

"This paper is part of my doctoral publication activities. It's one of those papers, in my future thesis. The thesis is not ready yet! (laughs)... I've developed this work further since this was published. This paper allowed me to reach one phase in the process. I've then progressed to other phases."

The second variant of requirements-fulfilling concerns research project funding. Two of our respondents mentioned this issue. A professor described his case:

"This article is a part of a three-year European Union FP7 funded research project. We had submitted this article to a journal earlier, but that version was not mature enough [to get published]. In EU-projects you need to get publications while the project is running. That's why we didn't try any journals after that rejection, but we submitted to SCIS instead."

The same professor discussed also how the national publication rankings are one requirement he had to meet. This issue was brought up by another professor as well.

"One of the reasons [for why we targeted SCIS] was that it provided me to go to IRIS. The SCIS publication provided me the funding to go. SCIS is on that level [in the national publication rankings] that we get monetary support from the Swedish government. The SCIS proceedings is published in the Springer series. Participation in IRIS only does not provide this advantage."

5.2 Establishing Oneself

The next category concerns *establishing oneself*. Åkerlind [1] states that the "primary focus in this category is on the personal discovery of something new in the academic's disciplinary area that leads to becoming known and recognised in their field" (p. 26). We identified two variations of this category: (1) establishing oneself in a network and (2) establishing oneself by face-time.

One author noted that SCIS was the first conference where she presented, and thus the first occasion when she did serious networking with other/senior researchers. Hence the variation *establishing oneself in a network*. In relation to the second variation, *establishing oneself by face-time*, a professor emphasized the opportunity for face-time:

> *"You get face-time in the plenum. That is very difficult to get at other conferences... Everybody hears it – everybody sees it. They go home with a sense of what we are working on. Whether you are keynote or present a paper doesn't make a big difference besides they [the keynotes] get more time... This is Allen Lee's concept of face-time that I didn't think about before [I presented]."*

None of the interviewed authors suggested that getting their work published in the SCIS proceedings would lead them to become known or recognized within the IS field. It was noted that SCIS was a less prestigious outlet compared to other conference proceedings. However, the newly introduced possibility of having the paper selected for fast tracking to the Scandinavian Journal of Information Systems was part of some authors' motivation for submitting to SCIS.

5.3 Developing Personally

Developing personally involves an "intrinsic focus to the experience of being a researcher" [1]. The role of publications is "seen primarily in terms of gaining feedback from peers to improve the academic's research and understanding of the issue". We identified three variations of this category: (1) ideational stimulation, (2) testing new research directions, (3) engaging with progressive research.

The view of *ideational stimulation* refers to an arena in which conversation about a novel topic can be held. For example, one Ph.D. student was very interested in hearing how the Scandinavian research community would react to this research. Another respondent discussed how her goal was to develop new understanding of a phenomenon:

> *"The idea was that co-creation was then a new concept. And the economy is moving towards an experience-based economy. [The purpose of the paper] was to show that it is possible to do such an analysis. ... [I think that SCIS] is an appropriate arena to stimulate ideas rather than to present work that is already finished."*

The second variant of developing personally is *testing new research directions* related to trying out new research topics as part of a personal research portfolio: *"I had never written anything about [this topic] before. It fit the conference theme that year, so I tried to tie it with that. This was sort-of-a new direction."*

The third variation is *engaging with progressive research*. One respondent said that the reason for him to submit to the first SCIS conference was that he "thought it was an interesting initiative and wanted to support it." A non-Scandinavian author argued that the paper provided a ticket of entry for engaging with a progressive group of researchers that are open to less traditional IS research. This helped him to develop as a researcher:

"The entire culture [of SCIS/IRIS] was very supportive and developmental. Although the setting that I gave this paper is very traditional – it is the meeting itself. Then of course you have to acknowledge there are fairly progressive and enlightening attitudes among this group that identifies as Scandinavian research in IS."

5.4   Enabling Change

The fourth category is about *enabling change*, [1] attending to "a more altruistic focus on benefits to a larger community" (p. 27). Examples of this stance may include "advancing a particular social cause in line with the researcher's personal ideology and values, for instance, encouraging conservation, combating racism, etc., or a more traditional focus on advancing the discipline" (Ibid). We identified two variations for how SCIS publishing was seen to enable change. These variations are: (1) scholarly boundary spanning and (2) identification within a tradition.

The *scholarly boundary spanning* is the first subcategory. When researchers are spanning scholarly boundaries they are promoting that a research topic that could fit in many disciplines should in fact be of interest within this particular research community. A Ph.D. student gave this argument about her research topic:

"When I was doing my literature review, I found out that IS researchers rarely study information security issues with children, even though information security is a central topic in IS research. I think we should include children. Why should researchers from other fields study children's information security? Why wouldn't this topic be relevant in our discipline?"

The second variation is *identification within a tradition*. This issue implies that conferences and research communities have their own history, and distinctive ways of doing and thinking. The majority of respondents referred to the "Scandinavian tradition" in one way or another. For example, a Ph.D. student said that their "research was conducted in a Finnish context, so it seemed fitting to present it in a Scandinavian conference." Another respondent said that their "topic was the reason [why they sent this to SCIS]: IS and the Scandinavian participatory design tradition." A professor mentioned that he prefers to go to SCIS/IRIS every year when possible, because he identifies with the community:

"I've participated in quite many IRIS conferences throughout the years. I try to participate whenever I have the possibility. ... For me, it's a way to serve the community. I think it is important."

In addition, another professor argued that the mainstream (American) research holds a different perspective from the Scandinavian view in his research area. Thus, he saw that SCIS was a good place to present an analysis from the Scandinavian perspective:

"Most of the [IT governance] literature is very much about top-down governance. I mean, it's adopted mostly from American frameworks. And in Scandinavia we are – not critical to top-down governance – but we would like to draw nuances in this picture. So we wanted to discuss how you can accomplish governance by a set of other means."

5.5   Other

In our interviews, plenty of answers did not fit in any of Åkerlind's [1] categories. We have organized these issues in this section, under three subcategories: (1) creating synergies, (2) practical convenience, and (3) achieving closure.

First, *creating synergies* refers to those activities that aim in bundling multiple goals and purposes into one. One of the clear synergies comes from the availability of two conferences at the same time: IRIS and SCIS. When asked about *publishing in SCIS*, the respondents discussed *participating in IRIS* instead. This shows how these two conferences – and publishing and participating in them – are intertwined. In addition, some respondents had planned going to the conference regardless if they had a paper there or not. That became then a motivating factor for paper submission, so that they could proverbially 'kill two birds with one stone.' For example, one professor described how one reason to participate was due to her editorial responsibilities: *"[2013] was the year when I became an editor of the Scandinavian Journal of Information Systems. Therefore I was going to [IRIS/SCIS] in any case."*

The next is *practical convenience*. Many respondents mentioned that it was convenient for them to go to the conference, that the location or the timing of conference suited their other activities. A Ph.D. student stated how *"SCIS was a natural choice, because it was organized here in Oulu."* Another Ph.D. student discussed how the conference deadline was conveniently synchronized with her research process:

> *"Schedule-wise it was convenient to submit this paper to SCIS. [The paper was based on] research that was finished at the end of 2013, and the SCIS deadline occurred in early 2014."*

Finally, there is *achieving closure*. In two cases, the respondents reported how their SCIS papers had been previously rejected elsewhere. The role of SCIS was then to provide the needed closure for their research effort, to get the work published. In a sense, this is the complete opposite to the popular "stepping stone" principle promoted in literature, that conference publishing is for presenting an initial version of an article that is later submitted to a journal. In contrast, reaching closure means that the paper finds its final home in the conference. An example of closure comes from a professor:

> *"I did not write this with SCIS in mind. The paper had a long history before that. I think I sent the first version [for a journal] already in 2009. ... The data was collected in 2008. ... When I got this paper finally accepted in SCIS [in 2013], I was satisfied, ... even though this ended up to be a shorter paper."*

6   Discussion

In this paper we have addressed the research question "What are the roles of conference papers in IS research?" We selected the first six years (2010–2015) of the *Scandinavian Conference on Information Systems* (SCIS) as the case of investigation. This conference has not been studied before.

Traditionally, Information Systems researchers study people, artifacts, and practices in groups and organizations. However, scholars such as Lee [15] have argued that we should also reflect on our own practices, that we should "undergo the same manner of diagnosis to which we subject others, and that we have a taste of our own medicine" (p. 21). In this paper we have done just that. Our analysis adds to the literature on reflections of IS research practice [13, 14, 57].

Information systems conferences are not a very much studied topic of research. We have provided central categories of previous research (Table 1). These previous studies of conferences analyze scientometrics and social networks. In turn, we have attempted to provide an engaged and reflective analysis that is grounded on interviews with conference authors themselves. In such way, this paper provides an alternative and a more nuanced view of the roles of IS conference papers. Additionally, we provided a bibliometric analysis of the first six years of SCIS in Sect. 4.

Through the analysis of the ten interviews we conducted, we provided an analysis of the roles of conference papers in IS research. These are provided in Sect. 5, and summarized in Table 4. The higher-level categories were adopted from Åkerlind [1]: fulfilling requirements, establishing oneself, developing personally, and enabling change. Under each of these main categories we identified two to three subcategories. We also identified issues that we could not fit under Åkerlind's categories, so we provided those in the 'Other' category. Underneath this, we provided three variations of 'other'.

We have explicitly targeted the role of conference *publishing*. Implicitly, this has separated the interest from conference *participation*. During the research process, it became clear that this dichotomy is not that clear in practice. Especially for senior scholars, the discourse of participation and publishing was highly entwined. This relates to what Desanctis [58] refers to as scholarly routines of interaction. These can be found "in repeat visits to conferences, ongoing conversations among members, and development of joint, repeated research projects among members with otherwise variant organizational ties" (p. 365). Indeed, within the Scandinavian IRIS tradition since the very beginning, many participants have developed a habit of visiting the conference every year, with or without a paper to discuss [34].

Concerning the limitations of our study, we have studied just one conference. Therefore our analysis may have limitations regarding its generalizability. SCIS is a regional conference primarily for the Scandinavian IS community. It is much smaller and less prestigious conference than, for example, ICIS and ECIS. However, many of the identified roles may still be valid in these large and international conferences. We also underline that generalizability has not been a priority in our investigation. We put emphasis on contextual sensitivity, paying attention to the particular rather than the general.

Finally, this very article that you are reading, is a manifest for how the IRIS/SCIS has served as a platform for socializing and idea generating. We two authors first met during the first SCIS conference (IRIS33) in 2010. We met for the second time in SCIS 2015 (IRIS38). The initiation for this paper occurred during the latter meeting. To put this in more general terms, conferences such as SCIS are venues that facilitate what Dutton and Dukerich [59] call *relational practice*: "the skilled ways of interrelating that create connections between people" (p. 21). They see that in such relational foundation "the quality of the connections that researchers form with each other … is key to developing and sustaining interesting research" (p. 21). We wish that the outcome of our effort has resulted in what readers will found as an instance of interesting research!

References

1. Åkerlind, G.S.: An academic perspective on research and being a researcher: an integration of the literature. Stud. High. Educ. **33**, 17–31 (2008)
2. Ioannidis, J.P.A.: Concentration of the most-cited papers in the scientific literature: analysis of journal ecosystems. PLoS ONE **1**, e5 (2006)
3. Adler, N.J., Harzing, A.-W.: When knowledge wins: transcending the sense and nonsense of academic rankings. Acad. Manag. Learn. Educ. **8**, 72–95 (2009)
4. Luke, R.H., Doke, E.R.: Marketing journal hierarchies: faculty perceptions, 1986–1987. J. Acad. Mark. Sci. **15**, 74–78 (1987)
5. Tourish, D., Willmott, H.: In defiance of folly: journal rankings, mindless measures and the ABS guide. Crit. Perspect. Acc. **26**, 37–46 (2015)
6. Bernroider, E.W.N., Pilkington, A., Cordoba, J.-R.: Research in information systems: a study of diversity and inter-disciplinary discourse in the AIS basket journals between 1995 and 2011. J. Inf. Technol. **28**, 74–89 (2013)
7. Alvesson, M., Sandberg, J.: Has management studies lost its way? Ideas for more imaginative and innovative research. J. Manag. Stud. **50**, 128–152 (2013)
8. Willmott, H.: Journal list fetishism and the perversion of scholarship: reactivity and the ABS list. Organization **18**, 429–442 (2011)
9. Recker, J.: Scientific Research in Information Systems: A Beginner's Guide. Springer, Berlin (2013)
10. Hardgrave, B.C., Walstrom, K.A.: Forums for MIS scholars. Commun. ACM **40**, 119–124 (1997)
11. Becher, T.: The significance of disciplinary differences. Stud. High. Educ. **19**, 151–161 (1994)
12. Harzing, A.-W.: Document categories in the ISI web of knowledge: misunderstanding the social sciences? Scientometrics **94**, 23–34 (2012)
13. Constantinides, P., Chiasson, M.W., Introna, L.D.: The ends of information systems research: a pragmatic framework. MIS Q. **36**, 1–19 (2012)
14. Klein, H.K., Hirschheim, R.: The structure of the IS discipline reconsidered: implications and reflections from a community of practice perspective. Inf. Organ. **18**, 280–302 (2008)
15. Lee, A.S.: Doctor of philosophy, heal thyself. In: Kaplan, B., Truex III, D.P., Wastell, D., Wood-Harper, A.T., DeGross, J.I. (eds.) Information Systems Research. IFIP International Federation for Information Processing, vol. 143, pp. 21–34. Springer, Heidelberg (2004)
16. Córdoba, J.-R., Pilkington, A., Bernroider, E.W.N.: Information systems as a discipline in the making: comparing EJIS and MISQ between 1995 and 2008. Eur. J. Inf. Syst. **21**, 479–495 (2012)
17. Dwivedi, Y.K., Kuljis, J.: Profile of IS research published in the European journal of information systems. Eur. J. Inf. Syst. **17**, 678–693 (2008)
18. Sidorova, A., Evangelopoulos, N., Valacich, J.S., Ramakrishnan, T.: Uncovering the intellectual core of the information systems discipline. MIS Q. **32**, 467–482 (2008)
19. Cheong, F., Corbitt, B.: A social network analysis of the co-authorship network of the Australasian Conference of Information Systems from 1990 to 2006. In: ECIS 2009 Proceedings (2009)
20. Gable, G., Smyth, R.W., Stark, K.: An archival analysis of ACIS research papers. In: 19th Australasian Conference on Information Systems, Christchurch, New Zealand (2008)
21. Takeda, H., Truex, D.P., Cuellar, M.: Evaluating scholarly influence through social network analysis: the next step in evaluating scholarly influence. In: AMCIS 2010 Proceedings (2010)

22. Serenko, A., Cocosila, M., Turel, O.: The state and evolution of IS research presented at ASAC: meta-analysis of the conference proceedings. In: ASAC, pp. 1–18, Halifax, Nova Scotia (2008)

23. Galliers, R.D., Whitley, E.A.: An anatomy of European information systems research, ECIS 1993 - ECIS 2002: some initial findings. In: 10th European Conference on Information Systems, Gdansk, Poland (2002)

24. Galliers, R.D., Whitley, E.A.: Vive les differences? Developing a profile of European information systems research as a basis for international comparisons. Eur. J. Inf. Syst. **16**, 20–35 (2007)

25. Stein, M.-K., Galliers, R.D., Whitley, E.A.: Twenty years of the European information systems academy at ECIS: emergent trends and research topics. Eur. J. Inf. Syst. **25**, 1–15 (2016)

26. Vidgen, R., Henneberg, S., Naude, P.: What sort of community is the European conference on information systems? A social network analysis 1993–2005. Eur. J. Inf. Syst. **16**, 5–19 (2007)

27. Whitley, E.A., Galliers, R.D.: An alternative perspective on citation classics: evidence from the first 10 years of the European conference on information systems. Inf. Manag. **44**, 441–455 (2007)

28. Chuan Chan, H., Kim, H.-W., Tan, W.C.: Information systems citation patterns from international conference on information systems articles. J. Am. Soc. Inf. Sci. Technol. **57**, 1263–1274 (2006)

29. Xu, J., Chau, M.: The social identity of IS: analyzing the collaboration network of the ICIS conferences (1980–2005). In: 27th International Conference on Information Systems, pp. 569–590, Milwaukee (2006)

30. Flynn, D., Gregory, P.: The use of social theories in 20 years of WG 8.2 empirical research. In: Kaplan, B., Truex, D.P., Wastell, D., Wood-Harper, A.T., DeGross, J.I. (eds.) Information Systems Research: Relevant Theory and Informed Practice, pp. 365–388. Springer, Boston (2004)

31. Dwivedi, Y.K., Levine, L., Williams, M.D., Singh, M., Wastell, D.G., Bunker, D.: Toward an understanding of the evolution of IFIP WG 8.6 research. In: Pries-Heje, J., Venable, J., Bunker, D., Russo, N.L., DeGross, J.I. (eds.) IFIP WG. IFIP AICT, vol. 318, pp. 225–242. Springer, Heidelberg (2010)

32. Henriksen, H.Z., Kautz, K.: Analysis of IFIP TC 8 WG 8.6. In: Avison, D., Elliot, S., Krogstie, J., Pries-Heje, J. (eds.) The Past and Future of Information Systems: 1976–2006 and Beyond. IFIP, vol. 214, pp. 143–152. Springer, Heidelberg (2006)

33. Molka-Danielsen, J., Trier, M., Shlyk, V., Bobrik, A., Nurminen, M.I.: IRIS (1978–2006) historical reflection through visual analysis. In: 30th Information Systems Research Seminar in Scandinavia (IRIS) (2007)

34. Nurminen, M.I.: Nurminen's column on IRIS: Part 1. Scand. J. Inf. Syst. **9**, 47–52 (1997)

35. Nurminen, M.I.: Nurminen's column on IRIS: Part 2. Scand. J. Inf. Syst. **11**, 5–12 (1999)

36. Trier, M., Molka-Danielsen, J.: Sympathy or strategy: social capital drivers for collaborative contributions to the IS community. Eur. J. Inf. Syst. **22**, 317–335 (2013)

37. Pouloudi, N., Poulymenakou, A., Pramatari, K.: A profile of information systems research in the mediterranean region. Eur. J. Inf. Syst. **21**, 345–357 (2012)

38. Cheong, F., Corbitt, B.: A social network analysis of the co-authorship network of the Pacific Asia conference on information systems from 1993 to 2008. In: PACIS 2009 (2009)

39. Esteves, J., Ramos, I.: A meta-analysis of information systems research diversity in Portugal. In: AMCIS 2003 (2003)

40. Cocosila, M., Serenko, A., Turel, O.: A scientometric study of information systems conferences: exploring ICIS, PACIS and ASAC. In: AMCIS 2009 Proceedings, San Francisco (2009)
41. Cocosila, M., Serenko, A., Turel, O.: Exploring the management information systems discipline: a scientometric study of ICIS, PACIS and ASAC. Scientometrics **87**, 1–16 (2011)
42. Ebeling, B., Hoyer, S., Bühring, J.: What are your favorite methods? An examination on the frequency of research methods for IS conferences from 2006 to 2010. In: ECIS 2012 Proceedings (2012)
43. Drott, M.C.: Reexamining the role of conference papers in scholarly communication. J. Am. Soc. Inf. Sci. **46**, 299–305 (1995)
44. Walsham, G.: The emergence of interpretivism in IS research. Inf. Syst. Res. **6**, 376–394 (1995)
45. Klein, H.K., Myers, M.D.: A set of principles for conducting and evaluating interpretive field studies in information systems. MIS Q. **23**, 67–93 (1999)
46. Carroll, J.M., Swatman, P.A.: Structured-case: a methodological framework for building theory in information systems research. Eur. J. Inf. Syst. **9**, 235–242 (2000)
47. Schultze, U., Avital, M.: Designing interviews to generate rich data for information systems research. Inf. Organ. **21**, 1–16 (2011)
48. Gregor, S., Bunker, D., Cecez-Kecmanovic, D., Metcalfe, M., Underwood, J.: Australian eclecticism and theorizing in information systems research. Scand. J. Inf. Syst. **19**, 11–38 (2007)
49. Weick, K.E.: Puzzles in organizational learning: an exercise in disciplined imagination. Brit. J. Manag. **13**, S7–S15 (2002)
50. Richardson, L., Adams St. Pierre, E.: Writing: a method of inquiry. In: Denzin, N.K., Lincoln, Y.S. (eds.) Handbook of Qualitative Research, pp. 959–978. SAGE Publications, Thousand Oaks (2005)
51. Kautz, K., Nielsen, P.A. (eds.): Scandinavian Information Systems Research, vol. 60. Springer, Berlin (2010)
52. Salmela, H., Sell, A. (eds.): Nordic Contributions in IS Research: Second Scandinavian Conference on Information Systems, SCIS 2011, Turku, Finland, 16–19 August 2011, vol. 86 (2011)
53. Keller, C., Wiberg, M., Ågerfalk, P.J., Eriksson Lundström, J.S.Z. (eds.): Nordic Contributions in IS Research, vol. 124. Springer, Berlin (2012)
54. Aanestad, M., Bratteteig, T. (eds.): Nordic Contributions in IS Research, vol. 156. Springer, Berlin (2013)
55. Commisso, T.H., Nørbjerg, J., Pries-Heje, J. (eds.): Nordic Contributions in IS Research, vol. 186. Springer International Publishing, Berlin (2014)
56. Oinas-Kukkonen, H., Iivari, N., Kuutti, K., Öörni, A., Rajanen, M. (eds.): Nordic Contributions in IS Research. Springer International Publishing, Berlin (2015)
57. Lanamäki, A.: A consideration for researcher career retrospectives in information systems and organization studies. In: Oinas-Kukkonen, H., Iivari, N., Kuutti, K., Öörni, A., Rajanen, M. (eds.) SCIS 2015. LNBIP, vol. 223, pp. 77–91. Springer, Heidelberg (2015)
58. Desanctis, G.: The social life of information systems research: a response to Benbasat and Zmud's call for returning to the IT artifact. J. Assoc. Inf. Syst. **4**, 360–376 (2003)
59. Dutton, J.E., Dukerich, J.M.: The Relational foundation of research: an underappreciated dimension of interesting research. Acad. Manag. J. **49**, 21–26 (2006)

IFIP 8.6 2016

Who is in Control in Crowdsourcing Initiatives? An Examination of the Case of Crowdmapping

Abdul Rehman Shahid[(⊠)] and Amany Elbanna

Royal Holloway, University of London, Egham, Surrey, TW20 0EX, UK
abdul.shahid.2012@live.rhul.ac.uk,
amany.elbanna@rhul.ac.uk

Abstract. The crowdsourcing literature is dominated by the view that the crowd can be controlled and that owners should adopt different technologies to control it and its output. This paper questions the agency and role of the crowd. Specifically, it questions how and to what extent can control over the crowd be exercised. To this end, the paper adopts an interpretive approach to the enquiry. It examines a case of crowdsourcing in the understudied area of humanitarian response. Concepts from structuration theory are adopted to interpret the data. The analysis reveals the paradox of crowd interaction and owner control in crowdsourcing. It shows the crowd to be made up of knowledgeable and reflexive groups that effectively tackle methods aimed at controlling them. The implications of the study are then discussed.

Keywords: Crowdsourcing · Crowdmapping · Structuration theory · Social theory · OpenStreetMap (OSM)

1 Introduction

Crowdsourcing is *"a type of participative online activity in which an individual, an institution, a non-profit organization, or company proposes to a group of individuals of varying knowledge, heterogeneity, and number, via a flexible open call, the voluntary undertaking of a task"* [1]. It is an emerging phenomenon, the wide applications of which are witnessed in practice and *"is yet to receive intense attention from the scholars"* [2]. In practice, crowdsourcing initiatives have shown exponential growth, with one popular platform (www.crowdsourcing.org), reporting a 100 % increase in the number of entities offering crowdsourcing services over a time frame of just two years [3]. It is surrounded by stories of crowd success in participating in and solving problems in many walks of life, varying from solving long-standing scientific problems (in a remarkably short time), to participating in the design of apparels and in urban planning [4, 5]. This is in addition to the crowd getting involved in innovation, generating commercial ideas, and swiftly providing disaster response [6–9]. Scholars find crowdsourcing to be a 'fascinating phenomenon', and have urged researchers to examine it both empirically and theoretically [10–12].

© IFIP International Federation for Information Processing 2016.
Published by Springer International Publishing Switzerland 2016. All Rights Reserved.
U.L. Snis et al. (Eds.): IFIP8.6 2016, LNBIP 259, pp. 135–148, 2016.
DOI: 10.1007/978-3-319-43597-8_10

Crowdsourcing initiatives typically begin with an organisation or group issuing an open call for unidentified individuals to participate in a particular task with a desired outcome. To differentiate them from the crowdsourcing participants—or, more simply put, 'the crowd'—we call these initiators the crowdsourcing owners. The crowdsourcing literature tends to side with the owners and largely adopts a managerial perspective to examine and prescribe how to manage the crowd, control the quality of its output, and keep it motivated [13–16]. Although a strand of literature exists that examines the crowd side of crowdsourcing, it centres on investigating the crowd's motivations. This is mainly done in order to harness the crowd for the benefit of the crowdsourcing owners and, hence, actually belongs to the managerial perspective of crowdsourcing. This research portrays the crowd as a potentially controllable multitude of individuals that owners only need to manage in order to harness its creativity and innovation [17]. This view of the crowd contradicts the few descriptive studies that show the crowd as being made up of individuals who are capable of taking surprising initiatives to respond and find solutions to problems [8, 18, 19]. It is not clear how the crowd could take action while the owners are exerting managerial control over it to achieve planned results, as described in the literature. This study aims at exploring this issue and specifically answer the following questions:

- Who is in control in crowdsourcing initiatives?
- How and to what extent can control over the crowd be exercised?

To do so, it examines a case study of crowdmapping during a natural disaster. As a theoretical lens, it adopts concepts from structuration theory, which takes a balanced relational view of control and hence provides an open lens for the enquiry. In this regard, structuration theory 'offers a valuable approach to theory development' [20].

In the following section, we review the crowdsourcing literature. Section three presents the concepts from structuration theory adopted by this study. Section four presents the research methods, including the description of the case study. Section five presents the analysis of the study. Sections six and seven respectively provide the discussion and the conclusion and implications of the study.

2 Literature Review

Crowdsourcing literature is dominated by research on controlling the crowd; it tends to adopt a descriptive and prescriptive managerial approach, and can be classified into two streams. The first highlights the importance of quality control and describes ways to effectively manage it. The second stream designs, tests or describes specific methods to control the quality of the crowd's output.

Among this existing research, Kittur et al. [15] developed the 'CrowdForge' framework. The authors highlighted the increasing role played by micro-tasking, in which organisations utilise a large number of workers for different purposes. Importantly, their study articulated the importance of quality control to avoid a bad contribution adversely impacting the task as a whole, when a complex task is broken down into a number of individual contributions. The authors proposed quality control methods which utilise human intelligence—namely, the map-reduce approach. Yung et al. [16]

built on the work of Kittur et al. [15] by proposing a crowdsourcing system architecture that enables a new quality control approach that utilises evolutionary computing and slow intelligence. Hansen et al. [14] explored the FamilySearch crowdsourcing initiative, in which contributors transcribe/index ancestral records, building up a comprehensive collection of genealogical records. The authors explored the effectiveness (accuracy) and efficiency (time) of two quality control mechanisms put in place by the crowdsourcing system—namely, arbitration and peer review. Hansen et al. [14] found that peer review is significantly more efficient than arbitration in terms of time, but is not as effective in terms of accuracy in certain fields. Interestingly, the authors found that arbitration of peer-reviewed contributions does not necessarily increase quality.

Hiltunen [21] highlighted training as an important component of an effective crowdsourcing system. The author explored the case of Finpro, an organisation that utilises crowdsourcing for its foresight activities, and argued that no foresight thinking can take place unless continuous and adequate training is provided to contributors. She asserted that *"there can be no successful results in crowdsourcing without training"* [21]. In their study, Le et al. [22] made an attempt at understanding how training crowdsourcing contributors could impact the quality of crowdsourced data and argued that those crowdsourcing systems that train contributors on relevance categorisation tasks achieve improvements in their overall data quality.

Other scholars explicitly connected effective training with quality control and went into more detail in regard to training methods. For example, Poesio et al. [23] argued for the importance of training and evaluation of contributors in ensuring quality data for Phrase Detectives, an online crowdsourcing game that utilises the crowd to create anaphorically annotated resources.

3 Theoretical Foundation

This study adopts concepts from Anthony Giddens's structuration theory [24] as the theoretical lens through which to trace and understand crowdmapping. Structuration theory is particularly suited because of its balanced view of structure and action (structuration theory refers to action as 'agency'). The sections that follow briefly present the concepts of agency, dialectic of control, knowledgeability, and reflexivity.

3.1 Agency and Control

Giddens argued that social agents possess and maintain the ability to 'make a difference' in the production of social outcomes, regardless of whether those outcomes are intended or unintended [24]. He also viewed social agents as being autonomous and having the ability to challenge structural control and domination. He emphasised that *"the seed of change is there in every act which contributes towards the reproduction of any 'ordered' form of social life"* [25]. Therefore, agency is associated with transformative capacity [26].

Structuration theory views human agency as being strongly voluntaristic, with social agents always possessing the ability to act otherwise; Giddens termed this the dialectic of control, where *"all forms of dependence offer some resources whereby those who are subordinate can influence the activities of their superiors"* [24]. Giddens argued that every social agent within a social system is involved in the dialectic of control, even if only nominally. For Giddens, if social agents do not participate in the dialectic of control, they cease to be agents. Only in the extreme case in which social agents were to be completely controlled and confined, would they not participate in the dialectic of control and therefore cease to be agents [24].

In essence, although certain power relations may be completely imbalanced, Giddens argued that social agents always have some degree of control or ability over conditions of reproduction even in the most imbalanced of relations, and that there is therefore always a dialectic of control that can potentially alter or shift the overall distribution of power, thus implying that power is never absolute [24, 27].

3.2 Knowledgeability and Reflexivity

Structuration theory emphasises that the production and reproduction of society has to be treated as a skilled performance by social agents. This implies that social agents are knowledgeable and aware of the social world around them. Social agents are not only active participants but also key composers of the social world. This is in contrast to the structuralist school of thought, which conceptualises social agents as being the product of the system in which they find themselves in. In other words, according to Giddens, social agents are not 'cultural dopes' (a term developed by Garfinkel), because the workings of society are known by knowledgeable social agents by virtue of their being part of the social world [24, 28, 29].

Giddens highlighted the reflexivity of social agents. This concept goes beyond the understanding of social agents as only being self-conscious, to their being able to actively monitor ongoing social life. This reflexive monitoring of action takes place when social agents attend to the ongoing flow of everyday social life. To clarify reflexivity and its relation to social practices, Giddens stated that *"it is the specifically reflexive form of the knowledgeability of human agents that is most deeply involved in the recursive ordering of social practices. Continuity of practices presumes reflexivity, but reflexivity in turn is possible only because of the continuity of practices that makes them distinctively 'the same' across space and time"* [24]. The reflexive monitoring of conduct mainly occurs in a continuous manner rather than in selective moments [24].

4 Research Methods

This study adopts an interpretive approach, which enables the in-depth exploration of social and cultural phenomena [30]. Interpretive research attempts to understand phenomena through the eyes of the participants. This study adopts a case study approach in order to develop rich insights [31, 32]. The adopted case study is that of the development of crowdmapping in the context of humanitarian response, and will be detailed in the next section. The data collection is comprised of voice and video interviews, and of a document, newspaper, and media review. Moreover, online data were collected from a mailing list/forum and through Skype instant messaging. Forty-three voice and video interviews were conducted in addition to email communication with nine other participants. Documents and online resources—including agency reports, news items, television interviews, and video recordings—were reviewed. The 43 voice interviews were conducted with various actors, including the Humanitarian OpenStreetMap (HOT) community and various humanitarian organisations, including the American Red Cross, United Nations Office for the Coordination of Humanitarian Affairs (UN OCHA), MapAction, specialists from the Philippines Government—the National Economic and Development Authority (NEDA)—and various crowdmapping contributors. Further interviews were conducted with relevant actors from DigitalGlobe and Mapbox. The voice interviews were conducted between August 02, 2014, and July 20, 2015, and ranged in duration between 16 m 40 s and 96 m 36 s, with an average of 47 m 31 s; they were recorded and transcribed verbatim. The interviews were semi-structured, as this provided greater flexibility. Guidelines were followed to ensure thick description whilst increasing the credibility and richness of the gathered data [31, 33, 34]. In terms of data analysis, this study followed the methodological guidance of Pozzebon and Pinsonneault [35] —namely, grounded, narrative, and temporal bracketing analysis—which the authors had presented having drawn and built upon Langley's [36] nine strategies for analysing process data. According to Pozzebon and Pinsonneault [35], data-grounded analysis provides a basis for inductive theorising that benefits from the structurational lens. Narrative analysis is where the empirical data are structured in a systematic manner in terms of detailing a chronology of all phases, and temporal bracketing analysis is the breaking down of events into the effects of action [35].

4.1   Case Description

The case study looks at crowdmapping during the powerful tropical cyclone, Typhoon Haiyan, which struck the Philippines between the 6th and 9th of November 2013. Haiyan resulted in 6,201 fatalities, 28,626 injuries and 1,785 missing persons in 591 municipalities and 57 cities [37]. The humanitarian organisation detailed in the case description and analysis will be kept anonymous and will therefore be simply named Humanitarian Organisation One. It is a large international humanitarian organisation that provides education, emergency assistance, and disaster relief.

OSM was a prominent crowdmapping platform that was engaged with in the response to Typhoon Haiyan through its humanitarian team—namely Humanitarian OpenStreetMap Team (HOT). The OSM Haiyan crowdmapping system was activated by HOT on the 7th of November 2013, around 24 h before Haiyan made landfall in the Philippines. The system was activated to initially focus on mapping Tacloban City, which an early analysis had predicted would sustain the greatest damage. An email was then sent out to the HOT mailing list, calling the OSM crowdmappers to participate in the mapping of Tacloban City. By the end of the activation, the mapping efforts went

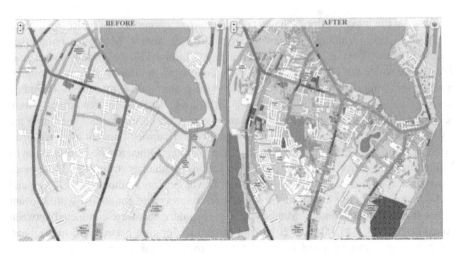

Fig. 1. OSM before and after the crowdsourcing initiative [39].

beyond Tacloban City, to cover the majority of the affected areas. Figure 1 shows the 'before and after' maps of Tacloban City to demonstrate the work done by the OSM crowdmappers in developing a richly detailed crowdmap. By the end of the OSM Haiyan effort, around 1,679 crowdmappers from 82 countries had been involved, and 4.7 million changes had been made to the relevant maps.

HOT played an intermediary role between the OSM crowdmappers and Humanitarian Organisation One. Humanitarian Organisation One was working on the ground in the Philippines and was continually advising HOT of what areas needed to be mapped. The activated crowdmapping system detailed a map of Tacloban City and other affected regions, broken down into small areas. The tasks were coordinated by HOT based upon the mapping requirements passed on by Humanitarian Organisation One; HOT would then list these online to be actioned by the OSM contributor community. The tasking manager allowed HOT to define the areas that needed to be mapped by the crowdmappers. The crowdmappers would select a task or randomly be given one and then pick the desired tool to edit using either of three available electronic editors—namely: JOSM, iD or Potlatch—and using satellite imagery that was provided by HOT. The tasking manager also allowed more experienced crowdmappers to undertake validation tasks in which they would validate or invalidate the contributions made by others. The three editors suited the different mapping abilities of the crowdmappers; whereas iD and Potlatch are browser based editors more suitable for beginners, JOSM is a desktop application that requires the contributor to download and configure various plugins. For the most part, Bing imagery was used to develop pre-disaster maps, whilst satellite imagery provided by DigitalGlobe was used to develop post-disaster maps [38]. Instructions on how to successfully complete the task were included in the tasking manager. Examples of tasks from Haiyan included tracing isolated buildings and road networks, with the mapping of entire cities helping to build up detailed basemaps.

5 Analysis

This section provides an interpretation of the findings obtained through the theoretical lens of structuration theory, and in particular the concepts of dialectic of control, knowledgeability, and reflexivity. It argues that, although the social structures of crowdsourcing owners dominated resources and exerted their control over the crowd through the tasking manager technology, this domination and control was contested. Shortly after the start of the Haiyan crowdmapping response, crowdmappers emerged as knowledgeable and reflexive agents, seeking the improvement of their participation. They contested the domination over resources and actively explored options to control them. The following sections present the detail of how the crowd, as a knowledgeable and reflexive agent, exerted power and negotiated control over resources.

5.1 Crowd Owners

During an activation, the HOT hierarchy carries out various tasks—e.g., imagery requests—while the platform activators drive the activation and accomplishment of the required crowdmapping tasks. The HOT community consists of these senior members, and of OSM crowdmappers.

As a beneficiary of HOT crowdmaps, Humanitarian Organisation One was involved in the redevelopment of the HOT tasking manager and also in the organisation of mapping events to train OSM crowdmappers. Therefore, the HOT hierarchy includes both platform owners and Humanitarian Organisation One's owners of outcomes; both will be referred to as 'owners' in the following section of the analysis.

5.2 Protesting Domination and Control

Satellite imagery is a crucial component in the undertaking of crowdmapping by OSM crowdmappers. Humanitarian Organisation One typically liaises with imagery providers—namely; DigitalGlobe—to obtain imagery and then make it available to the HOT platform. The latter, in turn, provides the imagery to the crowdmappers. Many initiatives have been developed to streamline the procurement process and obtain increasingly effective and swift access to imagery; this includes Imagery to the Crowd, where imagery would be purchased by the United States Department of State under specific licences that would allow its use for humanitarian purposes. However, DigitalGlobe remained the foremost organisation providing 'allocative resources'—namely, satellite imagery—to the OSM crowdmappers. During the Haiyan activation, OSM crowdmappers experienced delays of around seven to ten days in obtaining satellite imagery. As DigitalGlobe and Humanitarian Organisation One possessed the resources crucially needed by other actors, both controlled the imagery procurement process and held 'relational power' over the OSM crowdmappers. The latter were perceived to have little influence on any aspect of control of the activation, including the release of imagery, and to play a role of exclusively participating in mapping whatever tasks the owners provided.

```
Dear All,

You know how useful the geodata produced by OpenStreetMap contributors
is to help the relief effort in the Philippines after typhoon Haiyan.

This effort could be even more efficient if more imagery sources had
been made available more quickly, and for a longer period of time,
especially considering the magnitude of this crisis, and the time that
will be needed to recover.

So a petition has been setup, to give a way for the public to show its
support to this request.

https://secure.avaaz.org/en/petition/All satellite imagery providers Philippines open the satellite images/share/

Please sign it, and let the people around you know that they could do
something useful for the Philippines, and for the victims of future
major disasters, with a contribution as easy as a signature.

Best wishes,
```

Fig. 2. The call for petition in the OSM forum (OpenStreetMap, 2013a)

The delays with which DigitalGlobe released its imagery to OSM crowdmappers, coupled with an unclear release timetable, caused concern amongst the latter. In response, an online petition was initiated by a OSM crowdmapper who *"was frustrated with the pace at which imagery was being released, because it ended up taking a bit of time"* (OSM crowdmapper). The online petition specifically advocated the 'quicker release of imagery' for a 'longer period of time'. The announcement of the petition, which was made in the OSM forum, is shown in Fig. 2 below:

Once the petition had been launched, differences of opinion in regard to the form by which the protest had been made emerged. Senior members, both at HOT and Humanitarian Organisation One, found the petition to be less than courteous to the people working at the institutions involved in imagery procurement. A senior member of HOT remarked;

> *"It wasn't so much that it bothered them personally, but what happens is that you have institutions that donate imagery, and then this petition gets circulated calling for more imagery and it looks like the institution has screwed up or that the institution is attracting bad press and so, for the people that already kind of put their jobs on the line to help us out, it was kind of a slap on the face".*

However, others found the petition to have had a positive impact, despite its inevitable unintended negative consequences;

> *"It caused some issues, it kind of ruffled some feathers behind the scenes, because there are a lot people who have stuck their necks out to get us imagery and to help us and those people kind of took it the wrong way and they did not like this ... There was just a lot of bad blood between us and some of the groups, and it wasn't meant to be that way, but it just was the nature of these things; sometimes they don't go the way you want them to"* (HOT senior member).

Many crowdmappers thought that it helped push the agencies and imagery providers into re-thinking their approach and also push the community into reconsidering how they obtained their resources. This view was expressed by a crowdmapper;

> *"I think it somehow ruffled a lot of people and concerned some imagery providers, because some of the opinions were asking them to provide us with this kind of imagery".*

On the other hand, the HOT hierarchy found the community to be unrealistic in its expectations of and requests to the providers. One of the senior members commented;

"I think this petition—sort of—was a slap; like, there is no way in hell that the imagery providers are just going to put all their data online, open access for free. It costs two billion dollars to launch a satellite and that money doesn't recoup itself; like, it's not happening, the economics don't work. So, like, being kind of unrealistic like that just made the OSM community look dumb, instead of sort of being, like, good partners".

This view was also shared by Humanitarian Organisation One. A Geospatial Architect and Developer at Humanitarian Organisation One who was involved in the discussions argued that satellite imagery is not;

"A human right and that, as imagery providers are aware of their social responsibilities, the commercial model within which they operate should be respected".

He further remarked that;

"For me, it is a little disheartening; I wish people had focussed less on the petitions and more on the work itself".

Despite not being approved and being disliked by both the owners of the crowdmapping platform—namely, HOT and Humanitarian Organisation One—the petition was signed by over 400 active crowdmappers.

Importantly, the petition was successful in promoting the discussion about the overall role of the imagery providers and about how the HOT community could source imagery. It also positioned the crowdmapping contributors both as active agents, who reflect on the ways in which they participate in the crowdmapping platform, and as agents who have power to obtain and control their own resources.

5.3   The Diversification of Imagery Procurement

Some voices appeared to question the possibility of breaking away from being locked in the relationship with imagery providers altogether, and find other sources from which to obtain the imagery. These active discussions led the HOT community to consider their imagery sourcing, not only in terms of the time it took to obtain it, but also of the source from which they obtained it and how they could possibly control those sources. Possessing ownership of the sources was regarded as the ultimate control over the imagery. Hence, crowdmappers were motivated to think of alternative imagery sources that could be owned by the community members, such as Unmanned Aerial Vehicles (UAVs), commonly known as drones.

Whilst the effects of the online petition were unfolding, the OSM crowdmappers undertook a complementary move aimed at bringing about change in the imagery procurement process, tackling its dependency on imagery providers and increasing its control over resources. During the last few days of the Haiyan crowdmapping response, some of the OSM crowdmappers, who were affiliated to technology organisations and research centres, tested imagery obtained through UAVs to explore its suitability for the HOT platform. The positive results of the testing phase provided the crowdmappers with a complementary and inexpensive source of imagery that could be collected and owned by them, rather than having to rely solely on satellite imagery providers.

This change in the crowdmappers thinking of their own resources, in turn, led the owners to rethink the resources made available to the crowd. The HOT hierarchy started formally looking at different ways in which it could gain better access to UAV imagery. In addition, Humanitarian Organisation One began to consider the possibility of acquiring drones and using UAV images.

6 Discussion

The analysis shows that, under crisis conditions, the crowd were engaged in their practices and tried to find ways to improve them and make them more efficient, to the ultimate benefit of those affected by Typhoon Haiyan. They wanted to 'make a difference' in the production of detailed crowdmaps to help the agencies working on the ground in the Philippines. They questioned the resources offered to them by the owners, and their dependency on these resources. Moreover, they contested the *modus operandi* of the owners and loudly expressed the need for change. Moreover, while negotiating the times involved in obtaining existing resources, they took active steps to find alternative ones. In doing so, they depicted themselves as powerful actors who have the ability—to some degree—to control their means of production. The following sections discuss the dialectic of control in crowdmapping, and the knowledgeability and reflexivity of the crowd.

6.1 Dialectic of Control in Crowdsourcing

The study shows that, in a high-pressure situation, the crowd was able to reconsider the control on resources exercised by the owners. In an effort to challenge this control, the online petition was launched to protest against the delay in providing the lifeline resources to the crowd—namely, satellite imagery. This pushed the HOT and Humanitarian Organisation One hierarchies to find ways in which to obtain satellite imagery more quickly. It also initiated a wider discussion within the crowd regarding the control of resources, and led to initiatives aimed at obtaining alternative sources of imagery that went beyond satellite ones. Although the HOT hierarchy and various technological components—i.e., the tasking manager—attempted to maintain quality by controlling crowdmapping practices, the petition was still able to bypass the perceived control and have an impact on the community. The petition and the discussion, and the action it initiated, highlight the limitations in the owners' control, and the ability of the crowd to exercise control beyond the former's approval.

This finding shows that control is a double-edged sword that could be wielded by both the crowd owners and the crowd itself. It offers an alternative view to the existing crowdsourcing literature that depicts the crowd merely as entities to be controlled by the owners—e.g. Hansen et al. [14], Kittur et al. [15], and Yung et al. [16]. By contrast, this study shows that control in crowdsourcing initiatives in not a one-way force exerted only by the owners over the crowd, but it is a negotiation in which the crowd plays an active role in the end result.

6.2   The Knowledgeability and Reflexivity of the Crowd

This study shows that the crowd is aware of its practices, and knowledgeable and reflexive regarding their improvement. It sees itself as an active participant who is able to improve its social world. It is able to contest the resources offered to it, and obtain new ones.

This finding extends the literature beyond the current organisational perspective, to show that the crowd is not just some 'unidentified' workforce that can be controlled by means of codified methods [40, 41]. It is a knowledgeable actor who actively reflects on its circumstances and finds solutions to its own problems. It could have the desire to develop and advance further beyond the owners' plan, and might not be necessarily content with being controlled. It could aspire to gain power and control over its resources and contest the owners' domination. This shows that the crowd is not only an active participant but also a key composer of the social world [24]. This understanding of the crowd as a knowledgeable actor that could produce, reproduce, and change its social structure provides a fresh view of the crowd that goes beyond the current literature.

In essence, this study goes beyond a somewhat simplistic understanding of control by arguing that it cannot always be fully achieved or implemented despite the best efforts directed at achieving or implementing it. This is argued based upon the dynamics of the HOT and Humanitarian Organisation One hierarchies and their attempts at controlling crowdmappers, which were ultimately challenged by the online petition and its effects. The contrast between what is portrayed by the existing literature and the findings of this study raises important questions in regard to the type of control that can be achieved in crowdsourcing communities; in particular, this study doubts whether full control is ever even possible.

7   Conclusion and Implications

In conclusion, this study explored the following research questions:

• Who is in control in crowdsourcing initiatives?
• How and to what extent can control over the crowd be exercised?

To answer them, we examined a crowdmapping initiative in the humanitarian response context. Through the extensive collection of data from various actors and the application of concepts from structuration theory, the analysis revealed changes in structures of domination. Specifically, the paper articulated the knowledgeability, reflexivity and dialectic of control possessed by the crowd in effectively tackling methods aimed at controlling it. This analysis showed that it is not sufficient to simply state the ways in which the crowd can be controlled without giving due recognition to the agency that it itself possesses.

This study primarily makes a contribution to the IS crowdsourcing literature. Through its identification of the paradox of action and control, this study adds to the understanding of control afforded by the existing crowdsourcing literature. By identifying the knowledgeability, reflexivity, and dialectic of control possessed by the crowd in effectively tackling methods aimed at controlling it, this study provides a more thorough understanding of crowdsourcing and quality control, thus adding to the existing literature on crowdsourcing and quality control. This study calls for more appreciation and acknowledgement of the crowd and of the role it plays as a partner, as a possessor of its own skills, and as a knowledgeable actor, and not as a simple provider of solutions, ideas and innovation, as it is depicted in the literature.

Moreover, in terms of the wider IS literature, Walsham [42] argued that the IS literature needs to expand its agenda to understand whether ICTs are making the world a better place; this paper attempts to answer these calls through the exploration of the impact of crowdsourcing in a situation in which it 'made a difference' by enabling a humanitarian organisation to more efficiently respond in assessing damaged areas and allocating resources to relief efforts.

In practice, crowdsourcing owners need to be active communicators with the crowd and to be willing to listen to its voice regarding any improvement of its practices. This study presents a new perspective of crowdsourcing that can be further examined through additional research.

References

1. Estellés-Arolas, E., González-Ladrón-de-Guevara, F.: Towards an integrated crowdsourcing definition. J. Inf. Sci. **38**(2), 189–200 (2012)
2. Zhao, Y., Zhu, Q.: Evaluation on crowdsourcing research: current status and future direction. Inf. Syst. Front. **16**(3), 417–434 (2014)
3. Tarrell, A., et al.: Crowdsourcing: a snapshot of published research. In: AMCIS 2013 Proceedings (2013)
4. Brabham, D.C.: The myth of amateur crowds: a critical discourse analysis of crowdsourcing coverage. Inf. Commun. Soc. **15**(3), 394–410 (2012)
5. Savage, N.: Gaining wisdom from crowds. Commun. ACM **55**(3), 13–15 (2012)
6. Bergvall-Kåreborn, B., Howcroft, D.: The Apple business model: crowdsourcing mobile applications. Account. Forum 37(4), 280–289 (2013)
7. Djelassi, S., Decoopman, I.: Customers' participation in product development through crowdsourcing: issues and implications. Ind. Mark. Manag. **42**(5), 683–692 (2013)
8. Majchrzak, A., More, P.H.B.: Emergency! Web 2.0 to the rescue! Commun. ACM **54**(4), 125–132 (2011)
9. Goodchild, M.F., Glennon, J.A.: Crowdsourcing geographic information for disaster response: a research frontier. Int. J. Digit. Earth 3(3), 231–241 (2010)
10. Afuah, A., Tucci, C.L.: Crowdsourcing as a solution to distant search. Acad. Manag. Rev. **37**(3), 355–375 (2012)
11. Majchrzak, A., Malhotra, A.: Towards an information systems perspective and research agenda on crowdsourcing for innovation. J. Strateg. Inf. Syst. **22**(4), 257–268 (2013)
12. Zogaj, S., Bretschneider, U., Leimeister, J.M.: Managing crowdsourced software testing: a case study based insight on the challenges of a crowdsourcing intermediary. J. Bus. Econ. **84**(3), 375–405 (2014)
13. Allahbakhsh, M., et al.: Quality control in crowdsourcing systems. IEEE Internet Comput. **17**(2), 76–81 (2013)

14. Hansen, D.L., et al.: Quality control mechanisms for crowdsourcing: peer review, arbitration, & expertise at familysearch indexing. In: Proceedings of the 2013 Conference on Computer Supported Cooperative Work. ACM (2013)
15. Kittur, A., et al.: Crowdforge: crowdsourcing complex work. In: Proceedings of the 24th Annual ACM Symposium on User Interface Software and Technology. ACM (2011)
16. Yung, D., Li, M.-L., Chang, S.: Evolutionary approach for crowdsourcing quality control. J. Vis. Lang. Comput. 25(6), 879–890 (2014)
17. Majchrzak, A., Cherbakov, L., Ives, B.: Harnessing the power of the crowds with corporate social networking tools: how IBM does it. MIS Q. Exec. 8(2), 103–108 (2009)
18. Palen, L., Hiltz, S.R., Liu, S.B.: Online forums supporting grassroots participation in emergency preparedness and response. Commun. ACM 50(3), 54–58 (2007)
19. Palen, L., Liu, S.B.: Citizen communications in crisis: anticipating a future of ICT-supported public participation. In: Proceedings of the SIGCHI Conference on Human Factors in Computing Systems. ACM (2007)
20. Walsham, G., Han, C.-K.: Structuration theory and information systems research. In: International Conference on Information Systems (ICIS) (1990)
21. Hiltunen, E.: Crowdsourcing the future: the foresight process at Finpro. J. Futur. Stud. 16(1), 189–196 (2011)
22. Le, J., et al.: Ensuring quality in crowdsourced search relevance evaluation: the effects of training question distribution. In: SIGIR 2010 Workshop on Crowdsourcing for Search Evaluation (2010)
23. Poesio, M., et al.: Phrase detectives: utilizing collective intelligence for internet-scale language resource creation. ACM Trans. Interact. Intell. Syst. (TiiS) 3(1), 3:1–3:44 (2013)
24. Giddens, A.: The Constitution of Society: Outline of the Theory of Structuration. Polity, Cambridge (1984)
25. Giddens, A.: New Rules of Sociological Method: A Positive Critique of Interpretative Sociologies. Stanford University Press, Palo Alto (1993)
26. Cohen, I.J.: Structuration Theory: Anthony Giddens and the Constitution of Social Life. Macmillan, London (1989)
27. Tucker, K.: Anthony Giddens and Modern Social Theory. Sage, Thousand Oaks (1998)
28. Giddens, A.: Central Problems in Social Theory: Action, Structure, and Contradiction in Social Analysis. University of California Press, Berkeley (1979)
29. Giddens, A.: Profiles and Critiques in Social Theory. University of California Press, Berkeley (1982)
30. Myers, M.D.: Qualitative Research in Information Systems (2012). http://www.qual.auckland.ac.nz/. Accessed 9 Nov 2012
31. Walsham, G.: Interpretive case studies in IS research: nature and method. Eur. J. Inf. Syst. 4(2), 74–81 (1995)
32. Walsham, G., Han, C.K.: Information systems strategy formation and implementation: the case of a central government agency. Acc. Manag. Inf. Technol. 3(3), 191–209 (1993)
33. Schultze, U., Avital, M.: Designing interviews to generate rich data for information systems research. Inf. Organ. 21(1), 1–16 (2011)
34. Myers, M.D., Newman, M.: The qualitative interview in IS research: examining the craft. Inf. Organ. 17(1), 2–26 (2007)
35. Pozzebon, M., Pinsonneault, A.: Challenges in conducting empirical work using structuration theory: learning from IT research. Organ. Stud. 26(9), 1353–1376 (2005)
36. Langley, A.: Strategies for theorizing from process data. Acad. Manag. Rev. 24(4), 691–710 (1999)

37. NDRRMC: SitRep No. 108 Effects of Typhoon "Yolanda" (Haiyan) (2014). http://www. ndrrmc.gov.ph/attachments/article/1329/Effects_of_Typhoon_YOLANDA_(HAIYAN)_ SitRep_No_108_03APR2014.pdf. Accessed 21 Sep 2015

38. OpenStreetMap: Typhoon Haiyan - Tacloban Post-Disaster Imagery Mapping (2013). http:// tasks.hotosm.org/project/350. Accessed 27 Nov 2014

39. Hern, A.: Online Volunteers Map Philippines After Typhoon Haiyan (2013). http://www. theguardian.com/technology/2013/nov/15/online-volunteers-map-philippines-after-typhoon- haiyan. Accessed 7 April 2014

40. Saxton, G.D., Oh, O., Kishore, R.: Rules of crowdsourcing: models, issues, and systems of control. Inf. Syst. Manag. **30**(1), 2–20 (2013)

41. Oleson, D., et al.: Programmatic gold: targeted and scalable quality assurance in crowdsourcing. Hum. Comput. **11**, 11 (2011)

42. Walsham, G.: Are we making a better world with ICTs? Reflections on a future agenda for the IS field. J. Inf. Technol. **27**(2), 87–93 (2012)

Co-creation and Fine-Tuning of Boundary Resources in Small-Scale Platformization

Anna Sigridur Islind[1(✉)], Tomas Lindroth[1], Ulrika Lundh Snis[1],
and Carsten Sørensen[1,2]

[1] University West, Trollhättan, Sweden
{anna-sigridur.islind, tomas.lindroth,
ulrika.snis}@hv.se, c.sorensen@lse.ac.uk
[2] London School of Economics and Political Science, London, UK

Abstract. Most research on platform innovation studies the phenomena from a distance due to lack of access. This paper reports from within an action research case of platform development in a small-scale context. The case is based on a regional business initiative with the goal to establish an arena for mobile commerce and stimulate local industry growth. It was conducted in collaboration between researchers and third-party developers. The article shows how the initial phases of platformization are characterized by socio-technical arrangements, co-creation of boundary resources and intimate knowledge communication. The paper contributes to platform research by acknowledging a small-scale context for platform research. It further develops distributed tuning of boundary resources into an intimate fine-tuning process that we illustrate is valid for a small-scale context.

Keywords: Platform · Platformization · Knowledge communication · Fine-tuning · Co-creation · Boundary resources

1 Introduction

While research on mobile platforms in general has been the subject of research through the past decade and a half [1, 2] the recent explosive growth of smartphone apps on Apple and Google's app stores, along with a number of other notable examples, has elevated the issue of software and smartphone app platforms within the academic discourse. The iOS and Android app stores have jointly generated a total of 3 million different apps representing the development of around 150 billion lines of code since 2008 [3]. Apple alone has paid out $25 billion to its developer community the first six and a half years [4].

However, the examples of Apple and Google are far from the only ones, as the success of a range of services partly or entirely based on a generative Internet element [5] engages in complements from independent third-party developers through exposing Application Programming Interfaces (APIs), by providing Software Development Kits (SDKs), by relying on standard Internet technologies, and through providing quality assurance support.

In previous research, the platformization is viewed as primarily an exercise of innovation at arms length through a variety of boundary resources [6, 7]. Tilson et al. [8]

U.L. Snis et al. (Eds.): IFIP8.6 2016, LNBIP 259, pp. 149–162, 2016.
DOI: 10.1007/978-3-319-43597-8_11

reported from successful examples with significant installed bases of code and coders. The studies of mobile platforms generally do not have access to primary data sources, but tend instead to study the phenomenon indirectly. This paper, however, takes an exclusively inside-out view of the nascent phase of platform establishment with a particular focus on the initial creation of the boundary resources that will constitute a mobile platform. This process of establishing a platform will in this paper be called *platformization*. This paper reports from platformization in a small-scale context, as a contrast to the previously reported, large scale platformization studies mentioned above. In large-scale platforms the process of developing boundary resources does happen in an unprompted manner from an uncoordinated large group of third-party developers. This is not likely to happen in a small context since there are no uncoordinated large groups of developers. In a small scale context there are at the utmost small development teams or local SME firms that will engage in platform development and co-creation through various types of projects.

This article addresses two research gaps. First, the lack of accounts on how small-scale mobile platforms is established and how boundary resources are developed in such platforms. Second, there has been relatively little attention paid to how the role of knowledge communication in platform innovation influences the creation and use of boundary resources among the different actor groups. These research gaps imply that today's knowledge of mobile platforms cannot be directly applied to a small-scale context. Drawing on this, we describe the initial phases of platformization carried out in a small-scale context.

The paper is based on an action research case where a consortium of academics and practitioners developed a platform for local apps and services aimed at becoming a mobile commerce hub of a local Swedish community. The paper describes the main findings from the development process through a post-hoc analysis based on diary entries, email thread analysis, interviews and project documentation. The empirical analysis explores the effects from choices made during the platformization process, and seeks to understand these effects in terms of the communication and transfer of knowledge between the constituents.

Initial findings suggest that communication and knowledge transfer calls for a more intimate knowledge communication process where the embeddedness of knowledge into codes and software modules must be reconsidered. Therefore, this paper asks the question: How can small-scale platformization be understood in terms of the creation of boundary resources and the knowledge communication?

The following section outlines the theoretical constructs for our analysis. Section 3 briefly presents the research approach leading to the empirical results in Sect. 4. Section 5 discusses the findings and synthesizes our contribution. Section 6 concludes the paper.

2   Theoretical Concepts

2.1   Platforms and Generativity

Most of the literature on platforms and platformization is grounded within innovation management and explores the shifting interrelationships between internal production arrangements, external partners and independent complementors [2, 9–11]. Within platform research, there is a distinction between technical and socio-technical platforms [9].

A growing body of literature concerns research regarding mobile- and software-based platforms where the main focus is on platforms as two-sided markets [3, 6, 7, 12, 13]. Much insight can be gained from studying this body of work, the successful platforms with a significant digital element tends to fall into the category of two- or multi-sided markets where the platform brings parties together in open co-creation arrangements [14]. Such platform arrangements are based on the exposure of APIs, sourcing of SDKs, and relying on standard Internet technologies for the development of new services.

One of the core platform characteristics often discussed is the generativity emerging from the digital characteristics supporting independent developers engaging in producing new and interesting boundary resource recombinations [8]. Zittrain [5] claims that: "Generativity denotes a technology's overall capacity to produce unprompted change driven by large, varied, and uncoordinated audiences", and further characterizes the following five dimensions of generativity: 1. Leverage in performing some task; 2. Adaptability and built upon with ease; 3. Ease of mastery for broad audience; 4. Accessibility of tools; and 5. Transferability of results.

This paper focuses primarily on the socio-technical platform, that is, not only the technical components of the platform, the APIs or the SDKs. These are important parts but they need to be understood together with the so-called social dimensions or contexts, i.e. the information requirements and knowledge communication among different actor groups. In regard to Zittrain's [5] five dimensions, which are primarily of social character, we consider the social aspects as equal important in platform research and thus we draw attention to how boundary resources are co-created and how knowledge communication would have been facilitated.

2.2 Boundary Resources and Distributed Tuning

The research on software- and smartphone app platforms tends to explore features relating to the open and flexible models of collaboration facilitated by distributed development based on shared boundary resources, thus providing architectural leverage. To illustrate this, Ghazawneh and Henfridsson [6] introduce the boundary resources model.

Boundary resources are "the software tools and regulations that serve as the interface for the arm's length relationship between the platform owner and the application developer." [6, p. 174]. There are two forms of specific platform boundary resources [6]. First there are technical boundary resources typically consisting of software development kits (SDK) and application programming interfaces (APIs). Secondly there are social boundary resources, typically incentives, intellectual property and platform's documentation [9, 15]. These resources enable access to central modules of the platform [16]. This opens up for the necessary complementary innovation by third-party developers [17].

Generally, the third-party developers are those who develop applications that enrich a platform [6] and involve a heterogeneous group of app-developers (individuals or groups) who are disbursed and not a part of the same community as the platform owners. The platform owners are usually refereed to as the core management of the platform in terms of operating the platform and managing the boundary resources as assets for the third-party developers to (a) use in its existing form and (b) further develop the boundary resources.

Ghazawneh and Henfridsson's [6] model is primarily designated for large-scale platforms development contexts. The model emphasizes the distributed use of the boundary resources developed. Such processes are guided by principles of objectified and commodifying knowledge as well as the arms-length relationships.

The notion of tuning is originally built on Pickering [18] whereas Barrett et al. [19] have extended the concept of tuning. In Eaton et al. [7] the concept of tuning is further developed into a platformization approach of distributed tuning. Based an embedded case study analysis from Apple, their iOS service system and third-party developers they offer a process model that accounts for the power-oriented dynamics of using and designing boundary resources. "Distributed tuning emerges from on-going tensions among dispersed heterogeneous actors who deal with a set of technology artifacts in a network of dialectic interrelating as shown in all five themes." [7, p. 235].

To understanding the creation of sociotechnical platforms, tuning is a robust analytical lens to understand "the dynamic nature of boundary resources in service systems" [7, p. 221]. They also note that there is a power dimension in the relationship between the actors participating in a service system where they are not all equal in degree of agency over both material and other actors in the service system [7]. The relationships of tuning and influence function as fundamental characteristics of how boundary resources are resisted and accommodated [7]. They further highlight the distinction between boundary resources, auxiliary boundary resources and technology resources.

We apply Ghazawneh's and Henfridsson's model [6] for a detailed analysis of the nascent phases in the development of our small-scale platform and we specifically examine the platform development in terms of the relationship between platform owners, platform and third-party developers. The ambition is to argue for the communication of knowledge and capability to third-party developers in order to cultivate and contribute to the boundary resources of the platform.

2.3 Knowledge Communication in Innovation

If we then consider the social boundary resources and "management of knowledge at arms length" as a core function of design capability it highlights the importance of knowledge communication and learning for platform innovation. Much knowledge in today's society in general, but in platform innovation in particular, is based on technical knowledge [20]. This knowledge remains in the heads of the experts, or in software developer or innovation teams. The knowledge and skills are more or less built-in and embedded in a particular organization's processes and systems. Hence, the communication of knowledge mainly emphasizes the economic exchange of knowledge objectified in the boundary resources, which implies a knowledge communication through product-based economic transactions [20]. A too great focus on technical knowledge can lead to an expert-driven approach that might not be appropriate for dealing with tacit and distributed knowledge among various actor groups [21]. An opposite approach is that of knowledge communication through social processes of professionalization [20]. Herein knowledge is rather co-created and shared among different groups of individuals. It fits well when routines and standards are not yet set and when on-going interaction does not depend of a robust structure of relationships [22]. In the nascent phases of platform innovation we regard this latter approach as highly relevant.

3 Research Approach

The study is based on data collected over a 2.5 year action research (AR) project building a mobile app platform devoted to developing and harnessing local mobile commerce within a medium-sized Swedish city. The project was a regional business initiative with the goal of establishing an arena for mobile commerce and stimulating local industry growth. To reach the goal the project decided to design and build a socio-technical, mobile service cross-platform that should function as a bridge that should facilitate local entrepreneurship in mobile commerce.

The socio-technical platform was designed to support and manage the entire life-cycle of mobile app design, development and go-to-market strategies. In our case the socio-technical indicates a platform consisting of actors like programmers and managers, design processes, coding frameworks, SDKs and APIs, generic code modules as well as go-to-market and knowledge transfer strategies. App development processes were set up as a co-creative effort involving both platform owners, expert developers and local third-party developers.

To gain deeper insights conceptualized we applied qualitative approaches, conducted in close co-operation with industry. It was conceptually and methodologically framed using a variety of terms such as action research [23–25] and action case research [26–28].

The action-oriented activities in this research initiative were about the balance between involvement in the change process (the problem solving) and the research process [29]. We developed and conceptualized interventions in terms of introducing an artifact as a result of multiple perspectives on design, improvement, and use. The development process was organized between a group of platform owners including researchers and representatives from the municipality and third-party developers including technical consultants, teachers and local students, as further described in section four. The design process was constructed based on the principled outlined in the extant literature on action research, for example [30–32].

The action-oriented process generated a variety of data as the researchers (later on called platform owners) sought to be present in almost all activities concerning the project. Data was to a large extent captured through participatory observations at key points in the project cycles, such as: team meetings, discussion in on-line coordination tools, and education and training workshops. Furthermore, data was continuously collected through project documentation, such as, minutes and email conversations from project meetings and from ad-hoc interaction. At the end of the project, a series of 6 semi-structured interviews were conducted, 3 with expert developers and 3 with local third-party developers – in order to capture participant reflections on their experiences. It can, therefore, be argued that this data represents an inside-out perspective on platformization as opposed to the traditional outside observer perspective based on limited primary data or decontextualized secondary data.

For this paper, the data-set was re-analyzed specifically focusing on architectural choices, boundary resources, and knowledge communication within the project. Three main actor groups were involved, which will be explained more thorough in the result section. Three of the authors of this paper are a part of the group later called platform owners and the fourth, non-participant author of this paper served through this re-analysis the role of critical outsider seeking to challenge the analytical assumptions [33].

4   Results

In this section we describe the different roles and their activities in the project. The platformization process is visualized and exemplified with a senior citizen app. Additionally, the technological decisions are described as well as the so called knowledge transfer process from the third-party consultants to the local third-party developers.

4.1   The Roles

There were several different actors in the project. Here we describe their main roles. The roles of platform owners and third-party developers are both inline with the theoretical underpinning. In Fig. 1 the three major roles within the project are visualized.

Platform owners	Third-party developers	
Representatives from the local municipality and university including researchers.	Expert developers from a national IT-consultancy.	Local third-party developers: Faculty teachers and system developer students.

Fig. 1. The different roles

The Platform Owners: The platform owners were researchers at the university that were involved in a research project (see Fig. 1). The researchers contributed with user experience, service design as well as system analysis competence. Part of the platform owners group were also members from the local municipality contributed with access to the local business setting.

Expert Developers: In order to ensure the best possible design and execution of the platformization effort, a leading Swedish IT consultancy firm was hired to lead the technical development effort together with the platform owners. Consequently, the expert developers were employed at a large consultancy firm. The firm employed a great number of skilled management consultants and programmers with important platform related competences.

Local Third-Party Developers: Third-party developers used the boundary resources for utilizing the platform's capabilities in developing apps. In this local setting, the third-party developers were primarily local entrepreneurs, businesses and students at the university. The plan was that this group would subsequently use, enrich and develop the platform after the contract with the expert third party developers ended. This linked the general ambition of stimulating entrepreneurship and regional business. Herein, *the project* is used when referring to all three groups simultaneously.

4.2   The Platformization Process

Phase (A) Initiating and Exploring Platformization: The platform owners evaluated a range of different platform architectures from the researchers and expert developers point of view. A key consideration during this process was to come up with alternatives on what platform architecture and development arrangement to choose and design. The following options were available: (a) Open, web-based architecture with plain vanilla versions of HTML, CSS, JavaScript etc., allowing to build what in effect would be mobile websites partly cached on the handset, (b) Entirely native apps to be published across the two main smartphone platforms, iOS and Android, written using the respective SDKs and APIs (for example Objective C, Swift, etc.), (c) using more advanced high-level generator tools to produce a variant of (a), for example such as: PhoneGap, Angular.js, Telerik or Backbone.

The first choice to be made was between native apps or apps based on enriched HTML web-services. In this decision the consultants' standpoint was that the project should build hybrid (HTML) apps that would be modular and that the platform should be a self-supporting stand-alone entity. When it was clear that a native solution did not fit the project goals, other alternatives were considered. Different Platform as a Service (PaaS) solutions from Microsoft, Amazon and Google were evaluated and discussed.

Option (c) with a specific arrangement of Javascript environment and cloud provision was chosen. When the decision of (c) was delivered via e-mail written by the expert third party developers, to the platform owners, the reaction was a genuine surprise among the platform owners, who felt they had not been a part of that particular decision-making process as much as they would have liked. The motivation for this choice was that with (c), the project would be able to maximize the number of modules that were built, and the degree to which these modules would be reusable. Both aspects were regarded as central to the generativity of the platform. As one consultant expressed it: *"Considering the skills needed and learning thresholds for a student, which is an important issue, we propose a PaaS-solution. That is, the environment and systems are operated and monitored by the cloud owner and not by us."* The

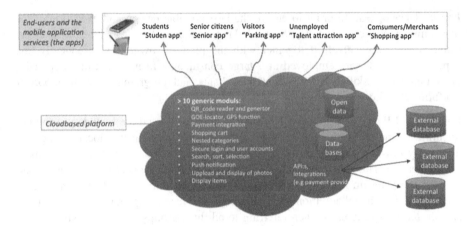

Fig. 2. An overview of the cloud-based innovation platform

argumentation from the consultant focuses on the PaaS choice. The chosen javascript framework and associated SDKs were downplayed both in the first e-mail that declared their choice and in the subsequent project presentation. The platform was, after these decisions, to be built in a cloud service called Cloudbees, which is based on Jenkins [34]. This particular service platform was set up to handle hybrid apps (HTML) with complex user interfaces and a Javascript library. This particular Javascript library is called Backbone and is fundamentally a Model View Controller (i.e. MVC) that enables the code to be modular and imposes calls to the server to be entirely done through RESTful API. This choice, the choice of Jenkins, Java and Backbone were never discussed, these were just silently implemented in the platform. An overview of the innovation platform is given in Fig. 2 below.

Phase (B) Creating the Apps and General Modules: To get the platform working, the expert developers started developing and creating relevant modules. Initially, it was decided to develop a set of apps and services with associated code modules that later could be combined and further developed by the third-party developers. The generic modules were common features regarding secure login, GPS-features and payment options, among others. In addition to these modules the expert developers developed three apps as proof of concepts in order to show the generativity of the general modules: (a) senior citizens app (b) talent attraction app (c) parking app. See Fig. 2 for an overview of the development process. The proof of concept apps is marked with orange boarders in Fig. 3.

Later, in the development process it was time for the local third-party developers to develop their first apps in the established platform (Green in Fig. 3). The generic modules were then used in several apps, which was in line with the general strategy to reuse the modules and code which were now ready for them to re-use as lego pieces. The plan was that this pwould be done in Scrum as well, and be a rather fast process. See Fig. 4 for an overview of the platform architecture, its content and the end-user groups of the developed apps.

The experiences of developing apps in the platform were mixed. A local third party developer working within the platform felt that: *"The advantages of the platform was that many modules and solutions from previous apps were available. It was also very modular, making it easy to reuse functionality."* But on the other hand, the third party developers also thought *"Cloudbees rarely gives the user feedback control. The feedback was not kind. You receive an error code which was about 700 lines, only of exception failures from Java"*. The module-based architecture was supposed to speed up the programming process. Instead, when the expert consultants successively handed over the platform and the programing to the local third-party developers, the time to create an app increased, as seen in Fig. 3.

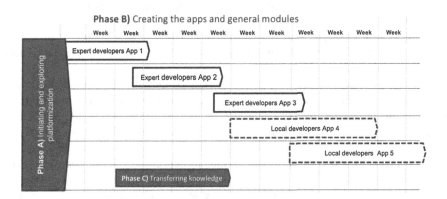

Fig. 3. The platformization process: phase A, B and C (Color figure online)

Phase (C) Transferring of Knowledge: In order for the platform to thrive and reach generativity it was central to have a knowledge transfer strategy from the platform owners and expert developers to the local third party developers. The aim was to lower the entrepreneurial threshold by providing the necessary prerequisites and components to cost-effectively build and manage apps and thereby stimulate industry growth.

The knowledge transfer phase occurred in parallel with the development phases as illustrated in Fig. 3. The third-party developers were able to sit at the consultancy and be present while the expert developers developed the boundary resources for the platform. To ensure the knowledge transfer for the local third party developers, there was a knowledge transfer series with lectures in how to develop new generative modules as well as in using the generative modules that were already in the platform. The knowledge transfer series was in a top-down manner where the technology was introduced and pushed onto the local third party developers. During these series, the consultancy wanted to ensure that they had done their part in the knowledge transfer obligation and to do that, they flew in and had lectures.

The students craved more of focused training: *"The visits of {the consultancy} made the work with {the project} feel like a real job. The training was quite okay, what I remember was that the focus was on delivery deadlines during the time I was with them. So there was more focus on the project than on the training and learning."*

A teacher felt that the process became so oriented towards limiting waste, that making mistakes was scaled down to the minimum, which left almost no space for the training to evolve into a real learning experience and competency.

As the local third-party developers consisted of students and teachers as a resource in developing apps for the platform, the chosen architecture implied a too steep learning curve due to the complex architecture of the platform. The students were overwhelmed with the technology framework, the rapid software development and knowledge transfer tempo.

The aspect of time, was therefore an important one, to overcome the barriers of the platform. However, due to the rapid sprints, there was no time available. The students and teachers' thoughts on the matter was the platform was too big, the platform interface was too messy and that other programming frameworks would have been a better fit. As one of the student said: *"So I think that the platform had too many templates and settings for what {the project} was doing, which made it messier."* Another student has a similar comment: *"The worst limitations that I experienced with Cloudbees was the lack of control."*

Pushing the expert developer's choice of technology onto the relatively inexperienced local third-party developers was not good, but pushing the compressed and front loaded learning cycles onto them as well with no time for reflection due to the time press and agility of the project, was worse. The lectures came to be in a monolog form where the consultancy (expert developers) fed the third-party developers information during a specific timeslot and there was no time for reflection. The third-party presence at the consultancy and the lecture series both happened before the actual handover of the programming responsibility to the local developers. When they were in the middle developing their first apps, they were on their own. At that time the knowledge transfer process had ended and the consultants had moved on to another project.

5 Discussion

As we stated in the introduction, platform innovation is a complex arrangement of *both technical and social boundary resources* that need to be critically considered [6, 9]. Diverse stakeholders are involved and different technical boundary resources become important such as application platforms, cloud services, code bases, programming knowledge, etc. Zittrain's [5] principles of generativity, where the capacity of general-purpose technology is utilized as boundary resources at arms length by groups of third-party developers, was backgrounded in this research initiative. Through the nascent phases in this platformization study, architectural leverage was not easy to master as it turned out to have a number of consequences for the communication of knowledge and skills requirements. There were several vital decisions made by the expert developers, which possibly were motivated by their pre-existing set of technical knowledge. In general, these were not bad decisions, the technical platform is a modern, state-of-the-art development suit, but it turned out to be a poor match of requirement and skills for the local third party developers and the project in its nascent phase.

The more socially oriented resources, like knowledge about platform innovation remained in the heads of the experts, innovation teams as well as organization's processes and systems [20, 21]. Furthermore, the social relations were not coordinated towards the overall purpose of the actual project. The platform owners were interested in seeing the local context blossoming from a two-sided market perspective [14], whereas the expert developers interest was to produce as many generative modules as possible [5].

As [7] imply, at an arm's length relationship, much knowledge is embedded into the APIs and SDKs as commoditized knowledge aimed to be directly used by distant third-party developers. But in the small-scale setting, there were no critical mass of developers that could act as the other side in a two-sided market. The genuine co-creation process of boundary resources did not occur as the communication and sharing of knowledge was hard to engage in for an outsider, i.e. a local third-party developer. There was no ease of mastery for accessibility or "reuse" [5] for the third party developers.

Hence, the architectural leverage was not yet achieved, as the tension between the communication of knowledge and the commodification of knowledge was not considered carefully [3, 20, 21]. How knowledge is produced and how skills are being trained for the purpose of platform building was one such important aspect in the context of this case. This meant, in a small-scale project, aiming for generativity is less essential than getting the right skills and competencies to match the technical choices made and to the boundary resources that needs to be established. In the forefront was the primary challenge of coordinating the social relations and knowledge communication, which in retrospect is key consideration that should have been done more carefully with a gentler fade out compared to the mid project "prompt stop" in fifth week, as visualized in Fig. 3, phase C.

Thus, for the nascent stages of platformization, establishing the foundation and negotiating best choices should all activities be governed by social arrangement and knowledge communication in accordance with [20] notions of professionalization and sedimentation.

5.1 Towards an Intimate Fine-Tuning Approach

This actual platform innovation initiative, with scarce resources and diverse participants, demanded a more advanced type of knowledge communication process that can bridge multiple types of actors in an open and efficient manner. Facilitating a more intimate climate for tuning the knowledge communication was in hindsight the most critical challenge. In retrospect, we can realize that the tuning process in a small-scale platform project cannot be of a distributed character with arms-length relationship [7]. For a small-scale platform, the relationship should instead be characterized by intimacy. With intimacy we mean close collaboration over an extended period of time during the whole development process. We argue for a *fine-tuning process* where intimacy and knowledge communication in a co-creation process are key characteristics. In the following we summarize this discussion in more detail.

In a small-scale context, a platform cannot simply be brought in from the outside and placed within the local setting in terms of commodified boundary resources [6] and expected to grow; it takes intimacy and nurturing. Seeing code as value, as well as seeing knowledge as value is vital. There is a need for fine-tuning knowledge communication to accommodate the intimacy of professionalization and sedimentation. Frameworks, code and developed modules do not have an intrinsic value of their own especially if there are not skills and competency on how to enhance them. In a small scale platform context co-creation needs to be a goal, and offshoring or outsourcing may not be a viable alternative. Thus, the platform boundary resources needs to be co-created and locally legitimized in order to achieve architectural leverage and make it be cultivated in the local platform ecology. Without this co-creation and communication of knowledge, the code and modules lacks value [14, 35].

The code-base was from the expert developers point of view the main knowledge needed to be progressively transformed into new, commoditized mobile application services. The human craft of socially produced knowledge out of code bases was neglected. This stands in contrast to what Scarbrough [20] points out when stating that technological innovation needs social communicability and that the commodification of hardware and software knowledge has actually "provided a platform for increasing demand for human expertise." [20, p. 1000]. De Reuver and Bouwman [35] point out the importance of balancing dependencies and power in the development phase. At the same time, they state the challenges for "too many small parties" without any power-based governance often prevents entering the implementation phase. We experienced the strong dependency to the consultancy firm (the expert developers) as a resource to be used more intimately, as in alignment to [21]. The local third party developers involved called for more training and knowledge communication, rather than the delivery of modules. There was a clear need for professionalization aligning the remote expertise and architectural choice to the local expertise and competency. Viewing the students and teachers as boundary resources and boosting their knowledge, might have lead to a less dependency with the expert developers. The arm's length relationship was not valid. Involving the students and teachers more in the selection of architecture and taking into account the students and teachers pre-existing programming skills and the teachers background in selection of architecture, would in retrospect, have delivered a different outcome for the local setting. Lean approaches also played a role in this case. Both focus on short sprints and limiting waste is a central aspect. With longer sprints and with a more forgiving process regarding mistakes both teachers and students could have played a more central role in the development process.

Following Zittrain's [5, p. 1980] notion of generativity: "Generativity denotes a technology's overall capacity to produce unprompted change driven by large, varied, and uncoordinated audiences" might need a re-consideration. In this case, as a small-scale platform establishment, it is much better characterized in terms of the opposite context, namely, prompted change through a small, possibly homogenous, and coordinated set of socio-technical arrangements [9, 14] to establish the platform and its complements. The communication of knowledge emphasizes a fine-tuning process of intimacy in professionalization, sedimentation of skills and competency but also a different view of time as well as goals. This fine-tuning approach is fitting for a small-scale platformization, rather then the arms-length relationship that fits for a large-scale platformization discussed by Eaton et al. [7]. However, we acknowledge that as a platform grows from small to large the importance of social arrangement and knowledge communication decrease in favor for commoditized knowledge into code, SDK's and API's.

6 Conclusion and Further Work

The aim of this paper was to shed light on the initial phases of platformization in a small-scale context. We have argued for acknowledging small-scale contexts as a part of the platform research. The models presented in prior research do not fit the purpose of the platformization processes observed in our case. The biggest challenge regarding the models is concerning the arms-length relationship between the platform owners and the third-party developers, which is the key in a large-scale platform. Through our research, we have illustrated that in a small-scale platformization, the relationship needs to be formed differently. The intimacy in the relationship between the platform owners and the third-party developers is the core. From an evolving small-scale platformization perspective, this relationship must be supported by an intimate and co-creative process of knowledge communication, herein called fine-tuning.

From this, we call for further research regarding fine-tuning of boundary resources for similar small-scale contexts. Research tends to cover platformization efforts once they have become successful and by definition are past their nascent phase. We would, however, argue that the first steps in the life of a platform are just as essential as its later race for global domination, and that perhaps we can learn from those baby-steps that result in falls rather than running.

References

1. Ciborra, C.U.: The platform organization: recombining strategies, structures, and surprises. Organ. Sci. **7**(2), 103–118 (1996)
2. Gawer, A., Cusumano, M.A.: Platform Leadership: How Intel, Microsoft, and Cisco Drive Industry Innovation. Harvard Business School Press, Boston (2002)
3. Sørensen, C., de Reuver, M., Basole, R.: Mobile platforms and ecosystems. J. Inf. Technol. **30**(4), 195–197 (2015). Forthcoming Special Issue Editorial
4. Ranger, S.: iOS versus Android. Apple App Store versus Google Play: Here comes the next battle in the app wars. ZDNet (2015). http://www.zdnet.com/article/iosversus-android-apple-app-store-versus-google-play-herecomes-the-next-battle-in-the-app-wars/
5. Zittrain, J.: The generative Internet. Harv. Law Rev. **119**, 1974–2040 (2006)
6. Ghazawneh, A., Henfridsson, O.: Balancing platform control and external contribution in third-party development: the boundary resources model. Inf. Syst. J. **23**(2), 173–192 (2013)
7. Eaton, B.D., Elaluf-Calderwood, S., Sørensen, C., Yoo, Y.: Distributed tuning of boundary resources: the case of Apple's iOS service system. MIS Q. Spec. Issue Serv. Innov. Digit. Age **39**(1), 217–243 (2015)
8. Tilson, D., Sørensen, C., Lyytinen, K.: Change and control paradoxes in mobile infrastructure innovation: the Android and iOS mobile operating systems cases. In: 45th Hawaii International Conference on System Science (HICSS 45), Maui, HI (2012)
9. Gawer, A. (ed.): Platforms, Markets and Innovation. Edward Elgar, Cheltenham (2009)
10. Gawer, A.: Bridging differing perspectives on technological platforms: toward an integrative framework. Res. Policy **43**, 1239–1249 (2014)
11. Thomas, L., Autio, E., Gann, D.: Architectural leverage: putting platforms in context. Acad. Manag. Perspect. **28**(2), 198–219 (2014)
12. Tiwana, A., Konsynsky, B., Bush, A.A.: Platform evolution: coevolution of platform architecture, governance, and environmental dynamics. Inf. Syst. Res. **21**(4), 675–687 (2010)

13. Wareham, J., Fox, P.B., Giner, J.L.C.: Technology ecosystem governance. Organ. Sci. **25**, 1195–1215 (2014)

14. Boudreau, K.J., Lakhani, K.R.: How to manage outside innovation. MIT Sloan Manag. Rev. **50**(4), 69–75 (2009)

15. Ghazawneh, A., Henfridsson, O.: Micro-strategizing in platform ecosystems: a multiple case study (2011)

16. Yoo, Y., Lyytinen, K., Boland, R.J., Berente, N.: The Next Wave of Digital Innovation: Opportunities and Challenges, A Report on the Research Workshop of "Digital Challenges in Innovation Research" (2010). http://papers.ssrn.com/sol3/papers.cfm?abstract_id=1622170

17. Gawer, A., Cusumano, M.A.: How companies become platform leaders. MIT Sloan Manag. Rev. **49**(2), 28 (2008). http://www.ncbi.nlm.nih.gov/entrez/query.fcgi?db=pubmed&cmd= Retrieve&dopt=AbstractPlus&list_uids=7944406096486535532related:bBGH5EAzQG4J

18. Pickering, A.: The mangle of practice: agency and emergence in the sociology of science. Am. J. Sociol. **99**(3), 559–589 (1993)

19. Barrett, M., Oborn, E., Orlikowski, W.J., Yates, J.A.: Reconfiguring boundary relations: robotic innovations in pharmacy work. Organ. Sci. **23**(5), 1448–1466 (2012)

20. Scarbrough, H.: Blackboxes, hostages and prisoners. Organ. Stud. **16**(6), 991–1019 (1995)

21. Sørensen, C., Lundh-Snis, U.: Innovation through knowledge codification. J. Inf. Technol. **16**(2), 83–97 (2001)

22. Hislop, D.: Mission impossible? Communicating and sharing knowledge via information technology. J. Inf. Technol. **17**, 165–177 (2002)

23. Avison, D., Lau, F., Myers, M., Nielsen, P.A.: Action research. Commun. ACM **42**(1), 94–97 (1999)

24. Baskerville, R.: Investigating information systems with action research. Commun. Assoc. Inf. Syst. Res. **2**, 1–32 (1999)

25. Baskerville, R., Myers, M.D.: Special issue on action research in information systems: making IS research relevant to practice-foreword. MIS Q. **28**(3), 329–336 (2004)

26. Kristin, B., Richard, V.: Balancing interpretation and intervention in information system research: the action case approach. Information Systems and Qualitative Research, pp. 524–541. Springer, New York (1997)

27. Kristin, B., Richard, V.: Interpretation, intervention, and reduction in the organizational laboratory: a framework for in-context information system research. J. Account. Manag. Inf. Technol. **9**(1), 25–47 (1999)

28. Kristin, B., Richard, V.: From observation to intervention. Planet Internet, pp. 252–276. Studentlitteratur, Lund (2000)

29. McKay, J., Marshall, P.: The dual imperatives of action research. Inf. Technol. People **14**(1), 46–59 (2001)

30. Baskerville, R., Wood-Harper, A.T.: A critical perspective on action research as a method for information systems research. J. Inf. Technol. **11**, 235–246 (1996)

31. Hevner, A.R., March, S.T., Park, J., Ram, S.: Design science in information systems research. MIS Q. **28**(1), 75–105 (2004)

32. Mathiassen, L., Chiasson, M., Germonprez, M.: Style composition in action research publication. MIS Q. **36**(2), 347–363 (2012)

33. Lee, A.S., Hubona, G.S.: A scientific basis for rigor in information systems research. MIS Q. **33**(2), 237–262 (2009)

34. De Loof, N.: Cloud Development and Deployment with CloudBees. Packt Publishing, Birmingham (2013)

35. De Reuver, M., Bouwman, H.: Governance mechanisms for mobile service innovation in value networks. J. Bus. Res. **65**(3), 347–354 (2012)

Learning for Professional Competence in an IS Context

Peter M. Bednar[1(✉)] and Christine Welch[2]

[1] School of Computing, University of Portsmouth, Portsmouth, UK
peter.bednar@port.ac.uk
[2] Portsmouth Business School, University of Portsmouth, Portsmouth, UK
christine.welch@port.ac.uk

Abstract. This paper considers the nature of professionalism as an expression of more than technical competence. This is related to the incidence of failure in IS change projects. We discuss how professionalism may be displayed, relating this to learning processes. The essential qualities of desire, exercise of will and their role in professional judgment are considered in relation to transcendent values espoused by professionals. We note that organizational consumers of information are also professionals, and not simply passive 'users' of systems. We relate this to the environment of Information Systems research and practice, including recognition of the importance of contextual dependencies.

Keywords: Professional competence · Extra-role behavior · Organizational learning · Information systems · IS failures

1 Introduction

The main concern of this paper is to highlight some key concerns that must be considered by IS professionals/analysts. In the IS community, we need to prioritize a perspective on human activity systems as integrated wholes, and the needs of unique individuals within them, rather than focusing blindly on 'model users' [1]. We reflect upon the high incidence of reported failures of Information Systems innovations in organizations over recent decades, relating this to the nature of professional competence in IS development practice and the learning which underpins it. The discussion draws upon secondary material reporting on failures, including one particular case that has received much public attention in the UK – attempts to introduce Computer Aided Dispatch systems in the London Ambulance Service.

We begin by examining the nature of organizations as dynamic, open systems. This is relevant to the nature of professional IS practice and the requirements for professional competence, discussed in the next section. The paper goes on to examine instances of failure in IS innovation projects, before returning to consideration of appropriate learning to underpin improved professional competence and attempting to draw some conclusions.

© IFIP International Federation for Information Processing 2016.
Published by Springer International Publishing Switzerland 2016. All Rights Reserved.
U.L. Snis et al. (Eds.): IFIP8.6 2016, LNBIP 259, pp. 163–175, 2016.
DOI: 10.1007/978-3-319-43597-8_12

1.1   Organization as a System

Figure 1 shows an organization as a system, with a hierarchical structure of functioning sub-systems, interrelated via channels for monitoring, feedback and communication. A boundary has been set, differentiating this system from its environment, i.e. those aspects of the world which influence system behavior but cannot be controlled from within it. This is effectively a closed systems view, within certain parameters.

Let us imagine a systemic model of a health center for example. Sub-systems include operational systems for patient consultations, therapy sessions, booking appointments, etc. A practice management system resources the center, provides for rule setting to regulate its use, and ensure effective staffing and materials/equipment. A monitoring system measures levels of supplies, wear-and-tear on equipment, waiting times, etc. and alerts the management system to a need for further resources or actions to ensure continued effective functioning. The environment [forces affecting the system but not controlled by it] include local demographics, patient demands, policies of the Department of Health and Primary Care trusts, and current medical research.

We can recognize this generic picture of health centers. However, it does not enable us to distinguish characteristics of any particular center. The qualities, experience, attitudes, beliefs, professional dedication and interests of particular medical staff and therapists employed in a particular center [and, indeed, the individual characteristics of other stakeholders such as patients or health service administrators] create a unique organization that such a model fails to capture.

Checkland and Poulter [2, p. 56] point out that, at any particular time, organizational behavior subsists as an accommodation between differing perspectives of stakeholders. This suggests that the view shown in Fig. 1 represents only a 'snapshot' of a phenomenon that is dynamic and constantly changing. As Mumford points out, e.g. [3], an open systems perspective on organizations is preferable. Any organization subsists from moment to moment as an emergent property of the interactions among the people who are its members. In the context of networked organizations, dynamic complexity is not merely expanded but radically altered. In a networked society, therefore, ICTs support transformations in organizational life as it is lived.

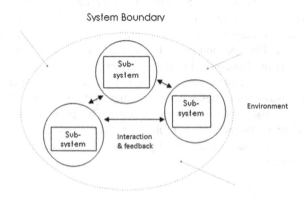

Fig. 1. Model of an organization as a system

Bednar [4] describes an alternative view of organizational emergence, recognizing that any individual component of a purposeful activity system may possess emergent properties that are greater than the 'whole'. Individual components may be participating in several perceived 'Systems' at the same time [reflecting our multifaceted experience of 'real' life]. Thus, a model of a system may be more akin to a set than a hierarchical model [see Fig. 2]. The system under consideration and any of its component systems are open and dynamic in a multidimensional way. Boundaries are not fixed but subject to continual re-drawing, depending on how the perspectives of interested observer[s] may shift to reflect fluctuating purpose[s] over time [5]. Organizational roles can also be seen to fluctuate - created and recreated as the perspectives/ intentions of individual actors and their interactions shift. Furthermore, individual actors may occupy multiple roles, creating an effect of 'flipping' perspectives, shaped by contextual dependencies in a constant state of flux. Any particular actor's experience of working life will differ from day to day, and the actor is continually creating and recreating him/herself, through experiences in multiple roles within various systems in which s/he is a participant member. As pointed out by Ulrich [6, 7] in his discussion of boundary critique, perception of a system varies with the stance of the observer. This highlights the importance of effective participation in organizational decision-making.

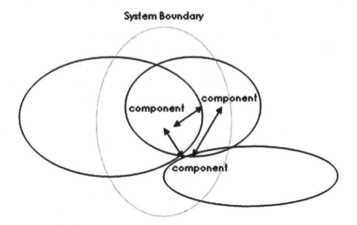

Fig. 2. An organization as a dynamic, open system

Langefors [8, p. 53] pointed out that organizations require direction from 'managers' in order to pursue their aims, and that managers require data about all activities and transactions conducted in order to provide appropriate direction. He concludes, therefore, that an Information System and the organization in which it is located must necessarily be seen as one and the same.

Recognizing this point, we now move on to consider the bases of professional competence, in relation to development of organizational information systems.

2 Professional Practice and Competence

Traditionally, management thinking favored a view that decisions can be derived rationally from objective analysis of relevant data. This view has been reflected in many approaches to Information Systems development, where 'users' are asked to specify their requirements from proposed systems, which professional analysts then translate into terms realizable by computing specialists. This perspective is subject to criticism [9, 10]. It is a mistake to regard organizational actors as passive 'users' or consumers of technologies [11, 12]. Distinguish scholar Borje Langefors, one of the founding fathers of IFIPWG8, suggested long ago that:

Nowadays the insight is spreading that to determine IS user needs ... requires a search-learning process through which the users develop an understanding of what their real needs are and what new opportunities have become available to them. As a consequence, the users emerge as the key persons in the task of analyzing user needs. Information analysts appear to have an important part in aiding the users in learning and analyzing, in doing the documentation in a way understandable to the users, while efficient as a design input for the data system design stages to follow [13, p. 6].

This view of 'professional' practice makes it clear that the term that must be extended to all organizational actors who are stakeholders in a proposed system, not just to IT specialists. Alvesson [14] has questioned the usefulness of modern views of 'professionalism'. Some occupations traditionally described under different terms [craft? job?] have now been reinvented under the label of 'profession'. This has often been accompanied by adoption of grandiose titles, unreflective of the real significance of the work to be accomplished. While this has sometimes helped to advance the status of participants, it has also, at times, complicated and confused ideas about practice and underpinning education for practice. However, in the context of IS development, it is preferable to regard all stakeholders as professionals within their own zones of competence, rather than consigning them to generalized obscurity under the title 'user' [11].

In relation to those actors primarily concerned to promote systems development, technical skills/knowledge relevant to the domain of competence are, of course, necessary; but these are insufficient in themselves without a desire to engage [15]. A professional is someone able to reflect upon practice of certain skills in context, and relate these reflections to a body of standards and values transcending his/her immediate job-role. Often, this involves membership of wider communities of practice – formal or informal [16], emphasizing the duality of tacit and explicit 'knowing' inherent in exercise of any professional expertise [16, 17]. Bruner [24] points out that people do not just learn about the world, they also learn to be in their world.

More recently, Wenger-Trayner adopted the concept of 'knowledgeability', [21, 25] which involves modulation by individuals of their identification among multiple sources of accountability [21]. Knowledgeability is gained through participation in multiple communities, some enduring; others more ephemeral. Individuals develop competence by negotiating a path through complex systems of communities and boundaries, possibly over a protracted period. Wenger-Trayner uses the metaphor of a 'landscape of practice' to denote this system [21].

How would the individual improve his/her professional practice over time? What motives would govern whether s/he complies with any particular instruction to act in a certain way? Engagement with the context of application leading to reflection upon practice can promote a productive learning spiral [10, 15, 22], or what Gherardi [23] refers to as 'the creative entanglement of knowing and doing'. It is through profound engagement with context and attachment to a transcendent system of values and standards that we recognize a professional at work, as opposed to, say, a capable amateur.

Within a formal organizational structure, a person may have a job description expressed in terms of appropriate skills, knowledge and roles. This is likely to bear only a loose resemblance to actual professional work carried out. Roles are created and re-created in conjunction with colleagues, taking into account professional standards. Desire to demonstrate skills in context according to particular standards and values is demonstrated in part through the informal organization [9, 24]. Exercise of judgment is an essential part of professional life. Sometimes, when faced with a dilemma, a person will justify an action by the words 'I had no choice!'. The suggestion that there is no choice here is a fallacy [5, 15, 25]. A person who habitually chooses a course of action that s/he knows will please 'the Boss' on these grounds is actually saying is that, weighing up the potential consequences of each available choice, s/he took the line of least resistance. Professionalism requires that we recognize the choices we make [including the choice to do nothing], their relationship to a wider value system, and their impact upon the contexts of professional life. It is important to remember that, in any context within which Information Systems development taking place, several/many different groups of professionals are at work, of which Systems Analysts are only one.

Drawing on work by Giddens [20] and Foucault [26], Walsham [27] reminds us that power relations pervade all organizational activity and discourse, and that continuous political processes impact upon any local change initiative. It is possible to perceive use of the term 'user' [denoting those professionals who are consumers of the proposed IS] as an effort to exercise power over them, both by initiating stakeholders - such as managers - and by IT specialists. However, those 'users' themselves exercise power of their own. It is important here to consider sense-making activities in relation to experience of work systems [28]. Vaast and Walsham [29] have considered how people make sense of their work practices through narratives that constitute shared social representations. Practices are reproduced where there is consonance between perceptions of action and these representations. Where gradual change in work context is experienced, adaptations in representations occur to maintain this consonance. Radical disruptions to context, such as IT innovation, may not be so readily assimilated. Devaujany [30] used a critical realist perspective to shed light on sociotechnical reflexivity, pointing out that internal conversations about technology and its use shape individual experiences on an on-going basis.

In understanding underpinnings of IS success or failure, it is important to consider agency of all groups of professionals upon project outcomes. The next section of the paper focuses specifically on the phenomenon of IS failure, using an illustrative case study.

3   Failure in IS Innovation

In 2007, the IT Governance Institute commissioned research into the incidence of IT project failure [31], gathering evidence from IT projects in a variety of organizations of differing sizes and fields. Out of almost 1700 projects, only 53 [3%] were formally cancelled, but 31% either delivered or were expected to deliver negative value.

Thorp comments that persistence with projects already known to be failing could be attributed to a culture of blame within many organizations, such that cancellation of a project prior to completion was seen as a sign of weakness. Williams [32], commenting on this survey, highlights a discrepancy between organizational discourse emphasizing rationality and decision-making grounded in the cognitive zone, when there is clear evidence that emotions, e.g. fear of blame and intransigence are impacting upon project status.

3.1   IT Innovation at the London Ambulance Service

Failures of two projects to introduce Computer Aided Dispatch [CAD] systems into the London Ambulance Service, in 1987 and 1993, have been well documented in the Press. An independent inquiry [the Page Inquiry] was conducted, whose terms of reference were to 'identify the lessons to be learned for the operation and management of the London Ambulance Service against the imperatives of delivering service at the required standard, demonstrating good working relationships and restoring public confidence'. Overall the operational issues identified by Page can be summarized as: technical problems, including software bugs and incompatibilities/hand-shake failures between units; poor user involvement in initial specification and lack of ownership of the solution; poor staff relations and communication; inadequate training; big bang approach from manual to automated system with concurrent changes to working practices.

Subsequently, LAS successfully implemented a CAD system [CTAK] developed in-house. In 2009, an initiative was undertaken to replace CTAK with a complete package [CommandPoint], employing a leading global security company. The remit was to install the software with minimal changes to work practices. An internal report, presented to the LAS Trust Board in May of 2011 [the Armitage Report] was intended to be an assessment of the state of readiness for the Service to implement CommandPoint, with particular reference to lessons learned and recommendations set out by Page. The first part of the report dealt with technical recommendations, pointing out that extensive testing had been done, surfacing a number of problems that had been dealt with. Some outstanding problems were highlighted, including tensions between different staff groups; requirement for changes to communication styles and terminologies; untested interface with Police systems; and a need to deal with some remaining bugs and faults. It was stated that 'users' had been fully involved in the project, under the auspices of the Deputy Director of Operations, who provided 'consistent and effective user input at a senior level throughout the procurement and implementation phase' - bringing in other users as and when their input was needed. The sense of staff ownership of CommandPoint was stated to be 'remarkable' and the feedback from training positive, as was feedback from 'staff-side representatives'.

Some modifications to working practices were deemed necessary, particularly to the layout of the Control Room. These changes were considered relatively minor, and based on 'sound reasons' of operational efficiency. Dry-run simulations had appeared satisfactory and a Readiness Checklist was provided and signed off by the Deputy Chief Executive prior to going live. It appeared that all was ready to go ahead with the project. Only in appendices to the report was a note of caution introduced. The section on Risks referred to the following: lack of user confidence in the solution; negative publicity for LS; and system performance not meeting user expectations.

In June 2011, the new system went live, and immediately collapsed. The Control Room operators were obliged to revert to pen-and-paper for a time. Delays in despatch during this failure contributed to the death of at least one patient and resulted in litigation by another. Many software 'bugs' emerged after going live. It emerged that, as the project progressed, it had slipped further and further behind schedule, creating budget pressures. In consequence, a freeze was placed on further changes or requirements. This was not mentioned in the schedule of risks and is likely to have had a grave impact upon likelihood of success. An investigation into the collapse suggested the root causes to be: failure of CommandPoint to deliver the system, technical and operational functionality expected; critical configuration issues not identified during testing; lack of operational procedures in place in the event of a critical system failure; failure to integrate the project into business as usual.

3.2 Discussion

Looking at the ways in which failure was experienced in 2011, there is a remarkable similarity to the conclusions of the Page Report on the earlier project failures. Since a great deal of effort and expense was undertaken to pursue a project informed by these recommendations, one must ask whether there are not more fundamental lessons to be learned. It may be significant that no mention is made of the team responsible for creation and implementation of the earlier CTAK system. It seems likely that many lessons were learned in the course of implementing and running this system over a period of several years. Was this useful information made available to the CommandPoint project team?

The internal report placed great emphasis on rigor of development processes – testing; training; involvement of 'users'. Subsequent events, however, cast this into question. The Trust Board met in anticipation of greater demand for ambulances during the upcoming London Olympic Games. Minutes indicated that risks reported to the Board included lack of user confidence in the solution, due to system performance not meeting user expectation; staff unrest and consequent poor publicity were anticipated. Thus, previous confidence about the level of 'user' involvement and positive 'user' feedback during training seem to have evaporated. The Board was of a risk that 'lack of confidence in the reliability and functionality of the system and data by operational users will alienate staff, undermine confidence and/or create suspicion leading to confused expectations'.

CommandPoint had previously been used successfully in the United States by both law enforcement and city fire services. On this basis, it was assumed that it could be

introduced into LAS with only a minimum of changes to work practices and cus-
tomization. Involvement of 'users' seems to have been limited to participation in
training and consultation via the Director of Operations. This suggests that those professionals whose work was involved in dealing with public calls for ambulance services,
triage of priorities and, significantly, those driving through London and providing
interim medical aid to patients, were only minimally involved in any decision-making
about the new system. Assumptions were made about the work practices of staff and the
impact upon them of changes to Computer Aided Dispatch. No opportunity was
available for any of the staff to reflect upon the usefulness of the changes and take
ownership of the new System – all decisions were made remotely at Trust Board Level.
In other words, the actors engaged in the work of the Service were not treated as
professionals in their own right, but as passive 'users'.

It is important here to distinguish between 'usefulness' in context and other terms
such as 'usability', which is concerned with ergonomic characteristics. This distinction
is one that may be overlooked when staff are offered training in new systems. Only
particular users, engaging with particular technologies in order to carry out work, can
decide whether they perceive them to be useful [33]. McGrath [34] discusses emotion
in the context of the earlier LAS projects, from the early 1990's. Here, it appeared that
the prevailing culture of public service and empathic support for patients within LAS
came into direct conflict with a rational planning ethic intended to increase 'efficiency'.
McGrath reflects that: "The case reveals that existing, even apparently latent, conflicts
and emotions may surface or heighten when IS innovation is attempted. In the LAS-
CAD case, these subjugated knowledges and emotions emerged during efforts to
achieve cultural change of the LAS through the use of ICTs inscribed with
government-driven efficiency logic" [34, p. 297]. It would seem that these lessons were
not learned in the interim.

Friis [35] Points to a need for engaged professionals to take ownership over their
own work systems, including change projects, in order to promote usefulness.
A 'symbiosis of knowledge' is needed between technical experts and working professionals who have tacit understandings of contextual dependencies. This can be
achieved through constructive and situated dialogue. She suggests an approach of
user-controlled information systems development, achieved when the future 'users' are
regarded not only as problem owners, but also as problem solvers, taking responsibility
for design and making binding decisions about the design project [35, p. 225]. Such an
approach, we suggest, requires professional engagement and commitment from both
communities of practice.

In the sections that follow, we discuss professional commitment to action as
involving more than rational, role-based activities but involving exercise of will to
adhere to a value system. The impact of extra role behaviour [36, 37] in this context will
be highlighted as a key factor in promoting creation of productive learning spirals [15].

4   Engagement and Competence

Rogers [38], in his discussion on diffusion of technology, distinguishes between different types of threshold, e.g. the difference between ignorance and knowledge of how a
technology might be applied as a solution for a particular problem - a key aspect of

professional competence; or the distinction between theory espoused and theory in use [39]. Discourse about intention often fails to take into account the investment of personal resources needed to address the required 'unlearning' [11, 12, 40, 41] involved in innovative practice. There appears to be an unwitting belief in rational behavior as if professional life could be conducted without any emotion. In the LAS case [above], it appears that this belief has persisted through a catalogue of successive failures, even though successive inquiries have reported that staff engagement, confidence and morale were crucial factors, and recommended greater staff involvement in future projects.

Possession of relevant skills/knowledge for a work role is insufficient without ability to exercise judgment in exercising those skills, related to a system of values that transcend the immediate context. This is the essence of professional engagement. In relation to Information System, as in art, desire can only be realized as we open up creative spaces for ourselves [42].

In a professional context, reflection is needed to negotiate such spaces [12, 22, 40]. These can become blocked through inappropriate management assumptions [15, 43–45], such as are evident in the LAS case regarding modification of work systems. As we have seen, an organization may be viewed as a system, made up of interacting elements. If any one element leaves the whole, or is changed, then it is no longer the same system and all other elements are necessarily affected [8, 43]. There is a need for design practice to address whole work systems and not just systems for use of particular artefacts. It is necessary for engaged actors to reflect upon their professional roles, engagement in those roles, and on engagement of the 'others', in order to avoid becoming entrapped in a double bind [11, 15, 16, 41, 46] in which they cannot create those choices that would empower escape. It is possible to observe 'disconnectedness', i.e. failure to reflect [30]. Entrapment can occur where a person feels that there are no choices open to him/her that will satisfy desire [5, 15, 25, 41, 47, 48]. This might be due to a lack of recognition of choices that are available, or inhibition of ability to create choices, as in the case described by Thorp, above [31]. Competence in judgment is required. However, this will not necessarily lead to appropriate action on its own, without desire for engagement.

The next section of the paper discusses such professional engagement, and its relationship to extra-role behavior in organizations.

4.1 Extra-Role Behavior and Professional Development

Engagement, within a professional context, is related to the phenomenon of extra-role behavior [21, 51]. We are faced with complexity of multiple, competing desires in many contexts [4, 15, 33, 41], partly due to the impact of opportunity cost – any choice to expend finite resources, including time, involves choosing between priorities. Boundary setting [6, 8, 15, 41, 44] is also involved, however. Channeled desire comes about through commitment to certain values and consequences. Efforts to recognize boundaries of competence involve extra-role behavior or improvisation [49]. Ciborra comments on the MIR space station in relation to bricolage [50, p. 2]. 'Up there, revolving in space, one could find, hand-in-hand, advanced, robust engineering solutions, rustic deign, and widespread virtuoso tinkering.'

Such 'extra-role behavior' becomes possible only through commitment to on-going reflection upon competence. There is also paradox in that a professional engaged must reflect upon 'the future' whilst still involved in creating it. This involves higher orders of learning [12, 15] in which an individual is reflecting not only upon experience, but upon the process of reflecting on exercising judgment - an exercise in practical philosophy as part of professional competence in action [12].

The engagement of particular individuals in professional work roles is accepted as a key attribute of organizational life from many points of view [45, 52, 53]. When interviewing a job applicant, employers often ask about the candidate's hobbies and interests. A person who cannot offer anything beyond the strict requirements of the job may not be considered suitable. However, there is a possibility that we concentrate too much upon role performance when modelling organizations as human activity systems, to the exclusion of proper recognition of extra-role behaviour. This can certainly be seen in the context of the LAS case, where the boundaries of the project were very narrowly drawn and attention to wider work systems, or desires of engaged professional staff, were specifically excluded, even where known risks were at stake. Work roles are shaped through interactions with others – co-workers, collaborators and also family, friends and acquaintances - in multiple contexts. These matters have long been recognized in the fields such as organizational behavior and human resource management, through the concepts of formal and informal organizations [see, e.g. 54]. A professional's desire to demonstrate her skills in context according to particular standards and values is demonstrated in part through the informal organization, drawing upon wider communities of practice. Recognition has been given to this dimension within the field of Systems modelling too, e.g. in the Soft Systems Methodology [2] through focus on a cultural stream of inquiry.

It is also not uncommon for managers in organizations to suggest that they wish their staff to be creative or innovative - to go beyond their formal roles and skill profiles, to exercise all their personal resources in addressing messy and complex demands of organizational life [21]. Such personal resources will have been acquired and exercised through the individual's total life experience, not just those experiences that form part of their specific work roles. In this instance, the view of individual emergence adopted is that suggested in Fig. 2. While work roles typically involve multiple contextual dependencies, life experiences of individual people nevertheless transcend them. It is possible to argue that organizational sustainability is critically dependent upon creativity and extra-role behavior to generate innovation and drive the organization forward.

5 Conclusion

We have looked at the nature of professional commitment and how transcendent value systems and the exercise of judgment are important in creation of beneficial organizational developments. We argue a professional is therefore someone who is able to reflect upon practice of skills in context, and to relate these reflections to a body of standards and values transcending the his/her immediate job role. Often, this involves membership of a wider landscape of practice – formal or informal. It might be expected then that a professional would engage in extra-role behavior, e.g. suggesting innovative methods, or making efforts to help others in their professional roles.

The potential to go beyond basic requirements of a role to create new boundaries involves a higher level of reflection. Thus, extra-role behavior becomes possible only through commitment to on-going reflection upon competence. Such reflection involves higher orders of learning [15] in which the individual is reflecting not only upon experience, but upon the process of reflecting on exercising judgment. This development of a learning 'spiral' may be regarded as an exercise in practical philosophy. It follows that a rational planning model for considering organizational choices involves an inherent paradox for unwary actors. This is clearly demonstrated in the events unfolded in the LAS case. Since any observation must, by definition, be made by a particular observer, adoption of a 'neutral' stance cannot be achieved in practice. This means that those who espouse rational planning are unaware that any data they gather about a dynamic and constantly-recreating problem space is inherently misleading, since they are failing to recognize their own, situated assumptions [41]. Ability to act as a professional is, we argue, crucially dependent upon ability to exercise extra-role behavior.

Our conclusion is that it is of utmost importance that efforts made within IS communities must prioritize human activity systems, and engage contextual dependencies from a critical perspective, in order to promote systems that are experienced as contextually relevant [useful]. What Meyers and Klein [55] describe as an explicit critique and improvement of social condition is necessary to develop richer meanings and understandings.

References

1. Bednar, P.M., Welch, C.: Critical systemic thinking or the standard engineer in Paris. In: Proceedings of 4th European Conference on Research Methods in Business & Management Conference. University of Paris-Dauphine, Academic-Publishing International (2005)
2. Checkland, P., Poulter, J.: Learning for Action. Wiley, Chichester (2006)
3. Mumford, E.: The story of socio-technical design: reflections in its successes, failures and potential. Inf. Syst. J. 16(4), 317–342 (2006)
4. Bednar, P.: Individual emergence in contextual analysis. Systemica 14(1–6), 23–38 (2007)
5. Lee, Y., Kozar, K.A., Larsen, K.R.T.: The technology acceptance model: past, present, and future. Commun. AIS 50(12), 752–780 (2003)
6. Ulrich, W.: Reflective practice in the civil society: the contribution of critically systemic thinking. Ref. Pract. 1(2), 247–268 (2000)
7. Ulrich, W.: Critical Systems Discourse: Rethinking Critical Systems Thinking. Open University, Milton Keynes (2005). Seminar 9 May 2005
8. Langefors, B.: Essays on Infology. Studentlitteratur, Lund (1995)
9. Lindblom, C.E.: The science of muddling through. Public Adm. Rev. 19(2), 79–88 (1959)
10. Whitaker, R.: Applying phenomenology and hermeneutics in IS design. In: Nissen, H.-E., Bednar, P.M., Welch, C. (eds.) Use and Design in IS: Double Helix Relationships? Informing Science Press, Santa Rosa (2007)

11. Nissen, H.-E.: Challenging traditions of inquiry in software practice. In: Dittrich, Y., Floyd, C., Klischewski, R. (eds.) Social Thinking-Software Practice, pp. 71–89. MIT Press, Cambridge (2002)

12. Churchman, C.W.: The Design of Inquiring Systems. Basic Books, New York (1971)

13. Langefors, B.: Analysis of user needs. In: Bracchi, G., Lockemann, P.C. (eds.) Information Systems Methodology. LNCS, vol. 65, pp. 1–38. Springer, Heidelberg (1978)

14. Alvesson, M.: The Triumph of Emptiness. Oxford University Press, Oxford (2013)

15. Bednar, P.M., Welch, C.: Incentive and desire: covering a missing category. In: Proceedings of MCIS, Venice, October 2006

16. Lave, J., Wenger, E.: Situated Learning: Legitimate Peripheral Participation. Cambridge University Press, Cambridge (1991)

17. Brown, J.S., Duguid, P.: Organizational learning and communities of practice. Organ. Sci. 2(1), 40–57 (1991)

18. Brown, J.S., Duguid, P.: Knowledge and organization: a social-practice perspective. Organ. Sci. 12(2), 198–213 (2001)

19. Bruner, J.: The Culture of Education. Harvard University Press, Cambridge (1996)

20. Giddens, A.: The Constitution of Society: Outline of the Theory of Structuration. Polity Press, Cambridge (1984)

21. Wenger-Trayner, E. (ed.): Learning in Landscapes of Practice. Routledge, Abingdon (2015)

22. Nissen, H.-E., Bednar, P., Welch, C.: Double helix relationships in use and design of informing systems: lessons to learn from phenomenology and hermeneutics. Informing Sci. 10, 1–19 (2007)

23. Gherardi, S.: To start practice theorizing anew: the contribution of the concepts of agencement and formativeness. Organization (2015). Pre-publication on-line, 21 September 2015, doi:1350508415605174

24. Etzioni, A.: The Active Society. The Free Press, New York (1968)

25. Gilovich, T.: How We Know What Isn't So. The Free Press, New York (1991)

26. Foucault, M.: Discipline and Punish. Vintage Books, New York (1979)

27. Walsham, G.: Interpreting Information Systems in Organizations. Wiley, Chichester (1993)

28. Weick, K.E.: Sensemaking in Organizations. Sage, Thousand Oaks (1995)

29. Vaast, E., Walsham, G.: Representations and actions: the transformation of work practices with IT use. Inf. Organ. 15(1), 65–89 (2005)

30. De Vaujany, F.-X.: Capturing reflexivity modes in IS: a critical realist approach. Inf. Organ. 8(1), 51–72 (2008)

31. Thorp, J.: IT project cancellations: pay now or pay later. ISACA J. 1, 18–19 (2008)

32. Williams, P.: Make sure you get a positive return. Comput. Wkly 13, 18–20 (2007)

33. Bednar, P., Welch, C.: A double helix metaphor for use and usefulness in informing systems. Informing Sci. 10, 273–295 (2007)

34. McGrath, K.: Affection not affliction: the role of emotions in information systems and organizational change. Inf. Organ. 16(4), 277–303 (2006)

35. Friis, S.: Information system design: a user involved perspective. In: Gill, Karamjit S. (ed.) Human Machine Symbiosis: The Foundations of Human-Centred Systems Design, pp. 255–312. Springer, London (1996)

36. Nemeth, C.J., Staw, B.M.: The trade-offs of social control and innovation in groups and organizations. In: Berkowitz, L. (ed.) Advances in Experimental Social Psychology, vol. 22, pp. 175–210. Academic Press, New York (1989)

37. Organ, D.W.: Organizational Citizenship Behaviour: The Good Soldier Syndrome. Lexington Books, Lanham (1988)

38. Rogers, E.M.: Diffusion of Innovations. The Free Press, New York (2003)

39. Argyris, C.: Overcoming Organizational Defenses. Prentice Hall, New Jersey (1990)

40. Bednar, P.M.: A contextual integration of individual and organizational learning perspectives as part of IS analysis. Informing Sci. **3**(3), 145–156 (2000)
41. Bednar, P.M., Welch, C.: Bias, misinformation and the paradox of neutrality. Informing Sci. **11**, 85–106 (2008)
42. Mumford, M.D., Scott, G.M., Gaddis, B., Strange, J.M.: Leading creative people: orchestrating expertise and relationships. Leadersh. Quart. **13**(6), 705–750 (2002)
43. Friis, S.: User Controlled Information Systems Development. Lund University Publ., Lund (1991)
44. Checkland, P., Holwell, S.: Information, Systems and Information Systems. Wiley, Chichester (1998)
45. Mumford, E.: Redesigning Human Systems. IRM Press, London (2003)
46. Ulrich, W.: Critically systemic discourse: a discursive approach to reflective practice in ISD. J. Inf. Technol. Theory Appl. **3**(3), 55–106 (2001)
47. Churchman, C.W.: The Systems Approach. Dell Publishing, New York (1968)
48. Churchman, C.W.: The Systems Approach and Its Enemies. Basic Books, New York (1979)
49. Weick, K.E.: Improvisation as a mindset for organisational analysis. Organ. Sci. **9**(5), 543–555 (1998)
50. Ciborra, C.U.: The Labyrinths of Information. Oxford University Press, Oxford (2002)
51. Van Dyne, L., LePine, A.J.: Helping and voice extra-role behaviour: evidence of construct and predictive validity. Acad. Manag. J. **41**(1), 108–119 (1998)
52. Davenport, T., Prusak, L.: Working Knowledge. Harvard Business School Press, Cambridge (2000)
53. Mullins, L.: Management and Organizational Behaviour, 8th edn. Financial Times/Prentice Hall, Harlow (2007)
54. Krackhardt, D., Hanson, J.R.: Informal Networks: The Company Behind the Chart. Harvard Bus. Rev. **71**(4), 104–111 (1993)
55. Myers, M.D., Klein, H.K.: A set of principles for conducting critical research in information systems. MIS Q. **35**(1), 17–36 (2011)

ICT and Learning Usability at Work

Challenges and Opportunities for Physicians in Everyday Practice

Helena Vallo Hult[1,2(✉)], Katriina Byström[3], and Martin Gellerstedt[1]

[1] School of Business, Economics and IT, University West,
461 86 Trollhättan, Sweden
helena.vallo-hult@hv.se

[2] Fyrbodal Health Academy, NU Hospital Group, 461 85 Trollhättan, Sweden

[3] Department of Archivistics,
Library and Information Science Oslo and Akershus,
University College of Applied Sciences, Gaza City, Norway

Abstract. The medical profession demands training and lifelong learning to ensure patient safety and quality of treatment. Main barriers are lack of time and resources. Information and communication technology (ICT) has proven to be useful to support e-learning, but less focus has been placed on the potential role of ICT as support for continuous learning in everyday practice. The aim of this qualitative interview study was to explore physicians' perspective of learning and how ICT in various ways can support learning at work. The findings indicate that continuous learning to a large extent is case driven, and that ICT may play an important role and support reflection and learning for individual physicians and for the collective as well. We argue that such ICT solutions must be adopted to and integrated in the everyday work, save time and include learning usability.

Keywords: ICT information and communication technology · Informal learning · Information seeking · Physicians · Workplace learning

1 Introduction

The medical profession demands training and lifelong learning to ensure patient safety and quality of treatment. Patients who are more aware of their treatment options, the rapidly growing amount of accessible knowledge and new information and communication technology (ICT) poses challenges but also opportunities in terms of information, communication and learning.

The deficiencies of continued training for medical specialists, mainly due to lack of time and resources, is one challenge that has gained increased attention [1, 2]. Recommendation regarding physicians professional development emphasize that it should cover both clinical and non-clinical aspects and that continuous training needs to focus on daily practice [1]. Furthermore informal learning through i.e. collegial communication, learning by doing and peer-learning is considered an important part of lifelong

© IFIP International Federation for Information Processing 2016.
Published by Springer International Publishing Switzerland 2016. All Rights Reserved.
U.L. Snis et al. (Eds.): IFIP8.6 2016, LNBIP 259, pp. 176–190, 2016.
DOI: 10.1007/978-3-319-43597-8_13

learning [3, 4]. Despite the recognized importance of training and lifelong learning for health professionals, less attention has been paid to how physicians learn in the workplace [5, 6].

Along with keeping up with the latest medical knowledge, physicians have to face an increasingly digitalized workplace. Tablets and smartphones provide quick and easy access to up-to date information and are used in a variety of ways, including information management, decision support and medical education [7–10]. Rapid advances in medicine and technology also provide for innovative health services, such as use of mobile technology for patient information and new technologies for self-care. This has led to an increase of health related ICT (eHealth/mHealth) research [11–14] and practice [15–17]. Despite of documented benefits, many eHealth initiatives have failed to realize predicted benefits in practice, and as a result health professionals are often sceptical and less supportive of eHealth technologies [14].

Research show that use of ICT also has an important role and potential to support continuous training and learning [18, 19] especially on informal learning activities [18, 20, 21]. While social media is well established and used in the external communication, it is only in recent years that focus has been on the use of social technologies for informal communication, collaboration and learning within organizations [22–25]. Current research highlight that engagement in social media and use of online tools for knowledge sharing and collaboration can be a key way for health professionals to continuously learn and incorporate lifelong learning principles in daily work [26–28].

Successful design and implementation of ICT in health care demands an understanding of the context, both on an organizational level but also on an individual level [13, 14, 29]. Practical experiences point out that many IT systems are perceived as time-consuming, non-user friendly, poorly integrated in medical practice and incompatible with each other [25, 26]. As a consequence it is fundamental to examine individual physicians' perception and experience of ICT, its use and potential in practice.

The aim of this study is to gain a better understanding of physicians' perception of learning in the workplace, and to explore how ICT in various ways can support and contribute to information related activities such as collegial communication, collaboration, knowledge sharing and keeping up to date. The research question is: *How do resident physicians' experience everyday learning in connection to information related activities and ICT, both as individual specialists and as members of a community?*

2 Theoretical Background

Learning in the workplace may occur in different forms and takes place in different settings. It is common to distinguish between formal, non-formal and informal learning. Formal learning usually refers to learning that is organized and structured, leading to certification. Non-formal learning is structured but occurs outside the formal education system, for example courses organized by workplaces. Informal learning refers to learning acquired through every day work, not organized or structured in terms of objectives, time or learning support [3, 30, 31].

A review of the literature on informal learning in the workplace by Le Clus [32] showed that informal learning is often spur-of-the-moment learning and self-directed, highlighting the importance of social context for the learning and concludes that if informal learning emerges during everyday activities in the workplace, there is potential for this type of learning to occur more often than formal learning. According to Eraut [33, 34] most learning in the workplace is informal and consists of both learning from others and from personal experience, and although informal learning contributes to most of the learning in workplaces (70–90 %) it is often not looked upon as learning but instead occurs as a by-product of engaging in work activities.

The notion that learning is a social process embedded in everyday life and work, as opposed to merely the acquisition of knowledge and skills, is central for theories of situated learning and communities of practice [35, 36]. According to this perspective learning and knowing is related to engagement in practice through participation and interaction with others, and the informal learning that comes with it [37]. More recent work by Wenger et al. [38] introduce the concept of knowledgeability as an outcome of learning with respect to a landscape of practice rather than focusing on a single community of practice, referring to social learning capability and professional knowledge as something not only associated with competence in specific practices but a negotiation of identity and claim of competence in and across an increasingly complex landscape of practice.

Research on physicians learning has shown that traditional education focus on formal learning and medical or scientific knowledge, which might not provide the students with other skills necessary needed throughout their working life [39], such as evidence based practice and lifelong learning [40] or ICT skills [13, 41]. Hansson and Marklund [42] highlights in a Swedish study that resident doctors believe it is important to acquire a scientific and critical way of thinking in order to be able to examine their own practice and to respond adequately to the patients' questions and that the education should relate more to their own everyday practice. Reflection and reflective practice has long been recognized as an important part of continuous professional development in healthcare [43, 44]. According to Schön [45] there is a difference between reflection in action (during the experience, at point of care when treating patients in clinical practice) and reflection on action (in retrospective, after an experience or particular situation has happened, consulting colleagues or the literature). Although the original focus of this distinction was on individual reflection, as shown by Prilla et al. [46] it also applies to collaborative reflection.

Within research on information behaviour, there has been an increasing interest in health professionals' information seeking as a result of rapid growth of medical information [47]. Earlier studies have mainly focused on physicians' information needs and use, with emphasis on formal information sources related to either keeping up to date or clinical treatment and patient care [48, 49]. More recent studies have focused on information seeking in context, highlighting information access, usability issues and information overload [50, 51]. Also access to online health information is challenging the professional identity and redefining roles of physician and patient [52].

Many studies on ICT and information seeking in health care focus on how the new technology can help increase efficiency, patient safety and quality of care (from the individual doctor's point of view), and do not have learning as their focus. They do emphasize on the benefits of ICT for education purposes and training, but do not look at learning as such. Although not explicit, the new technology is seen as useful for learning purposes such as: search for information and answers to questions in everyday clinical practice (individual learning); communication, collaboration and peer-to-peer learning (collective learning); the introduction of standards, best practices, guidelines and recommendations (organizational learning).

3   Methodology

This study is based on 15 individual semi-structured interviews with Swedish resident physicians. The research approach is qualitative, which is appropriate since the purpose of the research is explorative, aiming at gaining deeper understanding of the meanings, experiences, and views of the physicians [cf. 53]. The interviews were transcribed and analysed first manually and later with the qualitative data analysis software NVivo 10 [e.g. 54].

3.1   Setting and Participants

Resident physicians are a typical specialized profession, which has long been committed to lifelong learning. They practice as physicians but are also engaged in a minimum of five years continued clinical training towards specialist competence. In Sweden this is the responsibility of the public health authorities, not the higher education [55].

There are a number of different documents and frameworks that directly or indirectly control and imposes on physicians to keep up to date and continuously learn in professional practice. All members of the health care staff are to carry out their work in accordance with science and proven experience, and the patient shall be given competent and attentive health care that meets these requirements [56]. Working with Evidence Based Medicine (EBM) means integrating individual clinical expertise with the best available external clinical evidence from systematic research [57].

3.2   Data Collection and Analysis

Semi-structured interviews were conducted with individual physicians, attending a course on scientific approach during the spring semester 2015, as part of their specialist medical training[1]. The research project was introduced to the physicians at the beginning of the course. Thereafter an invitation to participate was sent by email to all attendees. The invitation email was explaining the purpose and objectives of the study,

---

[1] The regulations and general guidelines for doctors' specialist medical training by the Swedish National Board of Health and Welfare (2008), stipulate that the trainee should acquire a scientific approach, by attending a course and by carrying out an individual written work.

also emphasizing that although the study was carried out in connection with the course, the intention was not to evaluate the course or knowledge level of participants.

There were totally 24 course attendants, 18 agreed to participate in the study and a total of 15 interviews were completed. Each interview lasted for about 1 h and was recorded on tape. Prior to the study two pilot interviews were carried out to test the interview guide, resulting in minor adjustments. Informed consent was obtained according to Codex Rules & Guidelines [58].

The interview guide was developed by the researchers, with expertise in scientific methods and workplace learning, together with a senior physician experienced in qualitative methods in the selected population. It was structured around three key themes, as shown in Table 1, with open, explorative questions, aiming to encourage the respondents to talk freely on the subjects.

Table 1. Semi-structured interview guide

Question themes	Aim/purpose
Continuous professional development (CPD) and learning in the workplace	Gain a deeper understanding on information seeking in relation to continuous learning, and to identify formal and informal networks for knowledge sharing and exchange of experiences
Information use and needs in the clinical practice	Obtain an understanding of problem solving in the clinical work, including the physician-patient relation, with regard to communication and information aspects
Information and communication technology (ICT) and views on the future	Identify what challenges and opportunities resident physicians relate with use of ICT, and explore their views on digitalization and use of mobile technology (for learning and information seeking) in the working life of today and in the future

Initial analysis was conducted manually by the interviewing researcher. All interviews were transcribed and read through multiple times with the purpose to obtain a sense of the whole material. Key words and interesting aspects were highlighted, and reflections, impressions and observations from the interviews were written down as field notes. All interview transcripts and field notes were formatted and imported into NVivo. Interview data were read and coded iteratively, followed by a process including multiple coding to different nodes and recoding nodes into broader/narrower themes during analysis. A basic coding scheme with was developed with descriptions of each node and secondary analysis were conducted by a second researcher.

4 Findings and Analysis

The results are presented according to the themes, as shown in Fig. 1: *patient cases as the engine for learning* (self-learning, collegial learning and evidence based learning), *Patient perspective* (googling patients pros and cons, pedagogical task) and *the promising potentials beyond the technical hassles.*

Thematic nodes

Name	Sources	References
⊟ ○ Patient cases as the engine for learning	17	389
○ Collegial learning	17	149
⊞ ○ Evidence based learning	17	103
○ Self-learning	17	126
⊟ ○ Patient perspective	16	156
○ Googling patient pros and cons	15	60
○ Pedagogical task	16	96
⊟ ○ The promising potentials beyond the technical hassles	18	534
⊞ ○ Challenges	17	211
○ ICT	16	104
○ Potential	17	192

Fig. 1. Thematic nodes, sources and references coded

4.1 Patient Cases as the Engine for Learning

Self-Learning. The participating physicians had a strong focus on their own respon-sibility for learning. Many of them expressed this as a matter of professional identity, being a doctor is about being reflective, analytic and continuously keeping up to date:*"...but it is also a part of work, to always trying to learn and keep updated and work from the best knowledge available"*. Also relating this to patient responsibility, as a doctor you need to make important and well informed decisions about your patients every day: *"And you want to sleep well at night, knowing you have treated your patient the best way possible, so you read, you search, you learn"*. Thus, underpinning this focus, and related to all patient cases were continuous ongoing learning activities, to prepare and study, consulting colleagues and experts, follow up etc. Related to self-learning the physicians also talked about the responsibility of always to be pre-pared to back up decisions with liable arguments based on evidence, not on personal opinion. On the one hand a critical approach is essential for making decisions based on individual experience and judgement, as well as listening to and learning from col-leagues and experts, and on the other hand following procedure and recommendations for treatment and common best practice. Throughout the interviews the physicians expressed this as being a balance in the progression of becoming a specialist: *"it used to be that I had to search because I didn't know, but now I have more experience and searching is more for confirmation"* But with experience comes also a risk to lose motivation for learning *"and you think you know because you learned it a long time ago, but now to take the time to search and keep updated on things you know, you just don't have that time"*. Several commented on reading medical news in trade press and journal articles at evenings or on the bus to work, but explicit or implicit not defining it as "real" work. Much the same as with patient administration which is a lot about self-learning, but were often not looked upon as learning as such.

Collegial Learning. The physicians talked also about how they participate in everyday collegial exchange with supervisors, colleagues and experts or consultants. They described how they learn in supervision, but also function as a source for new and updated knowledge for the supervisor: *"there is a desire from the supervisor, and also a stress I think, to learn from me, because I have the new updated knowledge"* Learning from and with colleagues were highlighted by many as an important part of day to day learning, also to a great extent driven by patient cases creating a learning situation:*"We have weakly staff meetings where we discuss patient cases, but we also have open doors and a lot of discussions during the day, and I think this is really how I learn the most"*. Informal learning in the workplace was often addressed from the individual physician's point of view, described in relation to solving problems or asking or questions ad hoc, as they occur in the daily work. From an ICT perspective it is interesting to note that the physicians also called for better structure and more systematic and organized forms for collegial exchange of experiences. They saw the need for collegial learning, confirming it as an important way of learning at work, but hard to maintain *"when the responsibility is imposed upon individual physicians"*.

Evidence Based Learning. The physicians expressed high awareness of the EBM approach to summarize and give recommendation for treatment, based on the best available research evidence: *"As a physician you are trained in critical thinking [...] and pretty used to stand upon summarized regulations and guidelines"*. Many expressed feelings of concern and anxiety as well as to frequently have bad conscience not doing or being enough when it comes to learning and information seeking: *"you don't have time to search for evidence based research, so you just have to go on your own knowledge, and be confident in yourself that you can stand for your decision"*

Condensed Information Site. All of the respondents described that they use the internet daily for seeking work related information, to check for facts or specific documents, or for confirmation: *"So I Google a lot, but it's not like I learn new things, It's more of relearning or refreshing of knowledge that I already have but have forgotten at the time"*. It was also common to use Google as an alternative to bookmarks in the web browser, i.e. to google things you use often both out of convenience and on purpose not to miss out on new search results. The physicians' information seeking and choice of sources had a lot to do with what type of information that was needed at the time which was mostly short and fast answers to specific questions related to the patients or work task at hand. Besides confirmation and fact-checking, Google was used for image seeking (e.g. dermatological) and for finding clips on YouTube. These were regarded as being useful for instructions on how to perform certain procedures, either as information for the doctor or to show to a patient. Systematic information seeking using scientific databases was less common in clinical practices. It was judged as important but was more for specialisation and something done separate from the day to day work. In the everyday working with patients the physicians in general preferred local information and information written in Swedish:*"It's not so advanced the daily work, I don't need PubMed for that, and in case it's more complicated, then there is always national guidelines or recommendation that I can trust"*.

Sources of Authority. Altogether the interviews present a similar picture with respect to online information seeking. The Swedish medical information sites internetmedicin.se and praktiskmedicin.se (practical medicine) were mentioned as the most important sources for information, often referred to as "sources of authority", and were commonly used for case related information seeking. Furthermore, trustworthiness and user-friendliness were highlighted by many of the physicians as important aspects, exemplified by Internetmedicin.se as having both reliable content and an information structure organized according to physicians working methods. Another common remark about internetmedicin.se was that the authors were selected as specialists and authorities in their field of expertise: *"Internetmedicin you can trust, because it's written by experts and then reviewed by other experts so you feel confident that you can go on those recommendations".* Because of that, and since it is such a common information source among doctors, with many professionals reading and using it every day, it ought to be self-correcting (someone would react on incorrect or controversial information). In general the respondents claimed to trust their own judgement and ability to have a critical approach and way of telling if an information needed is trustworthy and correct: *"I can also tell my own opinion based on experience and regulations"* Although collegial learning was highlighted as important, there was also the opinion that turning to trustworthy internet based sources, representing 'the common professional knowledge', may in fact be a better option than getting a subjective opinion from a colleague or specialist at work.

4.2   Patient Perspective

The physicians' major focus was on patient care, which is where and how you learn to be a doctor. Even though the subject was on ICT and physicians learning, it was significant how the patient perspective occurred as a cross-cutting theme throughout the interviews.

Googling Patient Pros and Cons. Patients who google their symptoms were pretty much seen as a common part of the daily clinical practice, and not perceived upon as particularly problematic. Several of the physicians commented from a patient perspective that it may cause unnecessary anxiety and worries for patients who misinterpret googled biased or incorrect information. Other than that most of them emphasized on the positive effects: *"I think it's better when they have searched, because then I don't have to explain everything and that saves time"* and *"you may even learn, and sometimes it might even be helpful with ideas for diagnoses".* Furthermore, when it comes to more unusual diseases, the patient always knows best and contributes with knowledge: *"and in those cases it is obvious that the patient knows more than me so I don't think that is an issue at all".* It was less common among the physicians to search together with patients, but yet something they seemed to do on a regular basis, for example searching for drug related side effects, or looking up something the patient referred to in consultation. Very few commented at all on experiences of quantified self, that is patient generated data i.e. activity bracelets or patient apps for self-care.

Pedagogical Task. Several of the physicians reflected on the doctor-patient relationship and commented on an ongoing change in the medical profession leading them to take on a more pedagogical or consultative role: *"a challenge is to help the patient to reach an understanding, to explain in a pedagogical way so there is no unnecessary worry, and to obtain compliance"*. This was described for example by how taking on responsibility and explain for patients is becoming an important part of the clinical practice. Also by comments that referred to patient information leaflets (1177, patientinformation.se) as a great way to inform the patient. They were aware that patients do not take in information during a consultation but now can go home and read and remember and come to a better understanding. Some of the respondents also commented on how patients may feel about the doctor using Google, that it might look unprofessional. But that neither was seen as a problem nowadays: *"you just explain that this is how we work now, we are modern doctors and have digital access to all this information, and everything is right here in the computer and as a patient you should worry more if we did not use it"*.

4.3   The Promising Potentials Beyond the Technical Hassles

Lack of time and IT-related problems are well known challenges among health professionals as well as in modern work life in general, and was confirmed by this study. In particular the physicians expressed concern about the future and how to find time for learning and reflection as a completed specialist, considering there is little time to study even when it is scheduled as part of the specialist medical training.

The physicians emphasized heavy on ICT related problems at work and information overload, but were at the same time positive towards the possibilities with modern technology. They shared feelings of frustration due to overall outdated IT-systems and information environment: *"I just think that we are so far behind that it's embarrassing, patients take for granted that I know, if they've been in the hospital to where I have sent them, but I don't until I get a letter three weeks later, if I don't ask them to fax, so it's not really the 2000 s"*. Also because there is much potential in the systems but it is not being put into practice. It was noticeable during the interviews a very separate view on private vs work, almost as if they take off their digital clothes, while change into work clothes, and also between "real" work as in patient care and health related ICT, and administration, such as intranet or reading e-mails. Something that also signals that caring and information work is very separate. They seldom mentioned social media or digital tools for collegial collaboration or patient communication spontaneously. But even so it was apparent that many of them did read and seek for information, as well as having work related discussion outside of work. They expressed a similar approach to social media as something private and not work related: *"well, a barrier is that it is, that I want it to be private, I don't want anything work related here"* several stressed the importance of patient confidentiality especially in digital media: *"Facebook? No no, that's only private, no patient discussions"* But then there is the fact that the physicians' social networks, although viewed upon as private, are built up by student contacts from medical school and colleagues, which means there are a lot of doctor's talking informally. It was also common to read and follow discussions online, not make any comments in social media but bringing it up with colleagues at work for discussion. When it comes to apps and mobile technology, a few of them mentioned patient apps they knew of but had not really used any work related apps. There were some mentions of initiatives for seminars using skype and webcasting, as well as podcasts on specific subjects. In general the physicians showed little experience or interest in use of mobile technology, mostly explained because there was not something they needed in the workroom where there is always a computer available. When commenting on ICT they related this to technological advances in patient care, such as tablets for visualizing anatomy or sending images for direct expert opinion. Some of the physicians also commented on technology itself as an obstacle: *"it's not possible to fully concentrate on the patient and at the same time looking at a computer screen"*. But on the other hand there were also examples described when the doctor and patient search and talk about what they read and learn together.

5 Discussion

It was evident that the physicians are well aware of that their occupation is highly specialized and undergoes rapid development. Consequently, lifelong learning and keeping up to date are regarded as a natural part of the profession. Professional development in terms of participation in formal training and acquisition of medical knowledge seems to almost go without saying. However, learning on the job was stressed as the most important form of professional development (i.e. clinical experience, treating the patient and informal collegial communication). This is in line with earlier research on informal workplace learning [cf. 34] and further underline the importance of finding ways to better incorporate work and learning and bring awareness of informal learning as part of physicians continuous training.

Findings from this study illustrate a shift that has taken place in recent years towards a more evidence based practice. An approach which now seems to be well integrated in the clinical work. Before EBM medical decisions were to a large extent left to the individual physician, who had to judge necessity of research evidence, and merge this with previous experience and beliefs, possibly with nearby colleagues as counsellors. It is clear that this process nowadays is done on a higher gear, where evidence is essential and collegial advice is available not only among local peers but also in a global collegial community, due to the Internet.

This study has shown that workplace learning activities prompted by handling patient cases were considered as a major aspect of all learning. The physicians clearly expressed that learning is strongly related to the frequency of patient cases. Patient cases can be regarded as an engine which demands that the physician merge EBM, own and collegial experience into a decision which takes account to the characteristics of the individual patient. This was described both as a blessing and a burden. The physicians seemed to find it difficult to navigate and relate between their own knowledge (practical and theoretical), patient preferences and collegial learning. Thus, the challenges are not caused by time and resources only, but also by a concern and anxiety about corresponding to the diverse aspects in a holistic manner, and that in turn is the engine for activating the learning.

Regarding ICT, there was a duality of views. Although the physicians brought up a lot of IT-related problems in the interviews, ICT was accepted as a central part of the information society, and there was a positive attitude towards the possibilities, especially in relation to access information. The dominant role of ICT for the medical practice is highlighted by the physicians' reflections over the technical development and how they had hard to understand how doctors used to work before, when there were no computers and no internet. There were also many suggestions for improvements, both with regard to the "personal working environment", where better use of ICT could facilitate access to patient related information as well as, and integrated with, easy access to decision support systems, evidence based information and more practical information for learning purposes and documentation of experiences.

Given this, one may wonder how ICT could support physicians in their profession and continuous learning. Obviously patient cases are the main core of the physicians' everyday work, and it is also the engine for a number of learning activities. From a workplace learning perspective it is easy to make a parallel to the use of case methodology in teaching. One final ingredient in working with a case in education is to review and reflect over the learning process [59, 60]. This also goes hand in hand with the concept of "reflective practice", which implies that the experience alone is no guarantee for learning, it must be complemented with reflection [45]. Some of the physicians mentioned the importance of collegial discussions regarding guidelines, regulations and also "ungoogleable" questions, i.e. questions that are more a matter of judgment than searching for facts or confirmation. However, beyond these comments most of the collegial discussions seem to be focused on finding the best decision for a specific patient. Perhaps a more reflective approach and reviewing of how decisions are reached could constitute an important part of the continuous learning for both the individual physician and the collective. Considering that ICT and use of social media have been identified as a way to support workplace learning [26] our findings suggest that there is potential for information systems that facilitate i.e. saving anonymised patient cases for learning purposes and integrate functions for sharing and storing experiences and knowledge in everyday work.

6   Conclusion and Implications

"Medical care is often said to be the art of making decisions without adequate information" [61]. This study has illustrated how evidence based practice, health related ICT and digitalization of working life and learning is changing the healthcare landscape and the role of the physician. Thereby, making modern medical care the art of knowing how to best navigate the vast amount of adequate information available; own experiences with recommendations, regulations and the collected knowledge of collegial expertise and the Internet, and then balance this with the new emerging role of patients as co-creators and partners in care.

Overall this study has contributed to a better understanding of how physicians engage in information activities related to learning at work, and the role and potential of ICT as support for learning in the working life of health professionals. Findings confirm some already known problems regarding lack of time and resources and

IT-problems as well, highlighting the need for better integration of continuous learning in physicians' everyday practice and information systems more adopted to physicians working methods. Moreover though, this study have shed some light on the complexity of digitalization and how it's affecting this group of young/newly trained resident physicians, who as it seems are facing day-to-day challenges, a new professional role and a changing healthcare landscape with confidence and careful optimism.

Due to the fact that there is an existing culture of mistrust regarding some of the old systems, it is important that the new era of supporting ICT must be based on the work and learning situation in daily clinical practice. Solving the problems with technical hassles and incompatible systems not adopted to daily work will save time and reduce a lot of stress, frustration and irritation. This has implications both for research and practice: How could we find more user friendly tools for supporting informal learning at work? In which ways can ICT contribute to information seeking, knowledge sharing and keeping up to date in clinical practice?

Even though new technologies and systems require more learning, they might actually be a part of the solution as well. We believe that ICT and social media technologies could play an important role for enabling new ways of learning and supporting continuous learning for physicians. Better integration of both health related and administrative ICT as well as learning in everyday work is an important aspect. Designing personal working environment (PWE) could be helpful for sorting and filtering information. Finally, we believe that ICT support for more reflective practice regarding patient cases, may increase the learning usability of the systems substantially.

References

1. European Commission: Study concerning the review and mapping of continuous professional development and lifelong learning for health professionals in the EU (2015). http://ec.europa.eu/health/workforce/key_documents/continuous_professional_development/index_en.htm. Accessed 02 May 2016
2. SLS: Continuing Professional Development (CPD). A summary of the state of knowledge about physician training (2012). http://www.sls.se/Global/cpd/cpd2012_english.pdf. Accessed 02 May 2016
3. Strimel, G., Reed, P., Dooley, G., Bolling, J., Phillips, M., Cantu, D.V.: Integrating and monitoring informal learning in education and training. (research report). Techniques **89**, 48 (2014)
4. Cobo, C.: Strategies to Promote the Development of E-Competences in the Next Generation of Professionals: European and International Trends. SKOPE Issues Paper Series (2009)
5. Dornan, T.: Workplace learning. Perspect. Med. Educ. **1**, 15–23 (2012)
6. van de Wiel, M.W.J., Van den Bossche, P., Janssen, S., Jossberger, H.: Exploring deliberate practice in medicine: how do physicians learn in the workplace? Adv. Health Sci. Educ. **16**, 81–95 (2011)
7. Boruff, J.T., Storie, D.: Mobile devices in medicine: a survey of how medical students, residents, and faculty use smartphones and other mobile devices to find information. J. Med. Libr. Assoc.: JMLA **102**, 22–30 (2014)

8. Mickan, S., Tilson, J.K., Atherton, H., Roberts, N.W., Heneghan, C.: Evidence of effectiveness of health care professionals using handheld computers: a scoping review of systematic reviews. J. Med. Internet Res. **15**, e212 (2013)
9. Sclafani, J., Tirrell, T.F., Franko, O.I.: Mobile tablet use among academic physicians and trainees. J. Med. Syst. **37**, 1–6 (2013)
10. Ventola, C.L.: Mobile devices and apps for health care professionals: uses and benefits. Pharm. Ther. **39**, 356 (2014)
11. Barello, S., Triberti, S., Graffigna, G., Libreri, C., Serino, S., Hibbard, J., Riva, G.: eHealth for patient engagement: a systematic review. Front. Psychol. **6**, 2013 (2015). pmid:26779108
12. Jacobs, R.J., Lou, J.Q., Ownby, R.L., Caballero, J.: A systematic review of eHealth interventions to improve health literacy. Health Inform. J. **22**(2), 81–98 (2014)
13. Li, S., Bamidis, P.D., Konstantinidis, S., Traver, V., Zary, N.: Prioritization of actions needed to develop IT skills among healthcare workforce. PeerJ PrePrints (2015)
14. van Gemert-Pijnen, J.E., Nijland, N., van Limburg, M., Ossebaard, H.C., Kelders, S.M., Eysenbach, G., Seydel, E.R.: A holistic framework to improve the uptake and impact of eHealth technologies. J. Med. Internet Res. **13**, e111 (2011)
15. Strategy for National eHealth (2016). http://www.nationellehalsa.com/nationalehealth. Accessed 02 May 2016
16. Kay, M., Santos, J., Takane, M.: mHealth: new horizons for health through mobile technologies. World Health Organ. **64**(7), 66–71 (2011)
17. European Union: eHealth action plan 2012-2020-innovative healthcare for the 21st century (2012). http://ec.europa.eu/newsroom/dae/document.cfm?doc_id=4188. Accessed 02 May 2016
18. European Commission: The use of ICT to support innovation and lifelong learning for all - a report on progress (2008). http://www.europarl.europa.eu/registre/docs_autres_institutions/commission_europeenne/sec/2008/2629/COM_SEC(2008)2629_EN.pdf. Accessed 02 May 2016
19. Vaona, A., Rigon, G., Banzi, R., Kwag, K.H., Cereda, D., Pecoraro, V., Moja, L., Bonovas, S.: E-learning for health professionals. Cochrane Database of Systematic Reviews, **2015**(6). Art. No. CD011736. doi:10.1002/14651858.CD011736
20. Hague, C., Logan, A.: A review of the current landscape of adult informal learning using digital technologies. Educational Research (2009)
21. Yaşar, Ö., Karadeniz, Ş.: The power of social media in informal learning. In: Education in a Technological World: Communicating Current and Emerging Research and Technological Efforts. Formatex, Badajoz (2011)
22. Brzozowski, M.J., Sandholm, T., Hogg, T.: Effects of feedback and peer pressure on contributions to enterprise social media. In: Proceedings of the ACM 2009 International Conference on Supporting Group Work, pp. 61–70. ACM (2009)
23. El Ouirdi, A., El Ouirdi, M., Segers, J., Henderickx, E.: Employees' use of social media technologies: a methodological and thematic review. Behav. Inf. Technol. **34**, 454–464 (2015)
24. Leonardi, P.M., Huysman, M., Steinfield, C.: Enterprise social media: definition, history, and prospects for the study of social technologies in organizations. J. Comput.-Mediated Commun. **19**, 1–19 (2013)
25. Song, D., Lee, J.: Has Web 2.0 revitalized informal learning? The relationship between Web 2.0 and informal learning. J. Comput. Assist. Learn. **30**, 511–533 (2014)
26. Kind, T., Evans, Y.: Social media for lifelong learning. Int. Rev. Psychiatry **27**, 124–132 (2015)

27. Brown, J., Ryan, C., Harris, A.: How doctors view and use social media: a national survey. J. Med. Internet Res. **16**, e267 (2014)
28. Grajales III, F.J., Sheps, S., Ho, K., Novak-Lauscher, H., Eysenbach, G.: Social media: a review and tutorial of applications in medicine and health care. J. Med. Internet Res. **16**, e13 (2014)
29. Lupianez-Villanueva, F., Hardey, M., Torrent, J., Ficapal, P.: The integration of information and communication technology into medical practice. Int. J. Med. Inform. **79**, 478–491 (2010)
30. Cedefop, E.U.: Terminology of European Education and Training Policy: A Selection of 100 Key Terms. Office for Official Publications of the European Communities, Luxembourg (2014)
31. Ala-Mutka, K., Punie, Y., Ferrari, A.: Review of learning in online networks and communities. In: Cress, U., Dimitrova, V., Specht, M. (eds.) EC-TEL 2009. LNCS, vol. 5794, pp. 350–364. Springer, Heidelberg (2009)
32. Le Clus, M.: Informal learning in the workplace: a review of the literature. Aust. J. Adult Learn. **51**, 355 (2011)
33. Eraut, M.: Informal learning in the workplace. Stud. Continuing Educ. **26**, 247–273 (2004)
34. Eraut, M.: Informal learning in the workplace: evidence on the real value of work-based learning (WBL). Devel. Learn. Organ. Int. J. **25**(5), 8–12 (2011)
35. Lave, J., Wenger, E.: Situated Learning: Legitimate Peripheral Participation. Cambridge University Press, Cambridge (1991)
36. Wenger, E.: Communities of Practice: Learning, Meaning, and Identity. Cambridge University Press, Cambridge (1998)
37. Wenger, E.: Communities of Practice: A Brief Introduction (2015). http://wenger-trayner.com/wp-content/uploads/2015/04/07-Brief-introduction-to-communities-of-practice.pdf. Accessed 02 May 2016
38. Wenger, E., Fenton-O'Creevy, M., Hutchinson, S., Kubiak, C., Wenger-Trayner, B.: Learning in Landscapes of Practice: Boundaries, Identity, and Knowledgeability in Practice-Based Learning. Routledge, Abingdon (2014)
39. Embo, M.: Integrating Workplace Learning, Assessment and Supervision in Health Care Education. Universitaire Pers, Maastricht (2015)
40. Teunissen, P., Dornan, T.: The competent novice: lifelong learning at work. BMJ: Br. Med. J. **336**, 667 (2008)
41. Bronsburg, S.E.: The Impact of an Osteopathic Medical Program on Information Technology Skills of Physicians Entering the Workforce (2011)
42. Hansson, A., Marklund, B.: ST-doctors believe scientific courses should relate more to everyday practice. Lakartidningen **110**, 1098–1099 (2013)
43. Jayatilleke, N., Mackie, A.: Reflection as part of continuous professional development for public health professionals: a literature review. J. Public Health **35**, 308–312 (2013)
44. Mann, K., Gordon, J., MacLeod, A.: Reflection and reflective practice in health professions education: a systematic review. Adv. Health Sci. Educ. **14**, 595–621 (2009)
45. Schön, D.A.: The Reflective Practitioner: How Professionals Think in Action. Basic Books, New York (1983)
46. Prilla, M., Degeling, M., Herrmann, T.: Collaborative reflection at work: supporting informal learning at a healthcare workplace. In: Proceedings of the 17th ACM International Conference on Supporting Group Work, pp. 55–64. ACM (2012)
47. Case, D.O.: Looking for Information: A Survey of Research on Information Seeking, Needs, and Behavior. Bingley, Emerald (2012)
48. Davies, K.: The information-seeking behaviour of doctors: a review of the evidence. Health Inf. Libr. J. **24**, 78–94 (2007)

49. Gorman, P.N.: Information needs of physicians. J. Am. Soc. Inf. Sci. **46**, 729–736 (1995)
50. Clarke, M.A., Belden, J.L., Koopman, R.J., Steege, L.M., Moore, J.L., Canfield, S.M., Kim, M.S.: Information needs and information-seeking behaviour analysis of primary care physicians and nurses: a literature review. Health Inf. Libr. J. **30**, 178–190 (2013)
51. Younger, P.: Internet-based information-seeking behaviour amongst doctors and nurses: a short review of the literature. Health Inf. Libr. J. **27**, 2–10 (2010)
52. Higgins, O., Sixsmith, J., Barry, M.M., Domegan, C.: A literature review on health information seeking behaviour on the web: a health consumer and health professional perspective (2011)
53. Pope, C., Mays, N.: Reaching the parts other methods cannot reach: an introduction to qualitative methods in health and health services research. BMJ **311**, 42–45 (1995)
54. Bazeley, P., Jackson, K.: Qualitative Data Analysis with NVivo. SAGE, London (2013)
55. Socialstyrelsen: Doctors' specialist medical training – regulations and general guidelines. Descriptions of objectives" corresponds to SOSFS 2008:17 (2015)
56. Socialstyrelsen: Health Care Report 2009. Socialstyrelsen, Stockholm (2010)
57. Sackett, D.L., Rosenberg, W.M., Gray, J.A., Haynes, R.B., Richardson, W.S.: Evidence based medicine: what it is and what it isn't. BMJ **312**, 71–72 (1996)
58. The Swedish Research Council: Codex Rules & Guidelines (2015). http://www.codex.vr.se/en/. Accessed 02 May 2016
59. Kjellén, B.: Cases as boundary objects: transfer and authenticity in work-integrated learning. J. Coop. Educ. Internships **44**, 26–31 (2010)
60. Kjellén, B.: The case method as seen from different pedagogical perspectives. Int. J. Case Method Res. Appl. **19**, 10–16 (2007)
61. Sox, H.C., Higgins, M.C.: Medical Decision Making. ACP Press, Sydney (1988)

Author Index

Printed in the United States
By Bookmasters